WILDLIFE OF SOUTHEAST ASIA

SUSAN MYERS

**PRINCETON
POCKET GUIDES**

D0916163

Princeton University Press
Princeton and Oxford

PRINCETON POCKET GUIDES

Wildlife of Australia, by Iain Campbell and Sam Woods

Wildlife of the Caribbean, by Herbert A. Raffaele and James W. Wiley

Wildlife of East Africa, by Martin B. Withers and David Hosking

Wildlife of the Galápagos, by Julian Fitter, Daniel Fitter, and David Hosking

Wildlife of Southeast Asia, by Susan Myers

Wildlife of Southern Africa, by Martin B. Withers and David Hosking

Coral Reef Fishes: Indo-Pacific and Caribbean, Revised Edition, by Ewald Lieske
and Robert Myers

A Field Guide to the Birds of New Zealand, by Julian Fitter

The Kingdon Pocket Guide to African Mammals, by Jonathan Kingdon

Mammals of China, edited by Andrew T. Smith and Yan Xie

Reptiles and Amphibians of East Africa, by Stephen Spawls, Kim M. Howell,
and Robert C. Drewes

———————

Copyright © 2016 by Princeton University Press

Published by Princeton University Press, 41 William Street, Princeton, New Jersey 08540
In the United Kingdom: Princeton University Press, 6 Oxford Street, Woodstock, Oxfordshire
OX20 1TW
press.princeton.edu

Jacket photographs: Fig. 1 (top left): Bar-bellied Pitta, courtesy of Parinya Padungtin, Fig. 2
(top right): Asian Golden Cat, courtesy of Kaeryn Stout, Fig. 3 (bottom left): Asian Elephant,
courtesy of Susan Myers, Fig. 4 (bottom right): Wallace's Flying Frog, courtesy of Susan Myers,
Fig. 5 (center right): Gold-ringed Cat Snake, courtesy of William Tan

ISBN 978-0-691-15485-5
Library of Congress Control Number: 2015950554

British Library Cataloging-in-Publication Data is available

This book has been composed in Myriad Pro
Printed on acid-free paper. ∞

Edited and design by D & N Publishing, Wiltshire, UK
Printed by Imago in China

10 9 8 7 6 5 4 3 2 1

To all my many dear friends and colleagues
in Southeast Asia.

Nature does not hurry, yet everything is accomplished.

Lao Tzu

CONTENTS

ACKNOWLEDGMENTS

I would especially like to thank the photographers who assisted me with images for this guide—Scott Baker, Irene Dy, Choy Wai Mun, Con Foley, Jon Hall, Sam Hopley, Neoh Hor, Rob Hutchinson, Pitchaya and Rattapon Kaichid, Kwan Choo, Ayuwat Jearwattanakanok, Jeremiah Loei, Bernie Master, Mohd Abdul Muin, Parinya Padungtin, Coke and Sam Smith, William Tan, Tom Tarrant, and Wong Tsu Shi. Thanks also to Will Russell, Greg Greene, Matt Brookes, Erin Olmstead, and Kathi McIvor of Wings Birding Tours for all their support. And to my family, friends, and my Akita—much love.

INTRODUCTION

Southeast Asia is one of the most biodiverse regions on the planet and a wonderful place to start exploring the natural world. This guide is intended to provide an introduction to the unique mammals, birds, reptiles, and other creatures that live on this fascinating continent. The guide does not provide complete coverage of all the wildlife of the region but rather a first taste of the many possibilities. It may be used on a visit to any of the countries of the region. In addition to the species covered, numerous others may be seen on any given visit. I mention a number of these in the section "Guide to the Best Spots for Viewing Wildlife in Southeast Asia," below. For those who are enticed to explore on a more in-depth level, there are many more detailed volumes available; these are listed in the bibliography.

The species included have been selected on the basis of their relative abundance and/or significance. Each entry discusses the diagnostic features, including the size, color, and behavior of the species, as well as habitat and distribution. My hope is that this introductory volume will foster a wider and more in-depth appreciation of the wildlife of Southeast Asia.

GEOGRAPHIC COVERAGE

This general guide covers all the countries of mainland Southeast Asia but does not include Borneo and Indonesia, although people with a general interest can still use it in those regions too. The guide is designed to give readers an overview of the wildlife of Burma, Thailand, Laos, Cambodia, Vietnam, West Malaysia, and Singapore. The term Malay Peninsula refers to the region that comprises the southern "tail" of Burma, southern Thailand, and West Malaysia (Peninsular Malaysia).

MEASUREMENTS

Measurements given in the species accounts refer to the length of the animal from snout/bill/nose to tail tip.

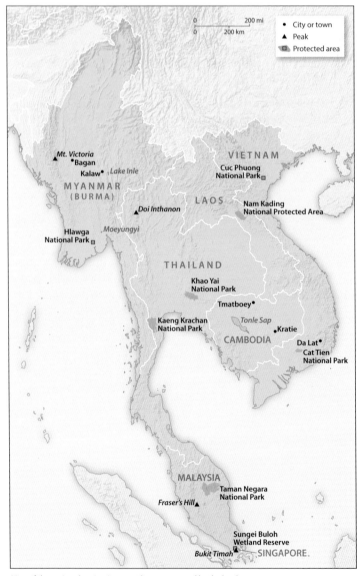

Map of the region showing in green the area covered by the book.

BASIC TIPS FOR VISITORS

Wildlife documentaries on television may give the impression that finding and observing wildlife is easy, but in reality this is not the case. Most creatures are wary of humans and will disappear from sight well before most people have any inkling that the animal is close by. Following are some tips for observing wildlife—suggestions for ways to approach animals or move through the forest that will increase your chances of finding some of the amazing wildlife of this region.

Be prepared
- Choose a good location to see wildlife; national parks or reserves are always good, but even urban parks can harbor many bird and insect species.
- Study before you go; know about the behavior, what habitats the species is likely to be found in, and how to identify the species you are likely to see.
- Have the right equipment; good binoculars are invaluable, and you may wish to carry a camera to record your sightings.
- Wear clothing suitable for the environment; subdued colors are recommended as they blend better into the surroundings. Avoid perfume and scented products.
- Be prepared—pack water, food, hat, sunscreen, and insect repellent.

Birding at Van Long, near Cuc Phuong National Park in Vietnam.

Find and observe

- Don't talk loudly or wear clothing that makes excessive noise, such as some rain jackets. Tread lightly to avoid breaking sticks and alerting animals to your presence.
- Listen, pay attention, and look for tracks and other signs of wildlife. If you are alert to certain signs, animals can signal their presence. Look for scats (animal droppings), tracks, nests, scratch marks, and other clues. Such signs are very often peculiar to a specific species.
- Be patient; remain still and wait in one place or walk slowly and quietly, always staying alert to sounds and movements. Choose a place that may attract wildlife, such as a water hole or fruiting tree, and plan to spend time quietly waiting and observing. When wildlife does appear, resist the urge to point or shout to companions.
- Don't sleep in. Most animals, especially birds, are more active early in the morning. The evening, just before dusk, can also be a great time to observe wildlife.
- Keep notes—what you see, where, when, and details of the animal's behavior. You may want to make sketches of what you see for later reference.

Respect wildlife

- Most important, respect the animals and the habitat. Don't approach wildlife too closely, and don't try to catch or prod an animal.
- Don't disturb wildlife; animals can be unpredictable and potentially dangerous. And you may be potentially dangerous to the animal.
- Never feed wildlife. It can create a dangerous situation for both you and the animal.

Respect other people

- Don't trespass.
- Don't leave the trails or get lost in the forest.

What you'll need

- Binoculars and/or a spotting scope
- A field guide
- A map
- A hat
- A camera
- Water
- Food
- A flashlight
- Rain gear—a jacket, poncho, or umbrella. Remember, it can get very hot inside a jacket in the tropics. At lower elevations a poncho or umbrella is preferable over a jacket, which will be more useful in mountainous areas.
- Suitable footwear for the often warm, humid conditions. Consider carrying a spare pair of socks.

GUIDE TO THE BEST SPOTS FOR VIEWING WILDLIFE IN SOUTHEAST ASIA

Throughout Southeast Asia, with the exception of Malaysia, forest and wildlife reserves were declared only after 1900; most were established from the 1920s onward. Thailand did not declare its first national park until 1962, the last nation on mainland Southeast Asia to do so. Happily, an excellent network of national parks and reserves now exists throughout the region, albeit with varying degrees of protection, which is dependent upon budgets, levels of corruption, and many other factors.

Many of these protected areas are important sources of revenue in the form of tourism dollars for local communities and national economies alike. Visitors can generally travel independently or with guided tours to all the spots mentioned below, as well as to a number of other possibly lesser-known reserves. Many small businesses in all the countries of Southeast Asia provide excellent services to foreign and local visitors, including wildlife viewing opportunities; these can be found with a simple Internet search. Tourism dollars can benefit local people and serve as an impetus to the continued protection of the wonderful wildlife and wild places of Southeast Asia.

BURMA (MYANMAR)

Burma is mainland Southeast Asia's largest country, stretching 2,100 kilometers from north to south. Biogeographically it is a meeting point of the South Asia, North Asia, and Southeast Asia regions. In the north, the snow-capped mountains of the Himalayas feed the mighty Ayeyarwady (Irrawaddy) River and other rivers that fan down through the wide, central plains to the coastal deltas of the Bay of Bengal. The northern forests constitute one of the largest contiguous forests in Southeast Asia.

The climate is heavily influenced by two subcontinental monsoons. The southwest monsoon brings the majority of the country's rainfall and takes place from June through October. During this summer wet season, the coastal and mountain areas receive the majority of the rain. The northeast monsoon usually arrives in November, lingers until March, and brings far less precipitation. The coolest season is November through February, while March through May, in the lead-up to the southwest monsoon, can be extremely hot.

Burma harbors some of the richest biodiversity in the region—well over 11,000 species of flowering plants, including 841 species of orchids; over 1,000 species of butterflies; and 1,017 species of birds.

BAGAN

The historic site of one of the most important ancient kingdoms of the region, this widespread area of temples and citadels, many dating back more than a thousand years, also harbors a plethora of birdlife. Located on the east bank of the famous Ayeyarwady (Irrawaddy) River, Bagan is one of the richest archaeological sites in Southeast Asia. Birding among the ancient ruins can be very rewarding, yielding

A view of Bagan in Burma.

sightings of four of the five endemic birds of Burma—White-throated Babbler, Burmese Bushlark, Jerdon's Minivet, and Hooded Treepie, together with many other interesting birds. A short boat ride along the Ayeyarwady River is a good way to look for Indian Sand Lark, Indian Skimmer, River Tern, Black-bellied Tern, Pied Kingfisher, Laggar Falcon, and White-tailed Stonechat, as well as Small Pratincole, along with other waterbirds.

Best time to visit: November through February, when birdlife is at its most active and abundant.

MOUNT VICTORIA

Nat Ma Taung National Park is a large protected area about 130 kilometers from Bagan in Chin State. The park surrounds the 3,053-meter-high Mount Victoria and is comprised of dipterocarp, pine, oak, and oak-rhododendron forests. This is one of the best areas to view wildlife in Burma—populations of Western Hoolock Gibbon, Bengal Slow Loris, Clouded Leopard, and Gaur. It is especially rich in birdlife. The national park falls within the Eastern Himalayas Endemic Bird Area, and 254 bird species have been recorded, including White-browed Nuthatch, which is endemic to the park. Other birds of special interest include Himalayan Cutia, Hume's Pheasant, Brown-capped Laughingthrush, Streak-throated Barwing, Chin Hills Wren-Babbler, and Mount Victoria Babax. This is also an excellent area for butterflies; almost 80 species occur here, including the rare Bhutan Glory.

Best time to visit: October through mid-May is fine, but November through February is ideal.

The view from Mount Victoria, Burma.

KALAW AND INLE LAKE

These two destinations lie on the Shan Plateau, a highlands area of hills, river valleys, and plains in the northeast. Kalaw is a hill station, a town founded by the colonial powers as a refuge from the stifling summer heat of the plains. Around the town, one can see Spectacled Barwing and White-browed Laughingthrush. The nearby remnant evergreen broadleaf and pine forests support a diverse avifauna, and a trip to Yay Aye Kan lake may yield sightings of the near-endemic Burmese Yuhina, Silver-eared Laughingthrush, Dark-backed Sibia, Common Green Magpie, and Pin-tailed Green Pigeon.

Inle Lake is the second-largest lake in Burma and famed for its "leg rowers" (the boatmen operate their crafts by standing with one leg wrapped around the long oar). A boat ride on the lake is worthwhile as it will allow you to search for the rare and local Jerdon's Bush Chat as well as a variety of waterbirds, including Ferruginous Duck and Pheasant-tailed Jacana. Groups of Brown-headed Gulls often follow the many boats on the lake, while Marsh Harriers regularly hunt over the lake edges and Striated Grassbirds call from the reed beds. Fascinating cultural traditions of numerous villages focus on the lake, and the distinctive houses, fishing boats, and floating vegetable gardens add to the unique experience of attending local events.

Best time to visit: October through April.

Wildlife watching on Inle Lake in Burma.

YANGON (RANGOON)

There are two good wildlife-watching sites near Yangon: Hlawga National Park and the Moeyungyi Wetland Wildlife Sanctuary.

Hlawga, located 35 kilometers north of the city, is a great introduction to the wildlife of Burma. In this 6-square-kilometer park of semi-evergreen and mixed deciduous forest surrounding several attractive small lakes, there is a healthy population of Rhesus Macaque as well as Hog Deer, Sambar, and Wild Boar. Almost 180 species of birds have been recorded, including Asian Openbill, Besra, Rosy Minivet, Racket-tailed Treepie, Black-naped Oriole, Greater Racket-tailed Drongo, Puff-throated Babbler, Lesser Necklaced Laughingthrush, Forest Wagtail, and Scarlet-backed Flowerpecker. Hlawga is also a good site for spotting the increasingly rare and elusive Pale-capped Pigeon. There is always a chance of seeing a Pangolin or Reticulated Python as well.

Moeyungyi lies 121 kilometers north of Yangon and encompasses an area of approximately 125 square kilometers. This reservoir was built during the British colonial period; the water is used for irrigating paddy fields. The wetlands include a large freshwater lake with extensive shallow margins, and one may see great rafts of ducks and large numbers of birds of prey. Some of the rich birdlife of the area includes Lesser Whistling-Duck, Cotton Pygmy Goose, Spot-billed Duck, the globally threatened Baer's Pochard, several species of egrets and herons, Indian and Chinese Pond-Herons, Cinnamon Bittern, White-breasted Waterhen, Pheasant and Bronze-winged Jacanas, Eastern and Western Marsh-Harriers, White-breasted Kingfisher, Blue-tailed Bee-eater, and Bluethroat.

Best time to visit: October through April.

THAILAND

Thailand is bordered to the north by Burma and Laos, to the southeast by Cambodia, and to the south by Malaysia. The north of the country is mountainous; the highest point is Doi Inthanon at 2,565 meters. The northeast flattens out into the Khorat Plateau, bordered to the east by the Mekong River. The Chao Phraya alluvial plain dominates the center of the country, and the south consists of the Isthmus of Kra, a narrow land bridge that connects to the Malay Peninsula.

The Thai avifauna comprises Sino-Himalayan, Indo-Burmese, Indo-Chinese, and Sundaic (Malaysian and Indonesian) elements, with large numbers of migrant visitors from the Palaearctic Region (northern Africa, Europe, the northern third of the Arabian Peninsula, and Asia north of the Himalayas). Thailand's extensive reserves and wild areas harbor some of the richest wildlife in Southeast Asia, including some of its most charismatic and endangered species, such as Tiger, Asian Elephant, Clouded Leopard, Gaur, White-winged Duck, and Green Peafowl. A very diverse range of habitats contributes to this rich fauna; in Thailand one can find montane and moist evergreen forests, deciduous and deciduous-pine forests, and swamps and mangroves. Thailand still faces many challenges in conservation, though, including habitat loss and fragmentation, as well as poaching.

Most of Thailand, including the north and west, has a savanna climate, with distinct wet and dry seasons, while the south and the east have a tropical monsoon climate. The dry season starts in November, with lower temperatures, which gradually climb until they rise dramatically in March, when the thermometer often reaches well over 38°C. The southwest monsoon arrives at some point between May and July, ushering in the rainy season, which lasts through October; this time of year is cooler but very humid.

DOI INTHANON NATIONAL PARK

One of the most exciting aspects of Doi Inthanon is that the central road transects the lowland dry dipterocarp forests and reaches moist evergreen forests and ultimately montane cloud forests. This allows observers to sample a wonderful variety of the wildlife of northern Southeast Asia. Starting at the top and working down, one can experience an array of habitats and the attendant wildlife. On the boardwalk at the Doi Inthanon summit, affectionately known as The Bog, one may encounter a number of skulking birds; as the sun rises, remarkable mixed flocks of birds take advantage of the warming rays. It is thrilling to experience the non-stop activity of Chestnut-tailed Minlas, Mrs. Gould's Sunbirds, Rufous-winged Fulvettas, Yellow-bellied Fantails, Blyth's Leaf Warblers, Dark-backed Sibias, and numerous other small, active birds. Moving down the mountain, you may find many species of barbet, forktail, babbler, bulbul, and plenty more, often accompanied by a background chorus of calling gibbons.

Best time to visit: May through November is the best time to see the many waterfalls here, but for wildlife watching March through June is ideal.

Entering Khao Yai National Park in Thailand.

KHAO YAI NATIONAL PARK

Well known for its abundance and diversity of birdlife, Khao Yai offers a fabulous representation of the Indochinese fauna, with arrays of small, mixed-flock bird species as well as many elusive ground-dwellers, not to mention raptors, hornbills, and nightbirds. The 300-square-kilometer area comprises dry deciduous and evergreen forests, tropical moist evergreen forests, hill evergreen forests, and grassland. A huge number of species has been recorded here—around 2,000 species of plants, over 300 bird species, 70 species of mammals, and 74 species of reptiles and amphibians. Thailand's third-largest national park, it is also the country's most popular. Its proximity to Bangkok makes it a popular destination for locals and foreigners alike. It is known for its waterfalls and forest trails, and wildlife-viewing opportunities abound. Two observation towers allow possibilities of encounters with Asian Elephant, Gaur, Golden Jackal, and Wild Pig. Gibbons are often heard, especially in the mornings; with luck, they can be found high in the treetops of the excellent forests here, maybe even in company with Great Hornbills.

Best time to visit: December through March, when it's a bit cooler.

KAENG KRACHAN NATIONAL PARK

Covering almost 3,000 square kilomters, Kaeng Krachan is the largest national park in Thailand and one of the most exciting nature reserves in Southeast Asia. It is contiguous with a forest reserve in southern Burma that covers an astounding 30,000 square kilometers. The only access to the park is via a 36-kilometer-long dirt road; it is in good repair, and the park provides jeep transport within the park. This huge area of evergreen forest on the southern Burmese border simply abounds with all sorts of exciting wildlife. The mixture of birds from the Sundaic region (Malaysia and Indonesia) and the Orient is one of the most exciting aspects of this superb reserve. Over 420 species of birds have been recorded here. The reserve also holds many charismatic mammal species, including Leopard, Tiger, Asian Elephant, Gaur, and Banteng, as well as a number of primate, deer, and civet species, among others. It is also one of the best places in Southeast Asia for butterfly watching, with over 300 species.

Best time to visit: November through February, when it is cooler and drier.

LAOS

A landlocked country bordered by Burma, China, Thailand, and Vietnam, Laos could be described as the center of the Southeast Asia region. With a population of just over 7 million, it is also the least populated country in mainland Southeast Asia.

The country is largely mountainous; elevations are mostly above 500 meters. The terrain is characterized by steep valleys, which are generally poor for agriculture. There are extensive plains in the southeast, which is primarily used for rice cultivation and livestock, but flat areas make up only about 20% of the total surface area. The western border with Thailand is demarcated by the Mekong River, while the Annamite Mountains form the eastern border with Vietnam. Laos has over 40% forest cover, and the Lao government has designated 24 national forest protected areas, known as National Biodiversity Conservation Areas, to conserve biodiversity. But despite nearly 5 million hectares of land lying within these protected areas, forest cover in Laos has declined dramatically over the years. Only about 4% of the land area is considered arable, and there is extensive forest cover, but this has declined significantly since the 1970s, mainly due to commercial logging and slash-and-burn agriculture.

Over 80% of the population of Laos is rural, and the people rely to varying degrees on natural resources. In recent times, there has been increasing foreign investment focused on exploiting the country's rich mineral and forest resources. Sales of endangered wildlife have also increased, and Laos has gained notoriety as a haven for the trade in wildlife, apparently driven increasingly by domestic demand from affluent politicians and urban residents, as well as Chinese tourists, who seek animal parts and meat for personal consumption. It also likely that many wildlife parts are used for traditional medicines.

The climate of Laos is influenced by the southwest and northeast monsoon air masses. It can be described as a tropical monsoon climate, with a pronounced rainy season—the southwest monsoon, from May through October—bringing 90% of the annual precipitation. The southwest monsoon is followed by a cool dry season from November through February, and a hot dry season in March and April.

With its extensive forest cover, Laos is host to a wealth of wildlife. But ecotourism is a new concept in this relatively poor country, and viewing opportunities are not widely available. That said, more and more tourists are visiting, and the opportunities are increasing. Many of the wildlife populations of Laos are depressed due to subsistence hunting, and growth in the ecotourism sphere can only benefit the wildlife, as well as the people.

Laos has around 700 species of bird species, including one endemic—Bare-faced Bulbul, which is found in the limestone karst forests of the Annamite Mountains in the central part of the country. Other species of note include Limestone Leaf Warbler and Sooty Babbler, both of which are endemic to the Annamite Mountains and were described as recently as 2009. Laos also has the largest population of Asian Elephants in Southeast Asia.

NAM KADING NATIONAL PROTECTED AREA

This large reserve protects an area of rich biodiversity roughly in the center of the country. The vegetation here is dry evergreen and semi-evergreen forest; the terrain is rugged and mountainous, with large rock outcrops, limestone formations, and rugged, boulder-strewn canyons. The elevations range from 500 to 1,200 meters. Four main rivers cut through the Nam Kading, an important watershed and fish breeding ground. The largest of these is the Nam Kading, whose name means "water like a bell." It is a major tributary to the Mekong River.

The park itself is largely inaccessible; there are no roads, and the rivers are impassable, so most visitors who wish to experience the area travel to the village of Na Hin, along Route 13 about 190 kilometers east of the capital of Vientiane, a journey of around three and a half hours. Route 13 skirts the southern boundary of the reserve, allowing some limited access, especially to the limestone pinnacles. For this reason, a visit to Nam Kading is recommended only for birders wishing to see the endemic bulbul and other specialties.

Forty-three species of mammals and 234 species of birds are found in the park. It is considered a highly important wildlife area with its populations of highly endangered animals, such as Tiger, Asian Elephant, and Gaur; however, these populations are not large. There are at least 13 globally and 12 regionally threatened mammals, including Gaur, Sun Bear, and both Northern and Southern White-cheeked Crested Gibbon. The Lao Langur is a range-restricted and increasingly rare primate; it is closely associated with forests in limestone karst environments, but also with non-limestone rock outcrops on steep or precipitous mountain slopes. It is folivorous (leaf-eating), both terrestrial and arboreal, and diurnal.

The limestone karsts of Nam Kading, Laos.

A view over Nam Kading Protected Area in Laos.

The endemic Bare-faced Bulbul can often be seen perched atop the pointed tips of the limestone pinnacles. Other birds include Moustached, Red-vented, and Green-eared Barbets; Red-headed and Orange-breasted Trogons; Limestone Wren-Babbler, and a variety of woodpeckers, maybe even the rare Red-collared and Pale-headed Woodpeckers.

Best time to visit: November through early March, when wintering species are present; starting in April it becomes increasingly hot, and the rainy season begins in May and continues through October.

CAMBODIA

This small country supports 24 threatened bird species—a remarkable testament to the extent and quality of the forests, grasslands, and wetlands. The landscape of the country consists of the lake and floodplains of the Tonle Sap Basin, the dry dipterocarp forests of the Northern Plains, the evergreen forests and grasslands of eastern Mondulkiri Province, and the rain forests of the Cardamom Mountains in the southwest.

About two-thirds of the country remains forested, but the land is increasingly being degraded by opportunistic slash-and-burn agriculture, logging, and poaching. Sadly, the rate of deforestation in Cambodia is now considered to be one of the highest in the world. Much of the Northern Plains is still covered with intact and extensive areas of deciduous dipterocarp forest, with scattered examples of the seasonal water holes called *trapeangs* in Khmer, dense riparian evergreen forests, and large grasslands. The forests of the Northern Plains once spread across much of the region and were home to an aggregation of large mammals and waterbirds that rivaled those of the savannas of Africa. These forests and their wildlife have largely disappeared, and the plains of Cambodia now represent the largest remaining contiguous block of this unique and critically important habitat.

As elsewhere in Southeast Asia, the tropical climate is dominated by monsoons, and Cambodia has a wet and a dry season of roughly equal lengths. Temperatures and humidity are typically high throughout the year. The cooler wet season runs from May through October, while the dry season, which starts in November, sees temperatures soaring over 38°C by the end of April.

TONLE SAP

The remarkable Tonle Sap lake and its surrounds support large breeding populations of Greater Adjutant, Sarus Crane, Milky Stork, and Bengal Florican—birds that are approaching extinction elsewhere in Asia. The Tonle Sap Biosphere Reserve, encompassing the enormous lake and the surrounding areas, hosts one of the largest waterbird colonies in Asia. The Prek Toal Bird Sanctuary, a core zone of the reserve, is located on the lake's northwestern shore. Small boats allow visitors to travel quietly up the small streams to platforms overlooking the breeding colonies; from these vantage points, one can be treated to great views of rare Greater Adjutants or Milky Storks perched on trees in the inundated forest. The reserve has been described as one of the most important breeding grounds in Southeast Asia for threatened waterbirds.

Best time to visit: During the dry season from October through April, when large numbers of migratory and breeding birds congregate. Later in the dry season the low water levels can make the reserve difficult to access.

KRATIE

The small town of Kratie is located on the banks of the mighty Mekong River. Taking a boat out onto the river is the best way to enjoy views of the delightful Mekong Wagtail, the river's only known endemic bird, and pods of friendly Irrawaddy Dolphins quietly cavorting in the muddy waters. Sadly, fewer than 80 dolphins remain in the river.

Best time to visit: December through March.

TMATBOEY

This small and isolated village in the Kulen Promtep Wildlife Sanctuary in the Northern Plains of Cambodia is the site of a very successful community conservation project, spearheaded by the Wildlife Conservation Society, that aims to link bird-watching tourism, bird conservation, and community development. The Tmatboey Ibis Project helps birders visit this area in order to observe two very rare birds—Giant Ibis and White-shouldered Ibis. Visitors who see one of these birds pay a small conservation contribution, which is used for infrastructure improvement in this very poor community. In return, birders and naturalists can experience a rich and endangered landscape and fauna with possibilities of observing not only the ibises but also the scarce White-rumped Falcon, Black-headed Woodpecker, Greater Adjutant Stork, Pale-capped Pigeon, Alexandrine Parakeet, and Rufous-winged Buzzard.

Angkor Wat in Cambodia.

Best time to visit: The best time to see Giant Ibis is from January through April, when the *trapeangs* (water holes) attract the birds during the dry season. White-shouldered Ibis can be found with reasonable certainty all year, but flooding during the wet season may restrict access to its habitat.

VIETNAM

This long, thin country is located on the eastern Indochinese Peninsula. Stretching between latitudes 8° and 24°N, with over 3,260 kilometers of coastline, Vietnam exhibits a wide variety of habitats and seasons. At its narrowest point, in the middle of the country, it is only 50 kilometers wide. Vietnam's north is dominated by the highlands and the Red River Delta. The Annamite Range delineates the country, running north–south parallel to the coastline, dividing the Mekong Basin from Vietnam's narrow coastal plain along the South China Sea. The densely populated Mekong River Delta dominates the south.

According to the United Nations Environment Programme, Vietnam is the 20th most biologically diverse country, with 12,034 amphibian, bird, mammal, reptile, and vascular plant species. Of its 1,534 known species of amphibians, birds, mammals, and reptiles, 8.2% are endemic. Sadly, the rate of forest loss in Vietnam is exceptionally high: between 1990 and 2005, the country lost a staggering 78% of its primary forests, leaving it with only 85,000 hectares of old-growth forest. Despite this, there are still excellent areas to observe wildlife, although these are now mostly confined to the numerous national parks. Vietnam also has a very rich culture and history, great ethnic diversity, and wonderful scenery, making this a very attractive destination.

Due to its wide latitudinal range, there is marked climatic variation throughout the country. Average annual temperatures are generally higher in the south than in the north. The winter (dry) season extends roughly from November through April, while the summer monsoon, from May through October, sees significant precipitation, especially in July and August. Seasonal variations in the mountains and in the north are more dramatic than in the south, with temperatures varying from 4°C in December and January to 38°C from July through August. The Mekong Delta exhibits a more stable range of temperatures from, 21°C to 28°C year-round. Because the climate varies so dramatically from region to region, there is really no overall best time to visit Vietnam.

CUC PHUONG NATIONAL PARK

The first national park to be established in Vietnam, Cuc Phuong is an area of limestone hills covered in primary rain forest and one of the most important sites for biodiversity in Vietnam. The park is located in the foothills of the Annamite Range, and its topography consists of karst mountains and valleys of subtropical forests. Almost 100 mammal species and well over 300 bird species have been recorded. Cuc Phuong holds some very special birds, including Bar-bellied, Blue-rumped, and Eared Pittas, Silver-breasted Broadbill, White-tailed Flycatcher, White-winged Magpie, Ratchet-tailed Treepie, Rufous-throated Fulvetta, Limestone Wren-Babbler, Fujian Niltava, and Pied Falconet. Sightings of mammals are relatively rare, but it is possible to visit the headquarters of three conservation projects located within the park boundaries near the entrance—the Endangered Primate Rescue Center, the Carnivore and Pangolin Conservation Program, and the Turtle Conservation Center. The park's proximity to Hanoi, a mere two-hour drive away, means the weekends are often very busy.

Best time to visit: Rainfall is generally high, so the dry season (from November through February) is the best time.

CAT TIEN NATIONAL PARK

Cat Tien contains the largest remaining area of lowland tropical forest in southern Vietnam and an incredible diversity of birds and mammals. Endangered birds found at Cat Tien include Germain's Peacock-pheasant, Green Peafowl, and the very elusive Orange-necked Partridge, while the mammal list includes Leopard Cat, Lesser Mousedeer, Sambar, Gaur, and two endangered primates: Black-shanked Douc Langur and Buff-cheeked Gibbon. Excellent trails start right at the park headquarters; for areas farther afield, such as Crocodile Lake, jeeps are used. The 5-kilometer walk through semi-evergreen forest to Crocodile Lake can be good for sightings of the near-endemic Germain's Peacock-pheasant and Blue-rumped and Bar-bellied Pittas, while the beautiful Siamese Fireback can often be seen on an early-morning drive to the start of the Crocodile Lake trail. Among the many other avian treats to be found at Cat Tien are Scaly-breasted Partridge, Woolly-necked Stork, Lesser Adjutant, White-bellied, Great Slaty, Pale-headed, Black-and-buff, and Heart-spotted Woodpeckers, three species of broadbill, and the Indochinese-endemic Grey-faced Tit-Babbler.

Best time to visit: December through May, during the dry season.

DA LAT PLATEAU ENDEMIC BIRD AREA

In the cooler climes of the delightful city of Da Lat, one can enjoy the old French colonial buildings and numerous outdoor cafés, restaurants, and markets. But the Da Lat Plateau is also one of three Endemic Bird Areas in Vietnam identified by BirdLife International. The area is home to a number of interesting endemics, including Collared Laughingthrush, Vietnamese Greenfinch, and Grey-crowned Crocias.

The two best places to find wildlife are Ta Nung Valley, a small but bird-filled area of remnant evergreen forest 10 kilometers from Da Lat, and Mount Lang Bian, a 2,167-meter peak about 20 minutes by road from Da Lat. The rare Grey-crowned Crocias, White-cheeked Laughingthrush, and the recently split Black-crowned Parrotbill can be found in the Ta Nung Valley, along with very distinctive subspecies of Blue-winged Minla, Rufous-backed and Black-headed Sibias, and Black-throated Sunbird. Target species on Mount Lang Bian may include wintering Mugimaki Flycatcher, Gray-crowned Tit, Vietnamese Cutia, Black-crowned Fulvetta, and Vietnamese Greenfinch. The most sought-after species at Lang Bian, however, is the beautiful and very secretive, endemic Collared Laughingthrush. Another site, Ho Tuyen Lam, is a man-made lake just 3.5 kilometers from the center of town. The pines here are home to Burmese Shrike, Slender-billed Oriole, Indochinese Cuckooshrike, and Vietnamese Crossbill, among many other species.

The flora of the Da Lat Plateau is also of interest, with two endemic pines—Vietnamese White Pine and Krempf's Pine, unique for its flat needles.

Best time to visit: Da Lat's temperatures range, on average, between a pleasant minimum of 15°C to 24°C. There are two seasons—dry from December through March, and wet from April through November, but neither of these is very pronounced.

WEST MALAYSIA

West Malaysia (also known as Peninsular Malaysia) is the part of the nation of Malaysia that lies on the Malay Peninsula and surrounding islands (the states of Sarawak and Sabah are located on the island of Borneo, which is outside the scope of this book). West Malaysia is bordered to the north by Thailand. To the south lies the island of Singapore. The region features coastal plains rising to hills and mountains, and extends 740 kilometers from north to south, with a maximum width of 322 kilometers. The Titiwangsa Mountains, with a high point

The rainforests of Southeast Asia are rich in mammal life that is often frustratingly difficult to find.

of 2,183 meters at Mount Korbu, extend north–south, forming the backbone of the peninsula. The highest mountain is Mount Tahan at 2,187 meters. Peninsular Malaysia retains an extensive forest cover and is dominated by lowland tropical rain forest; other forest types include montane, hill, mangrove, and swamp forests.

The Malay Peninsula is considered to be a megadiverse region, with over 10,000 plant species (compared with around 1,500 species, for example, in the United Kingdom), over 200 species of mammals, including 81 bats, 665 species of birds, 110 species of snakes, and many thousands of insect species. This is one of the last sites in all of Asia where Tiger, Asian Elephant, and rhinoceros still coexist.

The characteristic features of the climate of Malaysia are uniform temperature, high humidity, and copious rainfall. The climate, classified as equatorial, is characterized by two monsoons—the southwest from April through September, and the northeast from October through February. In the eastern states November to January are the months with maximum rainfall, while June and July are the driest months. Over the rest of the peninsula, the maximum rainfall occurs in October and November and in April and May. It is extremely rare to have a full day with a completely clear sky.

TAMAN NEGARA

A rather long and windy road trip takes one from Malaysia's capital, Kuala Lumpur, to the jetty for the boat trip up the Tembeling River to Taman Negara—the name means "national park," and it is Malaysia's largest. There are morning and afternoon departures; the morning boat is probably the best for seeing birds. Blue-throated Bee-eater, Common Sandpiper, Black-capped Kingfisher, Common Kingfisher, and others are usually easily seen; there is also the possibility of Black-and-red Broadbill and Small-clawed Otter.

A few days spent searching this spectacular lowland rain forest and its waterways for glimpses of the secretive and marvelous wildlife to be found here can be one of Asia's great wildlife experiences. An afternoon boat trip up the Tahan River may be one of the high points of your trip. Not only can one enjoy the stunningly beautiful riparian rain forest, but a number of sought-after species may be seen, including Blue-banded Kingfisher, Black-and-Red Broadbill, the endangered Straw-headed Bulbul, and the gorgeous Chestnut-naped Forktail. The trails around the accommodation repay numerous visits with possible sightings of Scarlet-rumped Trogon, Rufous-winged Philentoma, and Green Broadbill, among others. Some fruiting trees in the vicinity of the resort provide plenty of entertainment—lots of pigeons, hornbills, barbets, and bulbuls.

Best time to visit: February through September; the peak tourist season is from April through August.

FRASER'S HILL

The beautiful montane forests of Fraser's Hill harbor a wealth of high-elevation species, including the bizarre Fire-tufted Barbet, the elegant Red-headed Trogon, and the cheeky Chestnut-capped Laughingthrush. During the colonial era, the British would go to Fraser's Hill in order to escape the heat of the lowlands. The atmosphere is still one of laid-back relaxation; the pace of life is much more sedate here than down in the lowlands. The climate is considerably cooler and less humid; in the evening you may even need a sweater. The elevation is 1,300 meters, so the avifauna differs markedly from that at Taman Negara. One may encounter the bewildering but exciting-to-see mixed feeding flocks that characterize the Asian region; mixed flocks of Golden Babbler, Blue-winged Minla, Mountain Fulvetta, Bronzed Drongo, and others are often accompanied by Black-and-crimson Oriole, Blue Nuthatch, and other goodies. In the roadside vegetation one may find Lesser Shortwing, Streaked Wren-Babbler, and the simply fabulous Sultan Tit.

Best time to visit: Any time of year, though the best time is from March through May; note that the weather is always unpredictable.

KUALA SELANGOR NATURE PARK

Kuala Selangor is a reserve situated on the central-west coast of Peninsular Malaysia overlooking the Melaka Straits. An excellent park privately run by the Malaysian Nature Society, it is very popular with local and visiting naturalists and birders. It now harbors one of the last remaining tracts of relatively intact mangrove forest in Peninsular Malaysia and a large man-made lagoon encompassing 200 hectares. It is an important area for migratory waders and other waterbirds. Birds that may be found here include Grey Heron, the amazing Stork-billed Kingfisher, Coppersmith Barbet, and Laced Woodpecker. It is also a great place to get close-up looks at Silvered Leaf-Monkey. A nighttime boat trip on the Selangor River offers the unique opportunity to witness huge colonies of fireflies flashing by the thousands in synchrony.

Best time to visit: August through April, during the winter migration.

SINGAPORE

This ultra-modern island country lies off the southern tip of the Malay Peninsula just 137 kilometers north of the equator. While it is highly urbanized, close to 10% of Singapore's land has been set aside as parks and nature reserves—a network of reserves, parks, park connectors, nature ways, and tree-lined roads. Despite a 95% loss of forest cover in the past 180 years, Singapore retains a surprising diversity of fauna and flora. It is thought that over 28% of Singapore's plant and animal species have gone extinct, but there are still approximately 80 species of mammals, 395 species of birds, and almost 1,400 species of plants.

Singapore's climate is much the same as that of West Malaysia, with temperatures averaging from 22°C to 35°C and relative humidity around 75%.

BUKIT TIMAH NATURE RESERVE

Bukit Timah means "Tin Hill," and this small, 162-hectare nature reserve located near the geographic center of Singapore is the city-state's highest hill, standing at a height of 164 meters. This reserve represents one of the largest patches of primary rain forest remaining in Singapore. People use it for hiking, running, mountain biking, and other activities, but it also houses at least 840 species of flowering plants and over 500 species of fauna. The forest is lowland tropical rain forest dominated by 18 species of dipterocarp, as well as a number of species of palms, rattans, lianas, and ferns, of which there are still over 100 species. Commonly encountered birds may include Short-tailed Babbler on the forest floor, while Pin-striped Tit-Babbler, Olive-winged Bulbul, Cream-vented Bulbul, and Greater Racket-tailed Drongo dwell in the mid-levels. Yellow-vented Bulbul is common in the open areas. Happily, the endangered Straw-headed Bulbul still persists in small numbers.

Long-tailed Macaque is the most common mammal in the reserve, but Malayan Pangolin, Malayan Colugo, and Slender Squirrel also occur. Bukit Timah is now the only place in Singapore where the Red-cheeked Flying Squirrel can be found. Beware, though: The penalty for feeding the monkeys in Singapore is a $500 fine!

SUNGEI BULOH WETLAND RESERVE

This small, 129.5-hectare reserve in northwest Singapore is of global importance as a stop-over point for migratory shorebirds on the East Asian Flyway. Shorebirds such as Whimbrel, Common Greenshank, Common Redshank, Curlew Sandpiper, and Marsh Sandpiper, as well as other wetland species, like Striated Heron, Little Egret, and Yellow Bittern, utilize the extensive mudflats, freshwater ponds, and mangrove forests of the reserve. There are breeding colonies of Gray and Purple Herons. In the tidal zones, crabs and strange mudskippers are abundant. Water Monitors, up to 1.8 meters in length, patrol the area for crabs, frogs, carrion, and even small unwary birds. Fishlife is abundant; one may find Mullet, Halfbeak (so called for its elongated lower jaw), and the remarkable Archer Fish, which hunts land-based invertebrates by shooting them down (squirting them with water from its specialized mouthparts). Smooth Otters have been sighted here too, so keep an eye out.

EASTERN SPOT-BILLED DUCK *Anas zonorhyncha*

A winter visitor to the region, this Mallard-sized duck has a black crown with a prominent black eye stripe contrasting with a creamy-white supercilium, cheeks, and throat. The body is dark grayish-brown with pale edges to the feathers. The bill is black with a prominent orange tip. The sexes are alike. Inhabits freshwater lakes and marshes and can be found in Southeast Asia during the northern winter. The similar Indian Spot-billed Duck is lighter in color, and the bill has a red base. Length: 50–60 cm

PHASIANIDAE PHEASANTS, GROUSE, AND ALLIES

RED JUNGLEFOWL *Gallus gallus*

Commonly found throughout Southeast Asia, where it inhabits open forests, scrubby habitat, and grasslands, this medium-sized pheasant is the ancestor of the domestic chicken. The unmistakable male looks very similar to the familiar domestic rooster. In breeding plumage it is quite spectacular, with a distinctive bright red comb, golden plumage on the hackles, and a glossy, green arched tail. In the non-breeding phase the hackles disappear and the comb becomes smaller. The female, on the other hand, is quite dissimilar to the domestic hen—smaller than the male, with drab brown, finely patterned plumage and a short, laterally compressed tail. Usually seen in groups made up of a single dominant male and 2–5 females; often unaccompanied males are found nearby. The call of the male bird will also be familiar to most; it is almost identical to the crow of the domestic rooster, differing only in the last note being cut short. Resident. Length: M 70 cm, F 43 cm

SILVER PHEASANT *Lophura nycthemera*

A large, very beautiful pheasant; white plumage on the upperparts and a tail decorated with black lines and markings give the male a striking silvery appearance; the underparts and crest are glossy dark blue; the facial skin is bright red, as are the legs; the spectacular silvery-white tail is longer than the body and somewhat arched. The female is duller, with brownish upperparts, pale underparts with black markings, and a duller red face. Found from Burma through much of Thailand to Vietnam in healthy evergreen and deciduous forests. This generally secretive bird can be quite confiding in areas where it isn't harassed. Most often seen crossing narrow roads or feeding on the ground on roadside edges. As with many pheasants, it is most often found in groups of a single adult male and a harem of 3–5 females. Feeds on the ground, turning over leaf litter in search of invertebrates, seeds, grain, and fallen fruits. Resident. Length: M 120 cm, F 70 cm

Eastern Spot-billed Duck

Red Junglefowl, female

Red Junglefowl, male

Silver Pheasant

CRESTED FIREBACK *Lophura ignita*

A locally common species, found from the Malay Peninsula to Borneo and Sumatra; an inhabitant of lowland evergreen forests. The male is mostly glossy blue-black with white streaks on the underparts, bright blue facial skin, red legs, and a spectacular golden-red back often hidden by the wings. The other part of the bird's name derives from the floppy, tufted upright crest. The female has chestnut plumage with a slightly reduced crest, also with white streaks on the underparts, and a smaller, paler-blue facial patch. Most often found in harems with a dominant male and 3–5 females, sometimes with subadult males. Feeds on invertebrates, fruits, and seeds on the forest floor. Resident. Length: M 70 cm, F 57 cm

SIAMESE FIREBACK *Lophura diardi*

Found from Thailand throughout Cambodia, Laos, and Vietnam, this spectacular pheasant is an inhabitant of forests up to 800 meters. The male is unmistakable with smoky-gray upperparts, dark glossy blue underparts, an arched glossy dark-green tail, striking extensive red facial skin, and a floppy tufted crest of dark-blue feathers. The female is inconspicuous, with dark-brown wings, a tail with white barring, chestnut underparts, and a grayish head. The laterally compressed tail is much shorter than the male's; the facial skin is less extensive and duller red. Usually a shy bird of the forest floor, but is locally common; most commonly seen on quiet, narrow roads cut through forest. Usually found in harems with an adult male and 3–5 females; sometimes there may be more than one male. An endemic resident. Length: M 75 cm, F 58 cm

GREAT ARGUS *Argusianus argus*

One of the world's most spectacular birds, found in broad-leaved evergreen forests from the lowlands to the foothills in the Malay Peninsula and Borneo and Sumatra. The male has the second-longest tail of any bird (after the rarely seen Crested Argus); the plumage is generally brown with fine whitish vermiculations and spots on the upperparts. The central feathers of the laterally compressed tail are arched and extend beyond the exceptionally long secondary feathers. There is a short, spiky crest on the rear of the crown. The female is similar, with a much shorter tail and duller blue facial skin. The male makes a simple dancing ground in small clearings in thick forests, where he performs an elaborate display, rarely observed, in which he raises and fans the secondary feathers to the female. Feeds quietly on the forest floor in harems, usually with a single dominant male. Resident. Length: M 200 cm, F 75 cm

PODICIPEDIDAE GREBES

LITTLE GREBE *Tachybaptus ruficollis*

A locally common bird throughout Southeast Asia, an inhabitant of freshwater ponds, lakes, and wetlands. The sexes are similar. The bird is small and squat, with darkish-brown upperparts and paler buffish-brown underparts. The eyes are dark; the narrow, pointed bill is pale pinkish to yellow. In breeding plumage the eyes are yellow, and the bill is dark with a prominent yellow oval spot on the gape; the plumage of the face and neck takes on a deep reddish hue. Swims with rapid movements of the lobed feet, diving frequently. Feeds on small fish and invertebrates. Resident. Length: 27 cm

Crested Fireback, female

Crested Fireback, male

Siamese Fireback

Great Argus, male

Great Argus, female

Little Grebe

BIRDS | CICONIIDAE STORKS

ASIAN OPENBILL *Anastomus oscitans*

A relatively small stork. The non-breeding adult has dull-grayish plumage with a black tail and primaries, and a very distinctive bill with a large gap in the middle, rather like the shape of a nutcracker. In breeding plumage the plumage is much whiter, and the legs are bright red. The sexes are alike. A scarce to locally common resident in central Thailand, Cambodia, and southern Vietnam; a non-breeding visitor to Burma, most of Thailand, and southern Laos. This stork forms large colonies in marshes, lakes, paddy fields, and parks, where it is often very noisy and conspicuous. A resident and winter visitor. Length: 75 cm

WOOLLY-NECKED STORK *Ciconia episcopus*

A distinctive, large stork with all-dark glossy plumage, except for a bright white neck with woolly-like plumage. The legs are bright red; the bill and face are dark. In flight the underwings are all black. The sexes are alike. This stork does not form large colonies and is most often seen in pairs. It inhabits wetlands such as rivers, lakes, rice paddies, forest streams, and pools. Rare to locally common in Burma, western and southern Thailand, Cambodia, southern Laos, and southern and central Vietnam. Resident. Length: 80–90 cm

LESSER ADJUTANT *Leptoptilos javanicus*

This large stork is immediately recognizable with its heavy bill, bald head, and bare neck. The sexes are similar. In non-breeding plumage the head and face are pale pink, while the skin of the neck is yellow-orange. The upperparts are glossy black, the underparts white. In flight the broad wings, with widely splayed primaries, are black on the underwing, interrupted by a white axillary spur. The bill is a dirty yellow; the legs are gray. In the breeding season the facial skin turns a bright red, and the skin of the neck turns bright yellow; white scalloping appears on the tertial feathers. The juvenile of this species is duller on the face, neck, and upperparts, with woolly feathers on the neck. Inhabits mangroves, swamps, and riverine forests, often in small groups, where it forages on invertebrates. Often seen soaring on thermals. Found throughout Southeast Asia, but nowhere common. Resident. Length: 110–120 cm

PAINTED STORK *Mycteria leucocephala*

Rare to locally common in central Thailand and Cambodia. A winter visitor to south and central Burma, south Thailand, Vietnam, and Laos. A large, upright bird with a long neck and legs and a long, straight bill. The sexes are similar. The plumage is a dirty white, with black-and-white markings on the wings, and black primaries. One of the most striking features of this distinctive bird is the pink wash on the ends of the wing feathers. The bill is long and yellow, with a slight droop at the tip; the face is bare, with orange-red skin, and the legs are pinkish-red. In breeding plumage the bare parts all become more brightly colored. The juvenile bird is duller brownish-gray, with a dull-yellowish bill and face. The legs are dull pale pink. Usually found in flocks near swamps, lakes, riverine forests, and paddy fields. A resident and winter visitor. Length: 100 cm

Asian Openbill

Woolly-necked Stork

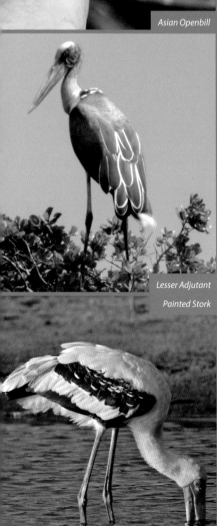

Lesser Adjutant

Painted Stork

Lesser Adjutant

Painted Stork

LESSER FRIGATEBIRD *Fregata ariel*

This very distinctive bird has all-black plumage with a glossy sheen on the upperparts in all forms and a deeply forked tail. The male is all black, with white patches on the underwings and a bright red gular pouch. The long, hooked bill is dark gray, and the legs are dull pink. The female has a white collar (giving it a hooded appearance) extending to a white upper breast and underwing patches. The juvenile bird has a rusty brown head and neck and a white patch on the center of the breast and underwings. This bird is found on oceans and inshore waters, where it feeds by pursuing other birds until they drop or regurgitate their prey, a feeding technique known as kleptoparasitism. Often found in large flocks; can be seen soaring high on powerful, broad wings. A common winter visitor from peninsular Thailand south to Singapore. Length: 70–80 cm

PHALACROCORACIDAE CORMORANTS AND SHAGS

INDIAN CORMORANT *Phalacrocorax fuscicollis*

A medium-sized cormorant, all black with a long, slender bill and whitish throat and pale face. The bill is black with a yellow base, and the eye is a deep blue. In the breeding season the plumage is blacker, with a white tuft behind the eye. The sexes are similar. This species inhabits any type of wetland and feeds on fish by diving; it swims partially submerged. Often stands with wings outstretched to dry after diving. The similar Little Cormorant is smaller, with a shorter, stubbier bill and shorter neck in flight. Indian Cormorant is a locally common resident in south Burma, central and southeast Thailand, Cambodia, and southern Vietnam. Length: 60–70 cm

ANHINGIDAE ANHINGAS

ORIENTAL DARTER *Anhinga melanogaster*

The long, snake-like neck of this diving waterbird makes it instantly recognizable. It is similar to cormorants in some respects but has a much longer neck with a distinct kink, a dagger-like bill, and a long body and tail. In non-breeding plumage the sexes are alike, with brown head, neck, and tail, pale throat, and glossy black upperparts with whitish streaks on the wings. In the breeding season the male has a rufous fore neck, with black spots on the white throat and a strongly demarcated white or buff stripe from the gape along the sides of the head and neck. The female is similar, but lacks the black spots on the throat. In all seasons the bill and facial skin are yellow. Darters are found in undisturbed oxbow lakes, watercourses, wetlands, and mangroves; they can be seen fishing with only the neck above water or perched on conspicuous branches, often with wings spread to dry. An increasingly scarce resident throughout. Length: 85–95 cm

Lesser Frigatebird, female

Lesser Frigatebird, male

Indian Cormorant

Oriental Darter

SPOT-BILLED PELICAN *Pelecanus philippensis*

This unmistakable large wetland bird with all-white plumage and a huge bill with a large extendable pouch can be seen in lakes, large rivers, and estuaries in Cambodia and southern Vietnam, where it is a locally common resident, as well as parts of Burma, Thailand, Laos, and the rest of Vietnam, where it is an uncommon winter visitor. The all-white plumage has a pinkish wash in the breeding season. The long, straight bill is yellowish-pink, with dark spots on the upper mandible. The pouch is pinkish, with darker mottling. The sexes are alike. The juvenile is similar to the adult, but browner on the head and upperparts. Length: 130–140 cm

ARDEIDAE HERONS, EGRETS, AND BITTERNS

YELLOW BITTERN *Ixobrychus sinensis*

A small, buffy-yellow bittern with a black crown and olive-brown upperparts. The underparts are pale yellowish-brown, with a pale gular stripe. In flight, the black flight feathers and tail contrast with lighter-colored back and wing coverts. The female is much more streaked than the male, with a browner crown, similar to the juvenile, which is even more heavily streaked. This shy bird is to be found skulking in reed beds, paddy fields, and thickly vegetated wetland edges. Most often seen when it takes short flights low over vegetation, only to disappear again quickly. Found throughout Southeast Asia, it is an uncommon resident and non-breeding winter visitor. Length: 30–40 cm

GRAY HERON *Ardea cinerea*

A striking, large, mainly gray heron with a black crown, a long, pendant crest, and a white face and neck. The fore neck is patterned with black streaks. In non-breeding plumage the bill and legs are yellowish. During the breeding season the bill and legs of adults brighten to orange. The sexes are similar. The juvenile bird has a grayer head and lacks the crest. Found in a variety of wetland habitats, from estuaries and lakes to paddy fields, where it slowly stalks small fish and other vertebrates. Usually flies low with slow, deliberate wing beats. An uncommon and local resident and winter visitor throughout Southeast Asia. Length: 90–98 cm

PURPLE HERON *Ardea purpurea*

A large, long-necked heron with distinctive purple-brown plumage, and a slender rufous neck with black stripes and spots. The bill and legs are yellowish. In flight, the neck is retracted, and the underwings are rufous. The sexes are alike. The juvenile bird is all rufous-brown with dark spots and streaks. It favors all wetland habitats, where it feeds on small fish and other vertebrates. A local resident throughout Southeast Asia. Length: 78–90 cm

Spot-billed Pelican

Yellow Bittern

Gray Heron   Purple Heron

GREAT EGRET *Ardea alba*

One of the largest herons in the region; a typical egret with all-white plumage, a dagger-like yellow bill, and long black legs. In breeding plumage the legs are pinkish-red, while the bill turns black; the facial skin turns a striking greenish-blue, and long black plumes develop. The sexes are alike. This bird can be seen in all types of wetland habitats, including estuaries, mudflats, swamps, rivers, and rice paddies. The flight is slow and heavy; often utters a gutteral *gwaa gwaa* in flight. An uncommon resident and common winter visitor throughout the region. Length: 80–105 cm

LITTLE EGRET *Egretta garzetta*

A small, all-white heron with a long, slender, black bill and black legs with distinctive yellow feet. During the breeding season the adults develop long white nape plumes and long filamentous plumes on the back and breast; the feet and facial skin take on an orange color. The sexes are alike. The juvenile is similar to the adult, but with duller bill and legs. An active feeder in shallow wetlands, it is often seen with other egrets and herons. Generally silent, but forms large, noisy breeding colonies. A locally common to uncommon resident and winter visitor throughout Southeast Asia. Length: 55–65 cm

PACIFIC REEF HERON *Egretta sacra*

This medium-sized egret found on rocky shorelines and beaches occurs in two forms—a white and a dark morph. Both forms have a blackish-brown bill and yellowish-green legs. The plumage of the white morph is pure white, while the dark morph has dark slaty-gray plumage with a white neck stripe. In breeding plumage long plumes develop on the nape and back. The sexes are alike. Can be mistaken for Cattle Egret, which is smaller with a shorter bill, and with Little Egret, which has a black bill and yellow feet. The habitat is also a clue to the identification of this species, as it is almost exclusively coastal. Usually seen singly or in pairs. An uncommon to common resident throughout. Length: 56–66 cm

CATTLE EGRET *Bubulcus ibis*

This very familiar bird is often seen in fields, shallow ponds, grasslands, and swamps associating with grazing livestock, such as cattle and water buffalo; feeds on insects disturbed by the larger animals. Usually in flocks. This small to medium-sized heron is generally all-white in non-breeding plumage, with a yellow bill and black legs. It can be confused with other small egrets, but has a shorter, thicker neck than either Little Egret or Pacific Reef Egret. In the breeding season adults develop a strong pinkish-buff hue on elongated plumes of the head, neck, and back, while the bill brightens to orange and the legs to yellow. During courtship, the legs turn bright red. The sexes are alike. The juvenile bird is like the non-breeding adult, but the bill and facial skin are a dull gray. A locally common resident and winter visitor throughout. Length: 46–56 cm

Great Egret

Great Egret

Little Egret

Pacific Reef Heron

Pacific Reef Heron
Eastern Cattle Egret

JAVAN POND-HERON *Ardeola speciosa*

Often seen feeding in fields as one travels in Southeast Asia, this small heron is found from central Thailand east to southern Vietnam and south to Singapore. It is also found in estuaries, mudflats, mangroves, and ponds. In non-breeding plumage the bird is whitish streaked with brown, and has solid brown upperparts. The wings are white, but this is quite inconspicuous until the bird takes flight. The facial skin and legs are a dull greenish-yellow. In breeding plumage the head and neck take on a striking orange-buff color, and the back darkens to black; 2 long white head plumes develop, and the bill changes to a bright orange with a black tip. The sexes are alike. The juvenile bird has many more spots and streaks, and brown wings. A common resident from central Thailand to southern Vietnam and south to Singapore. Length: 45 cm

STRIATED HERON *Butorides striata*

A widely distributed bird of wetland areas, inhabiting tidal flats, rocky shorelines, mangroves, and swamps. A small, inconspicuous heron with a hunched appearance. The adult is slaty gray, with a black crown and white streaking on the face. The facial skin is greenish-yellow, as are the legs. In the breeding season the legs become a much brighter yellow. The sexes are alike. The juvenile is brown, with buffy spots and scaling and greenish legs. It is generally solitary; most often sits motionless in or at the edge of thick vegetation; when flushed, it flies low. A locally common resident and common winter visitor throughout Southeast Asia. Length: 35–48 cm

BLACK-CROWNED NIGHT HERON *Nycticorax nycticorax*

Found throughout Southeast Asia, this chunky heron often forms very large colonies, usually near water—estuaries, swamps, mangroves, lakes, or rivers. They are distinctive in flight, with slow, steady wing beats. In non-breeding plumage the sexes are similar, with a black crown and back and pale-gray underparts; the wings and tail are a darker gray; 2 or 3 long white plumes extending from the nape are distinctive. In breeding plumage the male's normally black facial skin and legs take on a pinkish hue. The juvenile bird is altogether different, with bold buffish spots and streaks on brown plumage. A locally common to uncommon resident and non-breeding winter visitor throughout. Length: 56–65 cm

PANDIONIDAE OSPREY

OSPREY *Pandion haliaetus*

This large, highly specialized, fish-eating raptor is a common winter visitor throughout, and in summer can be found from northeastern Thailand east to southern Vietnam and south to Singapore. The white of its head and neck is broken by a dark band through the eye; the underparts are white, while the back and wings are dark brown. It has a short, shaggy crest. The larger female has a streaky breast band. In flight the underwings are white, with dark patches on the carpals and dark flight feathers. The wings are long and slender, with a distinctive angle from the carpals. The eye is golden yellow. Feeds exclusively on fish by diving onto the surface of the water and grasping prey with specially adapted feet. Length: 50–58 cm

Javan Pond Heron

Javan Pond Heron

Striated Heron

Striated Heron

Black-crowned Night Heron

Osprey

BLACK-SHOULDERED KITE *Elanus caeruleus*

This rather small, graceful raptor is a fairly common resident throughout the region, often seen perched and hovering over fields and open areas, hunting for small mammals, lizards, birds, and large insects. The flight is direct and graceful; it soars on raised wings. Overall the adult is clean white, with a gray crown, back, and wings, and a distinctive black shoulder patch. It has a dark eye patch with a deep-red iris. The cere and feet are yellow. The sexes are alike. The juvenile bird is streaked with brown on the upperparts. Length: 28–30 cm

ORIENTAL HONEY-BUZZARD *Pernis ptilorhynchus*

A common resident and winter visitor throughout, this raptor occurs in two forms; both have a longish tail, a very distinctive, pigeon-like head, a long neck, and a short crest. The pale-morph male has a white throat framed by dark malar stripes. The upperparts are dark, the underparts dark brown to white with rufous barring. The tail is dark with a broad pale band. The eye, cere, and legs are yellow. In flight the broad wings show rufous barring underneath and have black-and-white-barred flight feathers. The female is similar, but has brown sides of the head and narrower barring on the wings and tail. The dark morph is all dark brown, with a similar pattern on the underwings and tail, but dark underwing coverts. The juvenile is variable, but usually with a much paler head and underparts. Can be found in many types of forest, where it feeds on a variety of small prey items. Soars on flat wings and twists its head from side to side in a unique manner, often uttering a loud, high-pitched double whistle. Length: 52–61 cm

CRESTED SERPENT EAGLE *Spilornis cheela*

This distinctive bird of prey is a familiar sight throughout Southeast Asia, where it is resident. It is an attractive bird with a black crown, a short, rounded, fan-shaped crest, dark-brown back and wings, and a broadly banded black and white tail. The underparts are paler brown, with small white spots on the lower breast and belly. A prominent feature is the deep-yellow bare facial skin and cere. This raptor has a very distinctive flight in which the broad, rounded wings are held slightly forward and set upward in a gentle V-shape. The underwing is rufous, speckled with white; it has a black trailing edge bordered by a broad white band. The plumages of the sexes are alike, but the female is usually larger. The juvenile is paler, with a black face patch and buffish streaking. As the name suggests, this bird feeds on snakes, as well as small vertebrates. An inhabitant of primary and secondary forests, it can often be seen soaring over the canopy and is very vocal in flight. The call is a high-pitched, persistent *kek kek kweee kweee kweee*. Length: 55–74 cm

Black-shouldered Kite

Black-shouldered Kite
Crested Serpent Eagle

Oriental Honey Buzzard
Crested Serpent Eagle

CHANGEABLE HAWK-EAGLE *Nisaetus limnaeetus*

This large raptor occurs in two forms, a pale morph and a dark morph. The male of the pale morph has a short crest and brown plumage overall, with buff feather fringing on the upperparts and bold dark-brown streaks on the underparts. The tail has 4 dark bands. In flight the paler barred flight feathers contrast with the darker underwing coverts; the undertail has a broad, dark terminal band. The female is larger and more heavily marked below. The dark-morph male is similar to the pale morph, but the plumage is all dark blackish-brown. In flight, the dark underwing coverts contrast slightly with the slightly paler flight feathers, differentiating it from the similar-looking Black Eagle. The juvenile is quite different, with a whitish head and underparts, and mottled brown and white on the upperparts. Occurs in lowland and hill forests, where it feeds mostly on birds as well as reptiles and small mammals. A common to uncommon resident throughout. Length: 60–75 cm

BLACK EAGLE *Ictinaetus malaiensis*

A large, all-black eagle with yellow cere and legs. In flight, the broad wings show prominent "fingers" and a pale patch at the base of the primaries; the yellow legs are conspicuous. The sexes are alike. The juvenile is mottled brown on the upperparts. This spectacular raptor is found in primary lowland and hill forests; can often be seen in pairs soaring over forests, hunting for canopy-dwelling prey such as squirrels, birds, and reptiles. An uncommon resident almost throughout (absent from central and northern Thailand and from southern Vietnam). Length: 67–81 cm

EASTERN MARSH HARRIER *Circus spilonotus*

A fairly common winter visitor to marshes, paddy fields, grasslands, and pasture throughout. The adult male has black upperparts with white feather edging, and white underparts with black streaking on the breast; the face is rather owl-like, with a facial disk. This bird can be confused with Pied Harrier, which is solid black on the head and upperparts. The female is brown on the breast and upperparts with rufous streaks; the belly and thighs are solid rufous-brown. The eye is brown. The flight feathers are banded whitish and gray; the dark secondaries contrast with dark-tipped primaries. The legs are unfeathered. It typically flies low over open areas with the wings held in a distinctive, shallow V-shape, searching for small vertebrates and large insects. Length: 47–55 cm

CRESTED GOSHAWK *Accipiter trivirgatus*

A large accipiter with a short crest and a white throat with a broad gular stripe. The upperparts are grayish-brown, the underparts white with rufous streaks on the upper breast and rufous barring on the lower breast and belly. In flight the long white undertail coverts sweep up and give the impression of a white rump. The iris, cere, and legs are yellow. The female is larger and somewhat browner than the male, but otherwise similar. The juvenile is streaky on the head and underparts; its feathers have buffish edging on the upperparts. The spectacular display flight involves exaggerated shallow wing beats on stiff wings below the horizontal, alternating with normal flight. A common resident throughout, though rare in Singapore. Length: 40–45 cm

Black Eagle

Changeable Hawk Eagle

Eastern Marsh Harrier, juvenile

Crested Goshawk

Eastern Marsh Harrier, female

SHIKRA *Accipiter badius*

Found throughout the region, this distinctive goshawk is a fairly common resident in mainland Southeast Asia and an uncommon winter visitor on the Malay Peninsula. The adult male is pale gray on the head and upperparts, with dark tips on the flight feathers. The underparts are pale, with dense rufous barring, while the whitish throat has a gray central throat stripe. The undertail has 4 dark bands in the center. The eyes are red, the legs and cere yellow. The female is larger than the male, with more brownish upperparts, a yellow eye, and 7–8 bands on the tail. The juvenile looks quite different; has brown upperparts with paler fringing and brown streaking on the underparts. This species is found in many types of habitat, from forests to open areas, where it hunts aggressively for small vertebrates. The name Shikra derives from the Hindi word for "hunter." Length: 30–35 cm

BRAHMINY KITE *Haliastur indus*

Unmistakable, with contrasting white and rich chestnut plumage. The sexes are alike, with white head and breast, and rich brown upperparts and belly. The iris is dark red, the feet and bill yellow. The streaky-brown juvenile can be confused with Black Kite, but has a rounded tail. This raptor inhabits open areas and forests near estuaries, lakes, and rivers, where it feeds on fish, snakes and lizards, and carrion. The voice is a quavering, shrill *cheee-ee-ee* given in flight or, less often, when perched. It is a locally common, generally coastal resident in much of Southeast Asia, with the exception of northwest Thailand, northwest Vietnam, and much of Laos. Length: 45–50 cm

BLACK KITE *Milvus migrans*

A nondescript bird with streaky brown plumage and a longish tail with a distinctive fork, this is one of the most familiar raptors in the region. The sexes are alike. The juvenile is more heavily streaked whitish. In flight the shape of the tail is diagnostic; a former name for the bird was Fork-tailed Kite. It flies with hunched wings that show broadly fingered primaries, and frequently twists the tail; the underwings usually show a white patch at the base of the primaries. Inhabits cities, villages, rubbish dumps, burned fields, and almost any open area, where it can be seen soaring, often in large numbers. The distinctive call is a tremulous, high-pitched *pi-hyorororo* whistle. A common to uncommon resident in Burma, Thailand, Laos, Cambodia, and Vietnam, and an uncommon winter visitor to south Thailand, Peninsular Malaysia, and Singapore. Length: 55–60 cm

WHITE-BELLIED SEA EAGLE *Haliaeetus leucogaster*

A very large bird of prey with a distinctive wedge-shaped tail and gray-and-white plumage. The head, neck, and underparts of the adult are pure white; the back and wings are gray with black primaries. The legs are yellow. In flight the white underparts contrast strikingly with the black flight feathers. The sexes are alike in plumage; the female is slightly larger. The juvenile bird is dark brown with buffy streaks. It inhabits offshore islands, harbors, estuaries, lakes, and mangroves, feeding on fish, snakes, lizards, and carrion. An uncommon coastal resident throughout the region. Length: 75–85 cm

Shikra

Brahminy Kite

Black Kite

Black Kite

White-bellied Sea Eagle

LESSER FISH EAGLE *Ichthyophaga humilis*

An inhabitant of narrow, undisturbed rivers, this attractive species is almost exclusively a fish eater. It perches patiently for long periods in large trees overhanging water, stooping down to pluck fish from the water surface with powerful feet. The head, back, wings, and breast of the adult are gray, contrasting with the white belly and undertail. The tail is brownish, with a dark terminal band. The eye is pale yellow, and the bill and legs are gray. In flight, the base of the primaries appears paler, and the V-shaped white vent contrasts with the brown tail. The sexes are alike in plumage; the female is slightly larger. The juvenile is brownish with buffy streaks. A locally common resident in Burma (except the west), northwest Thailand through to Peninsular Malaysia, and western Vietnam. Length: 51–64 cm

GRAY-HEADED FISH EAGLE *Ichthyophaga ichthyaetus*

Similar to the Lesser Fish Eagle but larger, with a diagnostic white tail that is sharply demarcated with a broad black terminal band that can be seen when the bird is both at rest and in flight. The gray of the head and breast fades into brown on the back and lower breast. The sexes are alike in plumage; the female is slightly larger. It also favors a slightly different habitat, preferring wider rivers, lakes, and wetlands. Perches over water, swooping down to take fish from the water surface. A locally uncommon resident throughout. Length: 61–75 cm

RALLIDAE RAILS, GALLINULES, AND COOTS

WHITE-BREASTED WATERHEN *Amaurornis phoenicurus*

A somewhat chicken-like bird of wetland habitats, and a common resident throughout. The adult is instantly recognizable, with slaty black crown and upperparts contrasting with the white face and underparts. The flanks and undertail are rufous. The prominent bill is greenish-yellow, with a red patch at the base of the upper mandible; the legs are yellow, and the eyes are red. The sexes are alike. The juveniles are dull brownish-gray with paler underparts. Often seen feeding on worms, insects, and seeds in open near dense cover or on roadsides, and nearly always near water, especially after rain. Bobs its tail up and down. Gives a range of guttural calls consisting of loud grunts, croaks, and gurgles. The main territorial call is a characteristic *kwaaa kwaaa*; the onomatopoeic name in Malay is *wak-wak burung*. Length: 28–33 cm

BLACK-BACKED SWAMPHEN *Porphyrio indicus*

A large waterbird with a heavy red bill and a prominent red frontal shield. The head and upperparts are blackish-blue, the underparts greenish-turquoise on the throat and breast, fading to turquoise-blue on the belly; the undertail is white. The eyes and legs are red. The sexes are alike. The juvenile is dull gray. Found in marshes, lakes, ponds, fields, and parks; feeds on aquatic vegetation, snails, insects, and occasionally small vertebrates. Gregarious and often noisy, uttering a loud, rather screaming *grek* call. A locally common resident throughout. Length: 28–30 cm

Lesser Fish Eagle

Gray-headed Fish Eagle

White-breasted Waterhen

Black-backed Swamphen

EURASIAN MOORHEN *Gallinula chloropus*

An all-dark waterbird with blue-black head and underparts, and dark brown on the back and wings. The flanks are streaked with a thin white line, visible when the bird is on the water. The bill is red with a yellow tip, and the face has a prominent red frontal shield. The legs are greenish-yellow; the eyes are red. The sexes are alike. The juvenile is dull brown with no frontal shield. Usually seen swimming in lakes, ponds, paddy fields, and parks. Feeds on aquatic vegetation and small invertebrates. A locally common resident and winter visitor throughout, except northern Laos and Vietnam. Length: 30–35 cm

EURASIAN COOT *Fulica atra*

An all glossy-black waterbird with a prominent white bill and frontal shield. The eyes are brownish-red; the legs are greenish-gray with lobed toes. The sexes are alike. The juvenile is dull gray with a pale-gray bill and reduced frontal shield. It is usually seen swimming, often in large congregations, on lakes, ponds, rivers, and paddy fields. Its behavior is somewhat grebe-like as it dives and runs along the water surface when taking flight. Feeds on aquatic vegetation and insects. An uncommon resident, but absent from the Malay Peninsula and Singapore. Length: 40 cm

BURHINIDAE THICK-KNEES

GREAT THICK-KNEE *Esacus recurvirostris*

An uncommon to rare resident in Burma to northern Thailand, Laos, and central Vietnam in sandy habitats on lakeshores, riverbanks, sand flats, and salt pans. The plumage is sandy-brown on the crown and back, with a black band on the shoulder; the underparts are whitish. The face has strong black-and-white markings, and the large, slightly upturned bill is black with a contrasting yellow base. The legs are long and dull yellowish. The large eyes are strikingly yellow. In flight the upperwings are sandy-brown; the greater coverts are gray, while the flight feathers are black with large white patches. The sexes are similar. Mostly active at dawn and dusk. Roosts during the day under low trees, where it sits very quietly, relying on camouflage to escape detection. Length: 50–55 cm

BEACH THICK-KNEE *Esacus neglectus*

Similar to Great Thick-knee, but slightly larger, with a thicker, bulkier bill; the crown is black. The black band on the shoulder is more prominent. In flight the upperwing shows a different pattern, with gray greater coverts and secondaries, and mostly white inner primaries contrasting with black outer primaries. The sexes are alike in plumage. Strictly coastal, occurring on sandy and muddy beaches, coral reefs, rocky foreshores, and mangroves. Feeds on large invertebrates and small vertebrates. Crepuscular and nocturnal. A rare to uncommon resident in southern Burma, Thailand, northwest Peninsular Malaysia, and Singapore. Length: 53–57 cm

Eurasian Moorhen

Eurasian Coot

Great Thick-knee

Beach Thick-knee

BLACK-WINGED STILT *Himantopus himantopus*

A black-and-white wading bird with extraordinarily long legs and a long, needle-shaped bill. In breeding plumage the male's head, neck, and underparts are pure white, the back and wings black. The female is similar, but the back and wings are brownish. In non-breeding plumage the crown and hind neck are grayish to black. The eyes are red, and the legs are pink. Inhabits marshes, lake edges, and paddy fields, where it feeds on small invertebrates, tadpoles, and fish in shallow water. Often in large flocks. A locally common resident from central Burma and Thailand to southern Vietnam; a common winter visitor to Thailand south to Singapore. Length: 35–40 cm

CHARADRIIDAE PLOVERS AND LAPWINGS

RED-WATTLED LAPWING *Vanellus indicus*

A common resident throughout. This medium-sized bird with a short bill and long legs forages for invertebrates by running and stooping to pluck prey from the ground. Found, usually in pairs, in any area with open ground, such as edges of rivers and lakes, fields, and parks. The head and neck are black, with a large white patch behind the eye and a striking red wattle around the eye extending to the bill, which is red with a black tip. The upperparts are sandy brown, the underparts white. The eyes are deep red, and the legs are bright yellow. The sexes are alike. In flight the white underwing contrasts with the black flight feathers. The call is a very distinctive, sharp *dee-dee-do*. Length: 31–35 cm

LESSER SAND-PLOVER *Charadrius mongolus*

A medium-sized plover found on beaches, mudflats, estuaries, and mangroves. A winter visitor throughout, so seen only in non-breeding plumage in Southeast Asia. The crown and upperparts are sandy-brown, with an indistinct white forehead and supercilium. The underparts are white, with sandy-brown marks on the sides of the breast. The eyes and bill are black, the legs dark gray. The sexes are alike in non-breeding plumage. The Greater Sand-Plover is very similar but has a longer, bulkier bill, a more rounded forehead, and longer, paler legs, and is notably bigger (22–25 cm). Length: 19–21 cm

LITTLE RINGED PLOVER *Charadrius dubius*

A small, dumpy wader found throughout most of the region as a resident and winter visitor. The adult non-breeding bird has an olive-brown crown and upperparts, with a white hind collar and a broad, dark breast band on the white underparts. The eye is black with a prominent bright yellow eye ring. The legs are pinkish. In breeding plumage the male develops a black face mask extending over the forehead and a white patch above the base of the bill; the breast band thickens and darkens to black. The female has a narrower eye ring and a brownish breast band. Inhabits rivers, estuaries, paddy fields, and similar open areas. Usually solitary. Length: 14–17 cm

Black-winged Stilt

Red-wattled Lapwing

Lesser Sand-Plover

Little Ringed Plover

PHEASANT-TAILED JACANA *Hydrophasianus chirurgus*

A locally common resident and winter visitor throughout, except Singapore; inhabits swamps, marshes, lakes, and ponds with abundant vegetation. It has long legs and remarkably long toes adapted for walking on floating vegetation. The female usually occupies a large territory encompassing those of a number of males. The adult non-breeding bird has a brown crown and upperparts; a dull golden supercilium extends to a line down the hind neck; a brown line through the eyes and down the side of the neck extends to become a breast band; the rest of the fore neck and underparts are white. In breeding plumage the appearance changes dramatically: The brown of the back darkens, the underparts also turn brown, and there is a conspicuous white patch on the wings. The hind neck develops a large golden-yellow patch, and the central tail feathers are decurved and elongated, hence the name. The sexes are alike. Feeds on aquatic invertebrates and seeds gleaned from the water surface and aquatic plants. Length: 39 cm (up to 59 cm in breeding plumage)

BRONZE-WINGED JACANA *Metopidius indicus*

A locally common resident in much of Burma, Thailand, Cambodia, Laos, and Vietnam; its habits are much the same as Pheasant-tailed Jacana. The adult is glossy dark green on the head, neck, and underparts, with a thick, white supercilium and bronze-brown back and wings. The bill is yellow, with a small gray frontal shield and red gape. The sexes are alike. The juvenile is dull chestnut on the throat and breast fading into white underparts; the head and upperparts are brown. Length: 26–30 cm

SCOLOPACIDAE SANDPIPERS AND ALLIES

COMMON SANDPIPER *Actitis hypoleucos*

A small, short-legged shorebird with a habit of bobbing its tail. A common winter visitor and migrant. Usually seen singly or in small, loose groups, it inhabits beaches, mangroves, waterways, and paddy fields. The head and upperparts are olive-brown, with faint darker streaking and dark fringes on the wings. The neck and breast are paler brown, the rest of the underparts white. The white of the underparts extends around the curve of the front of the wings, forming a "spur." In flight a narrow white wing bar contrasts with the dark flight feathers. The eyes and bill are black, the legs yellowish-green to olive-gray. The sexes are similar. Length: 19–21 cm

COMMON GREENSHANK *Tringa nebularia*

A large shorebird with a thick, slightly upturned bill. In non-breeding plumage the crown and hind neck are grayish streaked with brown; the rest of the upperparts are grayish, with brown streaks and bars and pale edges; there is an indistinct pale supercilium. The underparts are all white. The bill is blackish with a yellowish-green base, and the legs are greenish-yellow. In flight the upperwings are all gray, and there is a white, wedge-shaped patch from the back to the uppertail. The legs extend slightly beyond the tail. The sexes are similar. A common winter visitor, it is usually solitary and inhabits coastal wetlands, mudflats, grasslands, and paddy fields. Length: 30–34 cm

Pheasant-tailed Jacana

Bronze-winged Jacana

Common Sandpiper, non-breeding

Common Greenshank, non-breeding

MARSH SANDPIPER *Tringa stagnatilis*

A fairly common winter visitor to coastal wetlands, mudflats, and paddy fields. A delicate sandpiper with a needle-like straight bill and long legs. In non-breeding plumage the crown and upperparts are grayish-brown with narrow, pale fringes on the feather edges contrasting with a white face and supercilium. The underparts are mostly white, with some pale-brown streaking on the breast. The eyes and bill are black, and the legs are greenish-yellow. In flight a long white patch extends from the back to the uppertail, and the legs project beyond the tail. The sexes are similar. Forages for small invertebrates in shallow water, often in mixed flocks with other shorebirds. Length: 22–25 cm

WOOD SANDPIPER *Tringa glareola*

An uncommon to common winter visitor to mudflats, wetlands, and paddy fields. In non-breeding plumage the crown and upperparts are grayish-brown barred and spotted gray and white. The face and breast are brown, with pale streaking fading to whitish underparts. A pale supercilium extends behind the eye; there is a dark line over the lores. The eyes are dark brown with a narrow white eye ring. The bill is dark gray with a paler base. The legs are greenish-yellow. In flight the upperparts are dark with contrasting blackish flight feathers and a white rump; the underwing is whitish. The sexes are similar. The similar Green Sandpiper is darker and has a pale supercilium that does not extend behind the eye; the underwing is dark. Length: 19–21 cm

COMMON REDSHANK *Tringa tetanus*

A relatively long-legged shorebird with conspicuous red legs. A common winter visitor and migrant to coastal estuaries, wetlands, mudflats, mangroves, and paddy fields. The head, fore neck, and breast are brownish with whitish streaking extending to the flanks. The rest of the underparts are white. The upperparts are brownish-gray with narrow white fringing. The lores are black. The bill is black with an orange-red base. The eyes are black with a white orbital ring. In flight there is a broad white trailing edge to the wings; the lower back to rump is conspicuous white, contrasting with the dark mantle. The primary flight feathers are black. The uppertail is white with narrow dark barring, and the red feet extend just beyond the tail. The sexes are similar. Often in mixed feeding flocks with other shorebirds. Length: 27–29 cm

WHIMBREL *Numenius phaeopus*

A common winter visitor to mudflats, estuaries, beaches, and mangroves throughout. A medium-sized shorebird with a long, decurved bill, long legs, and a distinctive call. The head is blackish with a pale-brown crown stripe and supercilium. The rest of the upperparts are brown with paler fringing and spots. The underparts are pale brown, with brown streaking on the neck and breast. The eyes are brown; the bill is dark gray with a pink base to the lower mandible; the legs are bluish-gray. In flight the dark upperparts contrast with a white back and rump (the scarcer race *variegatus* lacks this). The sexes are similar. The call is a tittering, musical *ti-ti-ti-ti-ti* … usually given in flight. Length: 40–46 cm

Marsh Sandpiper, non-breeding

Marsh Sandpiper, non-breeding

Wood Sandpiper, non-breeding

Wood Sandpiper, non-breeding

Common Redshank, non-breeding

Whimbrel, non-breeding

EURASIAN CURLEW *Numenius arquata*

An uncommon to locally common winter visitor to and migrant through coastal areas, including beaches, mudflats, estuaries, and mangroves. A large, grayish-brown curlew with a remarkably long, decurved bill. The head and neck are buffish with coarse blackish-brown streaks. The rest of the upperparts are blackish-brown with paler-buff feather edges. The underparts are buffish; darker streaking on the breast fades into white underparts, with blackish spotting on the flanks. The bill is dark gray with a pink base. The sexes are alike. In flight the underwing coverts are whitish, and the white lower back and rump contrast with the dark upperparts. The somewhat similar Far Eastern Curlew can be easily differentiated in flight by its uniformly brown upperparts and pale-brown underwings. Length: 50–60 cm

BLACK-TAILED GODWIT *Limosa limosa*

A common winter visitor to and migrant through mudflats, lakes, marshes, and paddy fields. A fairly large shorebird with a long, straight, pinkish, black-tipped bill and a plain black uppertail. In non-breeding plumage the upperparts are plain dark gray and it has a prominent pale supercilium. The sexes are similar. In flight there is a long, white bar on the central upperwing, and the white uppertail coverts contrast with the all-black tail. The underwing is white with a black border. Length: 36–44 cm

BAR-TAILED GODWIT *Limosa lapponica*

Very like Black-tailed Godwit, but the bill is shorter and slightly upturned, the upperparts are more brownish with paler feather edges, and the legs are shorter. In flight there is no wing bar, the underwings are barred dark brown and white, the uppertail coverts are grayish, and the tail is barred gray and white. The sexes are similar. Like Black-tailed Godwit, it probes in the sand with its long bill for molluscs and worms. Often in small groups. A common coastal winter visitor and migrant. Length: 37–41 cm

CURLEW SANDPIPER *Calidris ferruginea*

A common coastal winter visitor and migrant. A medium-sized shorebird with a long, decurved bill. The upperparts are grayish with paler feather edges. There is a long, whitish supercilium and darker lores and ear coverts. The underparts are white with a gray wash on the sides of the breast. In flight it is recognizable by the narrow white wing bar and the white rump and uppertail coverts. The sexes are similar. Inhabits mudflats and paddy fields, where it probes the soft substrate for small invertebrates. Often in large, mixed shorebird flocks. Length: 18–23 cm

LONG-TOED STINT *Calidris subminuta*

A tiny, long-necked shorebird with a slender build, long legs, and a short bill. A fairly common winter visitor and migrant (though absent from northwest Vietnam, north Laos, and northwest Burma). Inhabits coastal wetlands, marshes, grasslands, salt pans, and paddy fields. Usually seen singly, sometimes in mixed shorebird flocks. The head and neck are streaked brown and buff, while the back and wings are dark brown with broad pale-brown feather edges. The streaky neck and upper breast grade into whitish underparts. The eyes are brown with a narrow white eye ring. The black bill is slightly down-curved. The sexes are alike. Length: 13–15 cm

Eurasian Curlew, non-breeding

Black-tailed Godwit, non-breeding

Bar-tailed Godwit, non-breeding

Curlew Sandpiper, non-breeding

Long-toed Stint, non-breeding

RED-NECKED STINT *Calidris ruficollis*

An uncommon winter visitor and migrant to coastal mudflats, estuaries, and sandy beaches. A tiny, dumpy shorebird with gray upperparts with broad, dark streaking in non-breeding plumage; there is a faint white supercilium, and the underparts are white with gray streaks on the sides of the breast. The eyes, bill, and legs are black. As it comes into breeding plumage the upperparts and breast take on a rufous tinge. In flight the gray back contrasts with black flight feathers and a white wing bar. The sides of the rump and tail are white. The sexes are alike. Often seen in large flocks. Actively probes and pecks in wet substrates for small invertebrates. Length: 13–16 cm

PINTAIL SNIPE *Gallinago stenura*

A common winter visitor throughout, found in swamps, marshes, wet grasslands, paddy fields, and vegetated stream banks. Very cryptic plumage—mottled buff, brown, and white upperparts, finely barred whitish underparts, and buff crown stripe, supercilium, and eye stripe—provides excellent camouflage. The very long, straight bill is yellowish with a black tip. The legs are short and the body dumpy. The sexes are alike. In flight there is no white trailing edge on the wing, differentiating it from the very similar Common Snipe, also common throughout. It feeds on insects, worms, and aquatic insects by probing waterlogged soil with its long bill. Relies on camouflage, but when approached flushes explosively from cover. Length: 25–27 cm

GLAREOLIDAE PRATINCOLES AND COURSERS

ORIENTAL PRATINCOLE *Glareola maldivarum*

A locally common winter visitor to open grasslands, rice paddies, and wetlands. A fairly small shorebird with long, pointed wings and a short, pointed, decurved bill. The crown and upperparts are uniform grayish-brown. A thin black line extends from the lores both to above the eye and down to the upper breast, encircling a buffish-yellow throat patch. The upper breast is grayish-brown grading to a rufous lower breast. The belly and undertail are white. At rest the long black primary flight feathers extend well beyond the tail. The eyes are brown with a pale eye ring. The bill is black with a bright red gape. The underwings are rich chestnut in color, with a dark-gray leading edge and flight feathers. The white rump contrasts with the black, deeply forked tail. The flight is buoyant and graceful. The sexes are similar. Mainly crepuscular and gregarious; feeds by catching insects on the wing. Length: 23–24 cm

SMALL PRATINCOLE *Glareola lactea*

Somewhat similar to Oriental Pratincole, but noticeably smaller and paler; the throat is paler, but there is no demarcated throat patch with a border. In flight it also looks quite different, as the grayish-brown upperparts contrast with a black trailing edge and flight feathers on the upperwing, and there is a broad white band in the center of the wing. The rump is white and the tail black, but less deeply forked. The sexes are similar. A locally common resident. Inhabits the margins of lakes, large rivers, and marshes. Length: 16–19 cm

Red-necked Stint

Pintail Snipe

Oriental Pratincole

Oriental Pratincole

Small Pratincole

BLACK-HEADED GULL *Larus ridibundus*

A locally common winter visitor to large rivers, lakes, and coastal areas. In non-breeding plumage the head and underparts are white, with a black spot behind the eye and dark smudges on the head. The upperparts are pale gray with black wing tips. In flight there is a white leading edge on the gray upperwing and black tips on the primaries. The uppertail is all white. The bill is red with a black tip, and the legs are dull red. The sexes are alike. The first-winter bird is similar but has a paler bill and duller legs. The wing coverts are mottled with brown, and there is a black band on the uppertail. As with many gulls, it is an opportunistic feeder, and very gregarious and noisy. Length: 35–39 cm

BROWN-HEADED GULL *Larus brunnicephalus*

A locally common winter visitor throughout most of the region. Inhabits large rivers and lakes, and coastal areas. Similar in appearance to Black-headed Gull, but larger, with a thicker bill and pale eyes. In non-breeding plumage there is a dark, smudged spot behind the eye and there may be some black smudges on the head. In flight it shows broader, rounded wings, with more broadly black-tipped primaries with a distinctive white patch near the tips of the wings. The sexes are alike. The first-winter bird is like first-winter Black-headed Gull but with black on the wing in flight. Length: 42–46 cm

GULL-BILLED TERN *Gelochelidon nilotica*

A fairly common winter visitor to coastal areas and sometimes paddy fields. This large tern has a distinctive, heavy, gull-like bill. In non-breeding plumage the head is white with a dusky black mask extending to the sides of the head. The upperparts are pale gray and the underparts white. In flight the tail is shallow-forked and the wing tips dusky black. The eyes, bill, and legs are black. In breeding plumage the head and nape are black. The sexes are similar. It usually forages low over water, plucking prey from the surface, and seldom plunges. Length: 35–43 cm

CASPIAN TERN *Hydroprogne caspia*

The largest tern, easily recognizable with its huge, black-tipped red bill. The head and short crest are black, contrasting with the white face and the sides of the neck. The upperparts are pale gray, with a white rump and black flight feathers. The short, forked tail is pale gray. The underparts are white. At rest the primary flight feathers extend well beyond the tail. In flight the underwings are white with blackish primaries. The eyes and legs are black. In non-breeding plumage the crown is finely streaked with white. The sexes are similar. A locally uncommon winter visitor to southern Burma and central Thailand south to Singapore; recorded in summer in Peninsular Malaysia and Singapore. Inhabits coastal mudflats, sandbars, and estuaries. Length: 48–55 cm

Black-headed Gull, non-breeding

Brown-headed Gull, non-breeding

Gull-billed Tern, non-breeding

Gull-billed Tern, non-breeding

Caspian Tern, non-breeding

WHISKERED TERN *Chlidonias hybrid*

A common winter visitor to and migrant through coastal areas and inland wetlands at sea level, including paddy fields. In non-breeding plumage the forehead is white, grading into a white-streaked black crown and nape. A black streak extends through the eye to the crown. The rest of the upperparts are pale gray; the underparts are white; the eyes and bill are black, the legs blackish-red. In breeding plumage the forehead and crown are black, and the bill and legs are red. The sexes are alike. Usually seen in flocks foraging low over water. Length: 25–26 cm

GREAT CRESTED TERN *Thalasseus bergii*

A large, stocky tern with a robust yellow bill and dark-gray upperparts. In breeding plumage the forehead is white with a black cap that has a shaggy crest. The face, neck, and underparts are white. In flight the underwings are white with gray tips on the outer primaries. In non-breeding plumage the forehead and crown are white, the hind crown and crest black with dull white streaks. The bill is duller. The sexes are alike. The juvenile is duller than the adult; the upperparts are brownish with white fringing. Found in coastal habitats throughout the region. Can be seen flying rapidly with deep, slow wing beats, hunting fish by plunge-diving. Often sits on sandbars or floating debris in shallow estuaries. Length: 43–53 cm

COLUMBIDAE PIGEONS AND DOVES

ORIENTAL TURTLE-DOVE *Streptopelia orientalis*

A large, bulky, pinkish-brown dove similar in appearance to Spotted Dove but darker and shorter-tailed, with rufous scalloping on the plumage of the lower back and wings, and a gray rump. The patch on the side of the neck is striped black and white. The sexes are alike. Found in open forests, secondary growth and scrub, cultivated areas, and gardens. A locally common resident and uncommon winter visitor throughout, except in the Malay Peninsula. Length: 33 cm

RED COLLARED-DOVE *Streptopelia tranquebarica*

A common resident in cultivated areas and dry open woodlands throughout, except in the Malay Peninsula, where there is a feral population. A distinctive small dove with brownish-red plumage; has a gray head, a black half-collar on the back of the neck, black flight feathers, and a gray rump and tail. The female is similar to the male, but the plumage is mostly brownish-gray. Often seen perched on dead trees and power lines. Feeds on seeds on the ground with a bustling, shuffling walk. Length: 24 cm

Whiskered Tern, non-breeding

Great Crested Tern, non-breeding

Great Crested Tern, non-breeding

Oriental Turtle-Dove

Red Collared-Dove

SPOTTED DOVE *Streptopelia chinensis*

A medium-sized pigeon with a conspicuous, white-spotted black collar and a long, graduated tail with broad white outer tail tips that are conspicuous in flight. The head is pale gray; a narrow black line runs from the bill to the eye. The underparts are pinkish-brown. The upperparts are scalloped brown and buff, with gray outer wing coverts. The eyes are orange, the bill black, and the legs pinkish-red. The sexes are alike. Forages on the ground, feeding mostly on seeds, usually in pairs or small groups. The distinctive voice is a mellow *ku-koo-koor*. A bird of secondary forests, open woodlands, and cultivated areas, as well as parks and gardens, it is a common resident throughout. Length: 31–33 cm

BARRED CUCKOO-DOVE *Macropygia unchall*

A large, long, and slender brown dove with a long, graduated tail. The male's head is pale brown; the rest of the upperparts are rich rufous-brown with narrow black barring and a metallic-green wash on the back of the neck; the underparts are buffish-brown. The female is similar, with dense dark barring on the underparts. A common inhabitant of broad-leaved evergreen and semi-evergreen forests throughout. The voice is a distinctive, deep *woo-hoo* with the emphasis on the second note, repeated at intervals. Feeds unobtrusively in the forest canopy on fruits. Flight is powerful and direct, with strong wing beats. Resident. Length: 40 cm

EMERALD DOVE *Chalcophaps indica*

A medium-sized, ground-dwelling dove with a purplish-brown head; the underparts contrast with distinctive metallic-green wings. In the male the forehead and crown are grayish-white, and there is a small white patch on the shoulder; the lower back and rump are grayish-black with pale-gray bars; the flight feathers and tail are black. In flight the underwings are chestnut. The eyes are brown, and the bill and legs are pinkish-red. The female is duller and browner overall; the white on the head is restricted to the forehead; no white patch on the shoulder. This species inhabits primary and secondary forests, plantations, and gardens, where it forages on the ground, feeding on seeds, fallen fruit, and small invertebrates. When disturbed, it flies low, very fast, and direct. Voice is a slow, low-pitched, mournful *wup-woooo*. A common to uncommon resident throughout. Length: 23–27 cm

PINK-NECKED GREEN-PIGEON *Treron vernans*

A medium-sized, colorful green-pigeon found in lowland forests, plantations, and gardens, mostly in coastal areas from southern Vietnam, Cambodia, and peninsular Thailand south to Singapore. The male is green on the back and wing coverts. The tertials are edged yellow, and the flight feathers are black. The head is gray, the nape to upper breast purplish-pink, fading into burnt orange on the breast. The lower breast to belly is pale yellowish-green with broad yellow edges on the flanks and thighs. The vent is chestnut. The gray uppertail has a broad black terminal band. The eyes and legs are reddish, the bill pale gray with a greenish cere. The female is duller than the male, with an all olive-green head and neck and all yellowish-green underparts. Eats only fruit, feeding mostly on figs and *Melastoma* fruits. Usually found in small flocks. A common resident. Length: 23–28 cm

Spotted Dove

Barred Cuckoo-Dove

Emerald Dove

Pink-necked Green-Pigeon

ASHY-HEADED GREEN-PIGEON *Treron phayrei*

This common and widespread green-pigeon is very similar to Thick-billed Green Pigeon, but the male has a thinner, grayish bill, a yellowish tinge on the throat and an orange wash on the breast; it lacks the prominent eye ring of Thick-billed. The female is also similar to the female Thick-billed but similarly lacks the eye ring. An uncommon to locally common resident in evergreen and deciduous forests in Burma, Thailand (though absent from the center and south), Cambodia, Laos, and southern Vietnam. Length: 27 cm

THICK-BILLED GREEN-PIGEON *Treron curvirostra*

A medium-sized green-pigeon with a distinctive broad red cere and a broad greenish-blue eye ring in both sexes. The male has a pale-gray forehead and crown; the face and neck are grayish-green. The maroon back and wings contrast with the yellowish-green underparts; the thighs and vent show broad white edging, and the undertail coverts are chestnut. The female is like the male, but the back and wings are olive-green. An inhabitant of lowland forests, mangroves, plantations, parks, and gardens; usually found in flocks; often noisy and conspicuous. Feeds on small to medium-sized fruits. A common resident throughout, except Singapore. Length: 25–31 cm

GREEN IMPERIAL-PIGEON *Ducula aenea*

A large pigeon with all-gray head, neck, and underparts, contrasting with metallic green back, wings, and tail. The undertail coverts are chestnut. The eyes and legs are reddish, the bill gray with a red base. The sexes are alike. An inhabitant of lowland and hill forests, usually seen singly or in small groups. Eats fruit and feeds in the crowns of large trees. Flight is strong and direct, often high above the forest canopy. Performs a spectacular "roller coaster" display flight in which the bird flies steeply upward before stalling and suddenly dropping into a steep dive. Partially nomadic in response to fruiting events. The song is a loud, deep, growling *ka-koo*. A scarce to locally common resident throughout. Length: 42–48 cm

MOUNTAIN IMPERIAL-PIGEON *Ducula badia*

A very large, robust pigeon with deep-purplish upperparts and pale gray on the underparts. The head and neck are pale gray, the hind neck pale pink, and the throat white. The iris is grayish-white with a dark-red eye ring. The sexes are alike. The dark-red bill has a pale tip, and the legs are dull red. The juvenile is duller, with brownish upperparts. Inhabits lowland to montane forests, but is chiefly found in mountains up to 2,500 meters. Often found in small groups; feeds mostly on fruit. Has a very distinctive, low-pitched, growling vocalization. A locally common resident throughout. Length: 40–50 cm

Ashy-headed Green-Pigeon

Thick-billed Green-Pigeon

Green Imperial-Pigeon

Green Imperial-Pigeon

Mountain Imperial-Pigeon

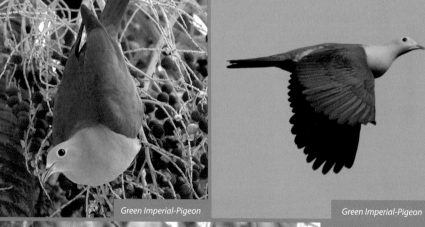

LARGE HAWK CUCKOO *Hierococcyx sparverioides*

A large cuckoo with a very hawk-like appearance. The adult has a slaty-gray face, crown, and hind neck; the throat is streaked white and dull rufous. The rest of the underparts are white with distinct, thin black bands. The upperparts are dull brown, and the long tail is barred with irregular broad black bands. The iris is yellow with a lemon-yellow eye ring; the bill is black and the feet are yellow. The sexes are alike. This is a bird of lowland primary and secondary forests, mangroves, and gardens, usually below 800 meters. Generally solitary; most often seen in the forest canopy. This brood parasite lays its eggs in the nests of species similar to their own size, such as laughingthrushes, whistling thrushes, and spiderhunters. Feeds on small invertebrates, bird eggs, and some fruits. Call a very distinctive, loud, 2-note *pi peewer*, repeated over and over, increasing in pitch and volume and sounding increasingly frantic. Outside of the breeding season it is usually silent. A locally uncommon resident in Burma, northern and western Thailand, Cambodia, Laos, and northern Vietnam; elsewhere it is a winter visitor and migrant. Length: 38–40 cm

MOUSTACHED HAWK CUCKOO *Hierococcyx vagans*

A small, hawk-like cuckoo. The adult has a dark-gray crown. The face shows a broad black moustache from the eye down the sides of the throat; the cheeks and throat are whitish, and it has a streaky, rufous-brown collar. The upperparts are dark brown, with lighter brown bars on the wings. The tail is barred gray and black with white tips. The underparts are white with clean, dark streaks. The dark eye is surrounded by a yellow eye ring, and the bill is black; the legs are yellow. The sexes are alike. A lowland specialist, it is usually found below 500 meters, but sometimes up to 900 meters, in primary and secondary evergreen forests. It is very shy and solitary, and known to feed on large insects. The song is a monotonous, 2-note *kang ko*; because of its secretive nature the song is the usual method of detection. An uncommon to rare resident in south Burma and the Malay Peninsula. Length: 26 cm

PLAINTIVE CUCKOO *Cacomantis merulinus*

A common to abundant resident throughout the region. This species is found in a variety of habitats—from lowland primary forests to plantations, parks, and gardens up to 1,000 meters; it is very often seen and heard. The adult male has a gray head and breast with pinkish underparts, and a grayish-brown back and tail; the undertail is barred black and white. Sometimes the female is like the male, but is most often seen in the "hepatic" form, with upperparts barred rufous and brown, and whitish underparts with narrow, dark-brown bars. Both male and female have a red iris with a black eye ring; the bill is black with a yellow base, and the feet are bright yellow. The juvenile is similar to the hepatic female, but the head is paler rufous, with more pronounced streaking, and the iris is brown. An active feeder, it forages in the tree canopies for insects and small fruits. Song is a plaintive *fi fi fi fi fi ... fi-fi-fi ... fififi...*, accelerating, then tapering off at the end. A brood parasite, it has been recorded laying its eggs in the nests of prinias, tailorbirds, and spiderhunters. Length: 18–23 cm

Large Hawk Cuckoo

Moustached Hawk Cuckoo

Plaintive Cuckoo

LITTLE BRONZE CUCKOO *Chrysococcyx minutillus*

This small cuckoo has a bright, glossy-green crown and upperparts. In the adult male the forehead and supercilium are dull white; a dark line runs from the lores through the dark-red eye to the sides of the head. The rest of the underparts are dull white with greenish-brown bars. The tail is bronze with white tips and broad black-and-white bands underneath. The iris is deep red, there's a red eye ring, and the bill and feet are gray. The female is like the male but not as glossy, and the iris is brown. The juvenile bird is duller on the upperparts, with less-distinct barring on the underparts. This brood parasite utilizes the nests of small birds such as sunbirds. The song given in the breeding season is an evenly pitched, 4- or 5-note *tiu tiu tiu tiu*. This cuckoo is found in secondary forests, mangroves, parks, and gardens up to 250 meters. A locally common to uncommon resident in the Malay Peninsula, Cambodia, and southern Vietnam. Length: 15–16 cm

FORK-TAILED DRONGO-CUCKOO *Surniculus dicruroides*

This cuckoo looks remarkably like a small drongo; it has glossy-black plumage and a slightly forked tail that is broad at the tip, but a typical cuckoo bill. The undertail coverts and undertail show narrow white barring. The iris is deep red, while the bill and feet are black. The sexes are alike. The juvenile is browner, with white spots on the body and wing coverts. Occurs in a variety of habitats and can often be found in clearings and forest edges in primary and secondary lowland forests up to 1,300 meters. Feeds on insects, spiders, and small fruits in the first canopy. The flight is typical of cuckoos—smooth and direct, unlike the dipping and looping flight of drongos. The song is a characteristic 5- to 7-note *pi pi pi pi pi* on an ascending scale, sometimes transcribed as *one, two, three, four, five, six, seven*. Can often be heard singing at night in the breeding season. A brood parasite, it lays its eggs in the nests of babblers, bulbuls, ioras, shrikes, and other birds. A fairly common resident throughout. Length: 24 cm

ASIAN KOEL *Eudynamys scolopaceus*

The distinctive call of this bird is one of the most characteristic sounds of tropical Asia. The territorial call suggests the name—a strident, piercing *ko-el* in a series of 5–10 notes increasing in pitch, volume, and pace. It also gives a distinctive, rapid secondary call that can be described as *wook kawook kawook kawook kawook*, each note rising and falling. The territorial call can often be heard at night as well as in the daylight hours. The adult male is glossy black all over, with a long, rounded tail; the iris is crimson, and the bill is pale green. The female is quite different—brown with rufous-buff streaks, bars, and spots; the underparts are buff with fine brown barring. The iris of the female is also red, while that of the similar-looking juvenile is brown. Mainly inhabits secondary forests, plantations, gardens, and parks, usually in coastal areas and at low elevations, but is sometimes found up to 1,200 meters. It feeds in tree canopies on small fruits, especially figs, and some insects. Known hosts of this brood parasite include crows and mynas. For a large, noisy bird it can be surprisingly inconspicuous and is more often heard than seen. A common to fairly common resident throughout the region. Length: 42–44 cm

Little Bronze Cuckoo, female

Little Bronze Cuckoo, male

Fork-tailed Drongo-Cuckoo

Asian Koel

BIRDS | **CUCULIDAE** CUCKOOS

BLACK-BELLIED MALKOHA *Phaenicophaeus diardi*

A large, long-tailed, non-parasitic cuckoo. The adult has dark-gray upperparts with glossy, dark-green wings. The tail is black with a green gloss and white tips. The iris is pale blue, and there is an extensive velvety, crimson facial skin patch around the eye. The sexes are alike. The juvenile is similar to the adult, but the iris is brown. This quite adaptable species can be found in lowland forests, mangroves, and plantations up to 1,000 meters. It is easily confused with the very similar-looking Chestnut-bellied Malkoha, which is found in the same range but has chestnut on the belly and a more orange-red facial skin patch. Black-bellied Malkoha is a quite secretive bird; it creeps around in thick vegetation in the mid-story and canopy, feeding on insects. The call is a short, inconspicuous, frog-like *kwak*. A locally uncommon resident in the Malay Peninsula. Length: 38 cm

GREEN-BILLED MALKOHA *Phaenicophaeus tristis*

The largest malkoha in the region, this long-tailed non-parasitic cuckoo has a grayish head and underparts with dark streaks, greenish-gray upperparts, and broad white tips on the tail, the latter very conspicuous on the undertail. The dark iris is surrounded by a bright red facial skin patch bordered with a white edge. The bill is green. The sexes are alike. The juvenile is duller overall, with a grayish bill. This common resident is found in a variety of habitats, from primary forests to secondary growth, plantations, and gardens up to 1,600 meters. As is typical of malkohas, it forages for insects in thick vegetation in a rather secretive manner. Length: 52–59 cm

RAFFLES'S MALKOHA *Phaenicophaeus chlorophaeus*

The smallest malkoha in the region. The male and female differ markedly. The male is rufous, with a black, finely barred tail that is tipped white. The iris is brown and surrounded by a pale-blue, bare facial patch. The female has a gray head, throat, and mantle; the back and wings are rufous, as is the tail, which is tipped white with a black subterminal band. This bird inhabits lowland forests and overgrown gardens up to 1,100 meters. It is usually solitary or in pairs and can be quite secretive as it forages in very thick vegetation in search of insects. The voice is a very distinctive, cat-like *kyar kyar-kyar-kyar-kyar*. It is a fairly common resident in southern Thailand and the Malay Peninsula. Length: 32 cm

GREATER COUCAL *Centropus sinensis*

A large, distinctively black-and-chestnut, long-tailed bird that inhabits forest edges, secondary growth, grassland, paddy fields, and gardens up to 1,500 meters. A common resident throughout the region. The body is glossy black all over, with chestnut wings and back. The iris is crimson; the bill and feet are black. The sexes are similar, although the female tends to be somewhat larger. The juvenile is blackish brown on the body with whitish bars and spots; the back and wings are rufous-barred black. These birds are often found in pairs. Feeds on a variety of prey—from small mammals, nestlings, and eggs to lizards, frogs, and large insects. Often seen clambering around in low vegetation or hopping on the ground. Usually hesitant to fly; when it does, the flight is laboured and slow. The call is a low-pitched, slow-paced *boo boo boo* … Length: 47–52 cm

Black-bellied Malkoha

Green-billed Malkoha

Raffle's Malkoha

Greater Coucal

BARN OWL *Tyto alba*

The adult has a heart-shaped white facial disc fringed with black, and golden-buff upperparts with black and brown spots and white tips on the scapulars and coverts. The underparts are white with black spots on the breast; the long legs are densely feathered to the toes. The sexes are alike. Strictly nocturnal, it feeds on mice, rats, and other small mammals. The flight is buoyant with legs dangling. Inhabits cultivated areas and open country up to 1,200 meters. An uncommon to locally common resident throughout. Length: 34–36 cm

ORIENTAL BAY OWL *Phodilus badius*

A very unusual and secretive owl, with a pale-pinkish, squarish facial disc and ear-like projections above the eyes. There is chestnut feathering around the eyes; the outer edge of the disc is fringed with brown. The crown, nape, and underparts are buffy speckled with black and brown. The rest of the upperparts are chestnut with black and buff spots. The powerful legs and feet are feathered to the toes. The sexes are alike. A very secretive, nocturnal inhabitant of primary and secondary forests and plantations up to 1,200 meters, it feeds on small vertebrates and insects, hunting from a perch in dense vegetation. The call is an ethereal, piercing 3- to 6-note *hwee hwee*. Nests in hollow trees and stumps. An uncommon to rare resident almost throughout. Length: 23–33 cm

STRIGIDAE OWLS

COLLARED SCOPS-OWL *Otus lettia*

This small owl occurs in two forms. One, a grayish variant, has a broad pale supercilium and obvious ear tufts; the upperparts are grayish-brown with buff markings; below it is whitish with fine vermiculations and streaks. The other variant has a buffish supercilium and collar, and is dark buff on the underparts. The sexes are alike. The juvenile is usually lighter, with darker, finer markings. Generally a common resident throughout, found in forests, woodlands, gardens, and plantations up to 2,200 meters. Length: 23 cm

ORIENTAL SCOPS-OWL *Otus sunia*

A tiny owl that occurs in two forms. The gray morph has a grayish-brown back with dark-brown streaks and bars, and bold white scapular marks; the underparts are paler with dark streaks; the eyes are yellow. The rufous morph has an overall rufous tone with black streaks on the crown and a whitish belly with dark streaks. The sexes are similar, but the female is slightly larger. An uncommon resident and winter visitor throughout the region; inhabits forests, mangroves, and plantations up to 2,000 meters. Strictly nocturnal, inconspicuous, and shy. Feeds on insects and small vertebrates in the mid-story. The voice is a clear and distinctive *tonk tonk tonk-tonkkk*. Length: 19 cm

Barn Owl

Oriental Bay Owl

Collared Scops-Owl

Oriental Scops-Owl

BUFFY FISH OWL *Ketupa ketupu*

A large, relatively conspicuous owl with long ear tufts held horizontally. The plumage is mostly a rich buffy rufous, with blackish-brown streaks on the head and underparts; the upperparts are dark brown with rufous streaks and spotted with brown and buff. The pale-gray legs are unfeathered. The sexes are alike. This owl frequents forested areas near water, including river and lake edges, estuaries, paddy fields, and mangroves, up to 800 meters. Nocturnal and sometimes crepuscular, it is usually seen hunting from a perch near water. Feeds on aquatic insects, crustaceans, and vertebrates. During the day it roosts in dense foliage in trees and palms. Among a variety of vocalizations are a long, wailing scream and a melancholy *pop pop* … A locally fairly common resident from southern Burma through Thailand, Cambodia, central and southern Vietnam, and Peninsular Malaysia. Length: 45–47 cm

COLLARED OWLET *Glaucidium brodiei*

A tiny, diurnal owl with a large, rounded head. Occurs in two morphs—rufous and gray, a distinction that occurs in the color of the upperparts. The head is gray with buffish spots; the supercilum and lores are white, and there is a white patch on the throat. There is a distinctive, eye-shaped yellow-and-black pattern on the back of the head. The upperparts are rufous brown or grayish-brown, barred buff and dark brown; the upper breast is brown barred with grayish-white. The rest of the underparts are white with broad, brown streaks. It lacks ear tufts. The sexes are alike. The species is often active during the day and is sometimes mobbed by small birds. Feeds on small vertebrates and large invertebrates. Inhabits evergreen forest up to 3,100 meters. The call, often heard during the daytime, is a rhythmic, piping *poo pu-pu poop* … ; the cadence varies regionally. A fairly common resident throughout. Length: 16 cm

ASIAN BARRED OWLET *Glaucidium cuculoides*

This small owl is a common resident of Burma, Thailand, Cambodia, Laos, and Vietnam. It has a large, rounded head with no ear tufts. The plumage is a dull brown with numerous pale bars; it shows a pale line in the center of the chest, and the belly and flanks are white with broad brown streaks. The sexes are alike. The juvenile is similar, but has less distinct barring; the crown is speckled. Inhabits open woodlands and forests, and is often seen perched during the day, when it hunts for large invertebrates and small vertebrates. Often detected by its call, as it vocalizes often during the daytime; typical call is a descending trill that gradually increases in volume. Length: 20–23 cm

BROWN WOOD OWL *Strix leptogrammica*

A very large owl; the buffish-rufous facial disc has a broad, dark-brown edge and rings around the eyes. It lacks ear tufts. The upperparts are chestnut with dark-brown barring; the throat and upper breast are rufous brown with fine dark bars; the rest of the underparts are buffish-white with fine brown bars. The legs are feathered to the toes. The sexes are alike. The juvenile is a much paler buffish color with fine rufous barring on the wings. Inhabits dense primary lowland and hill forests up to 2,600 meters. Strictly nocturnal. Roosts in the densest parts of tall trees. The call is a deep, mellow *boo boo-boo-booo*. An uncommon resident throughout, except for central Thailand, southern Vietnam, and Singapore. Length: 45–55 cm

Buffy Fish Owl

Collared Owlet

Asian Barred Owlet

Brown Wood Owl

GOULD'S FROGMOUTH *Batrachostomus stellatus*

This strange species belongs to a group of small to medium-sized, highly cryptic, nocturnal birds with extraordinarily wide, heavy bills and ornate head plumes. The adult male has dark-brown upperparts that are sometimes rufous, with a buffish supercilium and a narrow white collar; there are bold white spots on the wing coverts and scapulars. The eyes are yellow, and the legs pinkish. The female may have brownish eyes. Inhabits evergreen forest up to 200 meters. and is strictly nocturnal. Feeds on large insects; from low perches it pounces on its prey in thick vegetation and on the ground. Very difficult to detect due to its excellent camouflage and secretive nature. A scarce resident in south Thailand and Peninsular Malaysia. Length: 21–25 cm

CAPRIMULGIDAE NIGHTJARS AND ALLIES

GREAT EARED-NIGHTJAR *Lyncornis macrotis*

A large-headed, nocturnal or crepuscular insectivorous hunter with a very wide mouth for catching insects on the wing. The largest of the nightjars in the region. The upperparts are brown, speckled buff and cinnamon, with pale scapulars; its ear tufts are conspicuous (hence the name). A white collar divides the dark-brown face and breast. The sexes are alike. At dusk this bird hawks over open areas and forest clearings as it feeds on flying insects. Its distinctive flight has slow, leisurely wing beats. The call, usually given on the wing, is a pleasant, ringing *pit pee-yuw* … During the day it roosts very inconspicuously on the ground or on horizontal branches. A fairly common resident throughout, except for the southern part of the Malay Peninsula. Length: 40 cm

LARGE-TAILED NIGHTJAR *Caprimulgus macrurus*

The head is grayish-black and broadly streaked blackish, with a white malar stripe and a large white throat patch. The plumage of the upperparts is very cryptic— dark gray with blackish-brown lines and spots, and buff-and-white spots on the wing coverts. In flight it shows a white spot on the wings and broad white spots on the outer tips of the tail. The female is similar to the male but is more rufous overall; in flight the wing and tail spots are buffy. Found in open forest, secondary growth, and cultivation up to 2,000 meters. Its behavior is typical of nightjars: it is nocturnal and feeds by hawking for arboreal insects over open areas. The call is a loud, hollow-sounding *chonk chonk chonk* … A common resident throughout the region. Length: 31–33 cm

SAVANNA NIGHTJAR *Caprimulgus affinis*

A small nightjar with brownish-gray upperparts, vermiculated and speckled whitish and pale brown. The underparts are tawny brown, finally barred, and speckled grayish; there is a small white patch on the side of the throat. In flight it shows large white spots on the wings and white outer tail feathers. The female is more rufous; in flight, shows buffish-brown spots and no white in the tail. This nightjar is most likely to be found near towns and in cultivated areas, as well as in swamps and open forests in lowland areas. Nocturnal, it hawks and sallies with buoyant, acrobatic flight; roosts on the ground. The voice is a short, squeaky, repeated *kweek kweek*. A common resident throughout most of the region. Length: 25 cm

Gould's Frogmouth

Great Eared-Nightjar

Large-tailed Nightjar

Savannah Nightjar

BIRDS | **APODIDAE** SWIFTS

GLOSSY SWIFTLET *Collocalia esculenta*

A tiny swiftlet with distinctive glossy blue-black upperparts and a grayish breast that contrasts markedly with the white belly. In flight the underwings are pale grayish. The sexes are alike. The juvenile is duller, with pale fringing on the underparts. Can be seen in a variety of habitats, from forested areas and wetlands to human habitation up to 1,900 meters. A gregarious aerial insectivore often seen in very large numbers. The voice is a rasping twitter. An uncommon resident in south Burma and Thailand through Peninsular Malaysia. Length: 10 cm

HIMALAYAN SWIFTLET *Aerodramus brevirostris*

A slightly larger swiftlet with long, backswept, boomerang-like wings and all blackish-brown plumage, a grayish rump band, and a relatively deeply notched tail. The sexes are alike. Found in forested and open areas up to 3,100 meters. The voice is a low twitter. A gregarious arboreal insectivore, it hunts using echolocation. The nest is a tiny cup constructed from saliva and vegetable material attached to walls in caves. Forms large nesting colonies in caves, which it leaves during the day to hunt, returning at night. The flight is strong and acrobatic, on gliding wings. A locally common to uncommon resident and winter visitor throughout. Length: 13–14 cm

ASIAN PALM SWIFT *Cypsiurus balasiensis*

A small, all brownish-gray swift with long wings and a long, forked tail, usually held closed. The underparts are pale gray, with a paler throat and dark underwing coverts. The sexes are alike. In the juvenile the tail is shorter and less deeply forked. Gregarious, often in large flocks. Feeds on arboreal insects with highly acrobatic flight. Nests and roosts in palm trees, in the lowlands. The voice is a high-pitched trill. A common to uncommon resident throughout. Length: 11–12 cm

HEMIPROCNIDAE TREESWIFTS

WHISKERED TREESWIFT *Hemiprocne comata*

A fast-flying aerial insectivore with long, curved wings and very short legs and feet. Treeswifts often perch upright on horizontal branches. Whiskered Treeswift has a glossy dark-blue crown with a short crest and red ear coverts; its extraordinary facial plumage has white lores, a long narrow supercilium, a distinctive long, white line from the chin to the moustache that extends behind the head, and white whiskers. The body is chocolate brown with glossy blue wings and tail, and a white rump and vent. The female is similar, but the ear coverts are black. At rest the very long wings extend just beyond the tip of the tail. Typically treeswifts sally out from perches in clearings to catch arboreal insects. Inhabits open areas in primary and secondary lowland forests up to 1,200 meters. The call is a rapid, squeaky, high-pitched *pit-pit-pit-pit* … A common to uncommon resident in southern Burma and Thailand to Peninsular Malaysia. Length: 15–16 cm

Glossy Swiftlet

Himlayan Swiftlet

Asian Palm Swift

Whiskered Tree Swift

RED-NAPED TROGON *Harpactes kasumba*

This large trogon is an inhabitant of primary lowland forests; it perches upright in shady areas in the mid-story on horizontal branches from which it gleans insects from nearby foliage. It is quiet and unobtrusive, usually solitary or in pairs. In the adult male the head and breast are black with a thin white breast band and a conspicuous red neck stripe; the rest of the underparts are bright red. The back and tail are cinnamon, with black wing coverts vermiculated white and a broad black tail tip. The iris is reddish-brown surrounded by a broad blue facial patch; the bill is also blue. The female is quite different: olive-brown on the breast, head, and back; the rest of the underparts and rump are yellowish-brown; the bare parts are duller. The song is a slow, sad-sounding, 5- to 8-note *pau pau pau pau pau* … A locally uncommon resident in south Thailand and Peninsular Malaysia. Length: 31–34 cm

SCARLET-RUMPED TROGON *Harpactes duvaucelii*

A small trogon with habits typical of the family. The adult male has an entirely black head, with a bright-blue-skinned patch above the eye and a bright-blue bill and gape. The mantle and back are cinnamon brown, as is the tail with a black tip and black outer feathers. The wing coverts are vermiculated black and white, the underparts and rump bright scarlet. The female is mostly plain olive-brown, with a washed-out pale-pink belly and duller vermiculations and bare parts. This trogon can be found in primary and secondary forests, usually only up to 400 meters. It tends to be more active at lower levels than other trogons and is usually solitary. The song is a distinctive, rapid "bouncing ping-pong ball" series of 18–20 short, rapid notes that starts slow, then accelerates markedly. A locally fairly common resident in south Burma, south Thailand, and Peninsular Malaysia. Length: 23–26 cm

ORANGE-BREASTED TROGON *Harpactes oreskios*

The adult male has an olive-green head and upper breast; the back and uppertail are cinnamon brown, while the wings are black with fine white vermiculations. The underparts are a bright orange yellow; the undertail is mostly white. The iris is brown with blue orbital skin, the bill cobalt blue. The female is like the male, but duller with brownish-olive head and upperparts. Inhabits the middle to upper story of evergreen forests up to 1,200 meters. A common but inconspicuous resident in most of the area, except northern and western Burma, central Thailand, Singapore, and northern Vietnam. As with most trogons, it is usually detected by its vocalizations; the song is a fairly rapid, monotone, 5-note *tu-tau-tau-tau-tau*. Length: 26–31 cm

Red-naped Trogon, male

Scarlet-rumped Trogon, male

Orange-breasted Trogon, female

COMMON KINGFISHER *Alcedo atthis*

A common winter visitor and uncommon resident throughout, frequenting lakes, ponds, streams, mangroves, and ditches up to 1,800 meters. The crown, malar stripe, and wings are turquoise blue with dark-blue barring and a rufous loral spot and ear coverts. A white neck stripe divides the turquoise-blue head and bright-blue back. The chin and throat are white, the underparts rufous. The bill is black with a reddish gape. The female differs in having a reddish-orange lower mandible. The juvenile is similar but duller, with a grayish breast band and a white tip to the black bill. Length: 16–18 cm

BLUE-EARED KINGFISHER *Alcedo meninting*

A small kingfisher; the upperparts are ultramarine. The back and uppertail are brilliant turquoise blue, while the underparts are rufous. There is a rufous spot in front of the eye and a white patch on the side of the neck. The throat is white. In the male, the bill is black with a reddish base. The female differs in having an orange-red base to the mandible. An inhabitant of streams and rivers in lowland forests and mangroves up to 900 meters. It is solitary, sometimes seen flying very rapidly and directly along stream edges. Feeds by diving steeply into water to catch aquatic invertebrates and small fish. The call is a short, high-pitched *seet* uttered in flight. A fairly common resident throughout. Length: 15–16 cm

BLACK-BACKED DWARF-KINGFISHER *Ceyx erithaca*

This uncommon resident and winter visitor is a tiny, brightly colored, fast-moving kingfisher. The back and wings are black with bright-blue feather edges; the crown is lilac-rufous; the underparts are bright orange-yellow with a white throat. A blue patch on the ear coverts has a white spot below on the side of the neck. The sexes are alike. The juvenile is duller, with white underparts and paler bill. Very similar Rufous-backed Kingfisher, an uncommon resident in the Malay Peninsula, has a lilac-rufous back and mantle. Black-backed Dwarf-Kingfisher is found near small streams and ponds in evergreen forests up to 900 meters, it feeds alone, predominantly on insects and aquatic invertebrates as well as small vertebrates. Often sits quietly on a low perch and takes prey from the water, foliage, or the ground. The voice, usually given in flight, is a short, shrill, rather inconspicuous *seet* …. Length: 12–14 cm

BANDED KINGFISHER *Lacedo pulchella*

An unobtrusive, spectacularly plumaged forest kingfisher. The adult male has a rather long, shaggy, bright-blue crown with narrow black-and-white bands. The forehead and sides of the face are brown, contrasting with a white throat; the rest of the underparts are rufous fading to white. The upperparts are strikingly banded silvery-blue and black. The iris is brown and surrounded by a red eye ring; the long bill is bright red. The female is banded black and rufous on the head and upperparts; the underparts are buffish-white with narrow black bars on the breast and flanks. This secretive bird is usually detected by its calls. The song is a long, mournful series of *tu-wee* notes, somewhat reminiscent of the calls of a cuckoo. Usually solitary or in pairs in dense forest away from water. Hunts for large invertebrates, small fish, and lizards from perches in the mid-story. An uncommon resident in southern Burma, Thailand, Peninsular Malaysia, Cambodia, Laos, and southern Vietnam. Length: 20 cm

Common Kingfisher

Blue-eared Kingfisher

Black-backed Dwarf-Kingfisher

Banded Kingfisher

STORK-BILLED KINGFISHER *Pelargopsis capensis*

A very large kingfisher with a huge red bill and a conspicuous bright-blue rump in flight. The adult has a buffish-orange head, neck, and underparts, with a white throat. In some races the crown is darker. The back wings and tail are greenish-blue. In flight the bright-blue rump contrasts markedly with the darker blue-green of the upperparts. The iris is brown, and the legs are bright red. The sexes are alike. The juvenile has a dusky-brown band of vermiculations on the breast. This locally common resident is always found near water; favors rivers and lakes near evergreen forests, deciduous forests, and mangroves up to 800 meters. Feeds on fish, crustaceans, and small vertebrates, hunting from a concealed perch over water. Usually solitary, but forms pairs during the breeding season, when it becomes very territorial. The song is a piercing, plaintive 2-note whistle; the call is a rapid, raspy *kek kek kek* … of 10–15 notes. A locally common resident throughout. Length: 37–40 cm

WHITE-THROATED KINGFISHER *Halcyon smyrnensis*

A large kingfisher and common resident throughout the region in cultivated areas, secondary growth, and other open habitats up to 1,500 meters. The most distinctive feature is the white throat, which contrasts with the chocolate-brown head and underparts. The upper back is also brown; the wing coverts are brown and black, while the wings and lower back are turquoise blue. The large bill is bright red. In flight large white patches at the base of the primaries are visible. The sexes are alike. The immature is duller than the adult, with some vermiculations on the throat and breast. The territorial call is a repeated whinnying *ki-pipipipipi* on a descending scale. Length: 27–30 cm

COLLARED KINGFISHER *Todiramphus chloris*

A medium-sized, greenish-blue kingfisher with a white collar and underparts. There is a white spot in front of the eye, and the bill is black with a pale-pink lower base. The sexes are alike. The juvenile is duller, with greener upperparts and buffish underparts. A familiar bird of coastal woodlands, mangroves, paddy fields, plantations, and gardens, usually in the lowlands. The voice is a loud, slow-paced, and sharp *kek kek kek* of 2–6 notes, as well as a rolling *pri-pri-pri-pri* … Very similar Sacred Kingfisher, recorded only as a vagrant to Singapore, is smaller, with a buff loral spot and a buffish wash on the underparts. Collared Kingfisher is a noisy and conspicuous bird that feeds on crustaceans, insects, and small fish and vertebrates. A common resident throughout the region. Length: 23–26 cm

Stork-billed Kingfisher

White-throated Kingfisher

Collared Kingfisher

RED-BEARDED BEE-EATER *Nyctyornis amictus*

An extraordinary, brightly colored forest dweller with a heavy, decurved bill. The overall color is bright green, with a shaggy red throat. The undertail is bright orange yellow with a black terminal band. The iris is orange. In flight the underwings are rufous. In the male the crown and forehead are pinkish, and there is a narrow fringe of blue feathers at the base of the bill. The female is similar, but the forehead is red. The juvenile is all-green, except for a yellow undertail and blue feathers at the base of the bill. Found in primary and secondary lowland forest up to 1,500 meters. This sedentary bird hunts for arboreal insects from leafy perches in the mid-story. The call is a very unusual, throaty, and gruff *kwek-kwek-kwek-kwe-kwe-kwek*. An uncommon resident in south Burma, west and south Thailand, and Peninsular Malaysia. Length: 32–34 cm

BLUE-BEARDED BEE-EATER *Nyctyornis athertoni*

Similar in shape and size to Red-bearded Bee-eater, but with shaggy blue throat and breast. The crown is green, and the forehead is blue. The belly and vent are pale yellow with broad green streaks, and there is sometimes a blue wash on the green upperparts. The square-tipped tail is yellow underneath with only a narrow black terminal band. The sexes are alike. The juvenile is browner on the underparts. Resident throughout the region except in the south, where it is replaced by Red-bearded. Found in a variety of woodland habitats up to 2,200 meters. Length: 33–37 cm

GREEN BEE-EATER *Merops orientalis*

The smallest bee-eater in the region, the adult has a coppery rufous crown and mantle, black eye mask, and pale bluish-green throat with black gorget. The rest of the underparts are pale green, with a gray undertail. The upperparts are green. The sexes are alike. The juvenile is similar but duller overall and lacks the central tail feathers. Found in open country and cultivation, scrubland, and dunes up to 1,600 meters. Usually in flocks. Behavior is typical of the genus. A common resident throughout much of the region. Length: 19–20 cm

BLUE-TAILED BEE-EATER *Merops philippinus*

A large, greenish bee-eater with an orange throat and a bluish rump and tail. In the adult the crown is bronzy green; it has a black mask bordered blue above and below. The black bill is long and decurved. The tail has elongated central feathers. The iris is deep red. The sexes are alike. The juvenile is like the adult but duller, bluer; the throat is buffish-rufous. Inhabits a variety of open habitats, from cultivation to borders of large rivers and mangroves up to 2,800 meters. Often in flocks; feeds on flying insects, especially bees, wasps, and dragonflies. Nests in colonies, excavating burrows in sandy soils. The call is a short, liquid *bip bip* … Locally common and resident, though sometimes a winter visitor, throughout. Length: 23–24 cm

Red-bearded Bee-eater

Blue-bearded Bee-eater

Green Bee-eater

Blue-tailed Bee-eater

CHESTNUT-HEADED BEE-EATER *Merops leschenaulti*

A small bee-eater with a chestnut crown and mantle, and a pale-yellow throat bordered by a narrow black gorget. The rest of the underparts are pale yellowish-green. The wings and uppertail are bluish-green; the rump is pale blue. Lacks elongated central tail feathers. The sexes are alike. The juvenile is like the adult but duller overall. A local resident and winter visitor throughout. Found in a variety of forested habitats up to 1,800 meters. Usually in small flocks; in flight utters a soft, bubbling *prrt prrt* call that is repeated. Length: 22 cm

CORACIIDAE ROLLERS

INDIAN ROLLER *Coracias benghalensis*

This large, striking roller is common throughout the region except for the southern tip of Peninsular Malaysia. The crown and wings are turquoise, the upperparts olive-brown. The throat and breast are lilac, grading into a pale-blue belly and undertail. In flight the wings and tail show strikingly contrasting pale-blue and turquoise patterns. The sexes are alike. The juvenile is browner, with less turquoise on the crown. Found in open habitats, cultivated areas, and scrubby areas throughout the region, up to 1,500 meters. Hunts by dropping from a high, exposed perch onto the ground to find prey items such as mice, lizards, and large invertebrates. Length: 32–34 cm

DOLLARBIRD *Eurystomus orientalis*

A stocky, large bird with a broad, short, red bill and conspicuous white circles on the wings in flight. The head is blackish-blue, the throat purple. The body is mostly greenish-blue with purplish-blue flight feathers and tail. The iris is brown with a narrow, dark-red eye ring, the bill and legs red. The sexes are alike. The juvenile is similar to the adult but duller; the wing patches are smaller, and the bill is mostly black with a yellowish lower mandible. This bird can often be seen perching conspicuously in dead trees and on power lines in a variety of habitats, but especially on forested riverbanks, along forest edges, and on plantations. The voice is a short, raspy *chak* repeated slowly. Usually solitary or in pairs; feeds mainly on lizards and large insects caught on the wing. Flight is slow and leisurely on long wings. A common resident and winter visitor throughout. Length: 25–28 cm

UPUPIDAE HOOPOES

EURASIAN HOOPOE *Upupa epops*

A unique and colorful bird with a very long, slender, decurved bill and an extraordinary large, erect, black-spotted pink crest. The broad wings are striped black and white. The head, mantle, and underparts are pink. The sexes are alike. The juvenile is duller, with shorter crest and bill. Typically seen, usually singly or in pairs, foraging for insects and other invertebrates on the ground, using the long bill to probe and dig in leaves, dirt, and crevices. The eponymous call is a mellow *oo-po-po* or *po-po*. Inhabits open country, scrublands, open woodlands, cultivation, and gardens up to 1,500 meters. A locally common to uncommon resident and winter visitor. Length: 27–32 cm

Chestnut-headed Bee-eater

Indian Roller

Dollarbird

Eurasian Hoopoe

ORIENTAL PIED HORNBILL *Anthracoceros albirostris*

A small black-and-white hornbill. The male has glossy-black upperparts and breast; the rest of the underparts are white. The tail is black with a broad white tip. In flight the black wings have a broad white trailing edge. The iris is dark red, surrounded with a pale-blue skin patch. The bill is pale yellow, with a black base on the lower mandible and a cylindrical casque (a hollow outgrowth of the upper mandible of the bill). There is a pale-blue skin patch on the neck at the base of the bill. The female is smaller, with a less-pronounced casque. A locally common resident in all types of forested habitat throughout. Usually seen in large flocks; feeds mainly on fruit, but also insects, spiders, and small vertebrates. The call is a harsh, loud, yelping *kek kek kuck kuck* … Length: 55–60 cm

BLACK HORNBILL *Anthracoceros malayanus*

An uncommon resident of evergreen forest in the southern part of the region. The adult male is relatively small, with black plumage and broad white tips on the outer tail feathers, and sometimes with a broad white to gray stripe over the eye to the nape. The iris is red, and the bare facial skin is black. The bill and casque are all-yellow. The adult female is smaller; the bill and casque are brown and gray, and the casque is less pronounced. The bare orbital skin and submoustachial patch are dull pink. Usually in pairs; mainly feeds on large fruit, but also insects and small vertebrates. Length: 60–65 cm

GREAT HORNBILL *Buceros bicornis*

A very large, unmistakable bird with a huge yellow bill and a casque with some black markings. The plumage is mostly black with a white neck and vent, and a white tail with a broad, black central band. In flight the underwings show a broad white band across the greater coverts and a white trailing edge. The white parts may be variably stained yellow. The iris is red, the eye surrounded with black orbital skin. The female is smaller and lacks any black markings on the casque; has white eyes with red orbital skin. Usually in pairs or small groups in primary evergreen or mixed deciduous forests. A frugivore, dependent on large fruiting trees. The voice is a very large, deep *gok* leading up to a loud barking given by duetting pairs. A locally common resident throughout, except Singapore. Length: 119–122 cm

RHINOCEROS HORNBILL *Buceros rhinoceros*

A large, mostly black hornbill with a very distinctive casque. The upperparts are black with a white rump and a white tail with a black central band. The throat to belly is black, the undertail coverts white. In the male the iris is red with a black eye ring; the bill and casque are yellow, stained orange and red by preen oil, with black at the base of the casque to the base of the bill. The casque is cylindrical with a narrow black stripe on the sides and strongly curved upward at the tip. There is considerable individual variation. The female is smaller, with a white iris and red eye ring. Usually in male-female pairs, sometimes in small flocks outside the breeding season. Flies in flaps and glides, usually with the male leading. Feeds mainly on figs and other fruits, but also insects and small vertebrates. A locally uncommon resident in the south of the region. Length: 91–122 cm

Oriental Pied Hornbill

Great Hornbill

Black Hornbill

Rhinoceros Hornbill

BUSHY-CRESTED HORNBILL *Anorrhinus galeritus*

A small hornbill found in the southern part of the region. The only hornbill with no white in the plumage. The adult male is blackish-brown with a greenish gloss; a loose crown and nape feathers form a crest; the tail is grayish-brown with a broad blackish terminal band. In flight the underwings are all-dark. The iris is red, surrounded by a pale-blue, bare skin patch. The black bill with a low, inconspicuous casque has a pale-blue skin patch at the base. The female is similar but smaller, with a reddish-brown iris and a yellowish bill. Found in primary and secondary lowland forests up to 1,200 meters. Usually in noisy flocks of up to 20 birds. Feeds predominantly on figs but also large insects and small invertebrates. Forages in dense forest below the canopy. A locally common resident in southern Burma, Thailand, and the Malay Peninsula. Length: 60–65 cm

WREATHED HORNBILL *Rhyticeros undulatus*

A widespread, locally common species in much of the region. Usually in pairs or small flocks; inhabits evergreen and mixed deciduous forests. The male is mostly black, with a chestnut crown and nape; the face to the upper breast are white. The short tail is white. In flight the underwings are all-black. Iris red, with red orbital skin; bill yellow with ridges at base; low casque with reddish-brown ridges. The prominent gular pouch is yellow with a black central stripe. The adult female is smaller; head and neck are all-black, the eye ring pinkish-red; the gular pouch is blue. The voice is a loud, raucous, grunting *uk-guk*. Distinctive, very loud whooshing wing beats in flight. Length: 75–85 cm

MEGALAIMIDAE ASIAN BARBETS

COPPERSMITH BARBET *Psilopogon haemacephala*

An unmistakable species found throughout the region. The male's territorial *tonk tonk* call, reminiscent of a smith's hammer, is familiar to all. A small barbet with a red forehead, yellow patches above and below the eye, a black eye stripe, and a submoustachial stripe. The throat is yellow with a red band below; the rear of the crown and sides of the neck are black. Upperparts green; underparts pale green with dark green streaks. The sexes are alike. The juvenile is duller, with no red in the plumage. Inhabits deciduous forests, mangroves, open woodlands, plantations, parks, and gardens up to 900 meters. A common resident. Length: 17 cm

BLUE-EARED BARBET *Psilopogon australis*

One of the smallest barbets, a common resident throughout much of the region. Distinguished by its black forehead, red cheek patches, blue throat with narrow, black lower border, and blue ear coverts with red patches above and below. The bill is relatively small. The female has a duller head pattern. The race in Peninsular Malaysia has black ear coverts with more extensive red patches. Inhabits evergreen and deciduous forests, secondary growth, and mangroves up to 1,500 meters. Forages in the canopy, where it feeds mainly on fruit, especially small figs. The voice is a rapid, incessant, 2-note *tu-tuk* repeated over and over. Length: 16–17 cm

Bushy-crested Hornbill

Wreathed Hornbill

Bushy-crested Hornbill

Coppersmith Barbet

Blue-eared Barbet

GREEN-EARED BARBET *Psilopogon faiostricta*

Pronounced streaking on the head and neck, green cheeks and ear coverts, and green underparts. The bill is smaller and dark. The narrow orbital skin is gray. The sexes are alike. The territorial call of the male is a loud, ringing *took-took-a-rook* repeated endlessly. A common resident in Laos, Cambodia, and Vietnam. Inhabits evergreen and deciduous forests and open woodlands. Length: 24–27 cm

LINEATED BARBET *Psilopogon lineata*

A common resident except in southern Peninsular Malaysia and northern Vietnam. The head and underparts are brownish with paler streaks. The back, wings, and tail are bright green. The thick bill is yellowish with conspicuous bristles at the base. The dark eye has a broad area of yellow orbital skin. The sexes are alike. The territorial call is a loud, far-carrying, mellow *koo-ko*. Inhabits deciduous forests, open woodlands, and plantations up to 1,200 meters. Excavates nest holes in tree trunks or large branches. A specialist frugivore usually found in the forest canopy. Length: 27 cm

GOLDEN-WHISKERED BARBET *Psilopogon chrysopogon*

A common bird of lowland rain forests and hill forests in the southern part of the region. Large, with a large, strong, blackish bill. The overall plumage is green, with a complex head pattern: forehead yellow, crown, and lores red, broad black face mask bordered blue behind, and broad malar area yellow; the throat is gray below, bordered blue. The sexes are alike. Eats large figs and berries, and some insects. The call is introduced by a rapid *tu-tu-tu-tu* … followed by a resonant, mellow *tuu-tu-tu-tup* that increases in frequency and is often uttered endlessly. Excavates nest cavities in arboreal termite nests and rotting tree trunks. Length: 30 cm

BLACK-BROWED BARBET *Psilopogon oorti*

Found in the montane forests of the Malay Peninsula, this colorful barbet is mostly green with blue cheeks, red on the forehead above the bill, yellow crown and throat, and a prominent black brow. The sexes are alike. The very similar Indochinese Barbet, from eastern Cambodia, southern Laos, and central to southern Vietnam, was previously treated as the same species. Both species excavate nest holes in trees for breeding and feed mostly on fruits, although they are known to eat invertebrates. The voice is a monotonous and endlessly repeated *took-tk-tarook*. Length: 21–22 cm

PICIDAE WOODPECKERS

SPECKLED PICULET *Picumnus innominatus*

A tiny, olive-green woodpecker with spotted underparts and a short, triangular bill. The male has a barred orange-and-black forehead; the head and upperparts are olive, with a broad black-and-white supercilium and moustachial stripe. The throat is white, the rest of the underparts boldly spotted black. The adult female is similar, but the forehead is olive-green. Usually solitary or in pairs; may join mixed feeding flocks. Forages inconspicuously in dense undergrowth; eats insects and insect larvae. Often detected by the sound of its loud, persistent tapping when foraging. Found in evergreen and deciduous forests, secondary growth, bamboo. An uncommon resident throughout, except Singapore. Length: 8–10 cm

Green-eared Barbet

Lineated Barbet

Black-browed Barbet

Golden-whiskered Barbet

Speckled Piculet

RUFOUS PICULET *Sasia abnormis*

A tiny woodpecker with olive-green upperparts and rufous underparts; appears almost tailless. In the male the forehead is yellow; the forehead of the female is rufous. The iris and fleshy eye ring are red. The bill is gray with a yellow lower mandible. The juvenile is dull olive-green all over. A common resident in the southern part of the region, found in evergreen and bamboo forests, and plantations up to 1,400 meters. Usually seen singly or in pairs; often joins mixed feeding flocks. Feeds on insects, especially ants and insect larvae, which it gleans from bark, bamboo, rattan, and deadwood. Often detected by the sound of its loud, persistent tapping. The voice is a squeaky, high-pitched, 1- or 2-note *seet seet*. Length: 9 cm

SUNDA WOODPECKER *Dendrocopos moluccensis*

A small, brown-and-white woodpecker with heavy white barring on the back and brown streaking below. The crown is brown; the rest of the head and face shows a brown-and-white-striped pattern. The male has a red spot at the sides of the hind crown; the female lacks this feature. Juvenile duller and browner. Usually solitary or in pairs, found in secondary forests, coastal woodlands, mangroves, parks, and gardens in the lowlands. The voice is a trilled, high-pitched, rapid series of *ki-ki-ki-ki* notes. A locally common resident in Peninsular Malaysia and Singapore. Length: 13 cm

GRAY-CAPPED WOODPECKER *Dendrocopos canicapillus*

A widespread and common species of evergreen and deciduous forests, mangroves, and plantations up to 1,800 meters. A small blackish-brown and white woodpecker with orange-washed underparts. The forehead to hind neck is gray, with red spots at the sides of the crown; the female lacks this feature. A brown stripe from the eye to the sides of the neck is bordered above by a broad white line. The juvenile is darker and duller overall, underparts more heavily streaked. Solitary or in pairs. Forages in small branches of large trees and bushes, gleaning insects and small invertebrates from bark, lichens, and leaves. The voice is a sharp, relatively soft, high-pitched *kik*. A common resident throughout. Length: 13–15 cm

WHITE-BELLIED WOODPECKER *Dryocopus javensis*

One of the largest woodpeckers in the region. The male is black with a white rump, lower breast, and belly, and a crimson crest and broad crimson malar stripe. The iris is yellow. In the female, the crimson on the head is confined to the crest. The juvenile is duller and browner and has a gray iris. A bird of all types of forests, but more common in primary forests. The behavior is noisy and conspicuous; usually seen in pairs. Eats a variety of insects, which it gleans from the trunks and limbs of tall trees and fallen timber. The territorial call is a short, loud, far-carrying yelp. A locally uncommon to common resident in much of the region. Length: 37–43 cm

Rufous Piculet

White-bellied Woodpecker

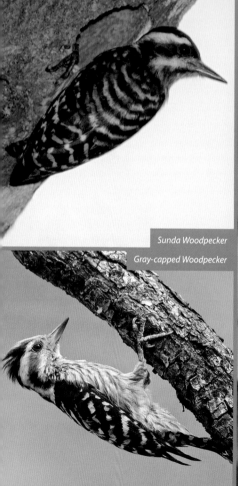

Sunda Woodpecker

Gray-capped Woodpecker

BANDED WOODPECKER *Picus miniaceus*

An uncommon to common resident in the southern part of the region. Predominantly reddish plumage with a yellow nape and narrow, dark-brown barring on buff underparts. The crown, face, and throat are brownish-red. The back is barred olive and buff, and the wings are red. The female is browner on the head, with buff spots on the cheeks. Similar Crimson-winged Woodpecker has greener unbarred upperparts and all-green underparts with little barring. An inhabitant of primary and secondary lowland and hill forests, mangroves, plantations, and gardens up to 1,250 meters. Relatively unobtrusive, usually solitary or in pairs. An active forager in dense vegetation, where it pecks, gleans, and probes predominantly for ants and ant larvae. The call is a short, explosive *kau*. Length: 23–26 cm

GREATER YELLOWNAPE *Picus flavinucha*

A widespread and common species throughout the region, with many varied subspecies. All are quite large with a pronounced yellow rear crest, olive-brown crown, black-streaked white throat, and olive-green body. In most races the male has a yellow throat or moustachial stripe, which is chestnut or lacking in the female. The juvenile has duller plumage. An inhabitant of evergreen and deciduous forests up to 2,750 meters. The call is a loud, sharp, 2-syllable *kiaow*. Usually solitary or in pairs. Resident. Length: 31–35 cm

COMMON FLAMEBACK *Dinopium javanense*

A large woodpecker with a distinctive black-and-white head pattern, yellow-green upperparts, and bright-red rump. The feathers of the underparts are buffish-white with narrow black fringes. The male has a crimson crown and crest, differing from the female, whose crown and crest are black with white flecks. The juvenile is like the adults, but with more brown on the breast. Favors more open habitats; found in deciduous forests, mangroves, gardens, and plantations up to 800 meters. Usually encountered in pairs. An uncommon to common resident throughout. Length: 28–30 cm

RUFOUS WOODPECKER *Micropternus brachyurus*

A medium-sized, all-rufous woodpecker with a short crest and black bars on the upperparts. The male has a crimson patch below and behind the eye; the female lacks red on the head. The black throat is scaled with chestnut and buff. The juvenile is less heavily barred. An inhabitant of all types of primary and secondary forests and woodlands, including plantations. Often encountered in pairs; feeds mainly on ants and termites; forages at all levels from ground to upper canopy. A very active bird with bounding and dipping flight. A common resident throughout. Length: 25 cm

Banded Woodpecker

Common Flameback

Greater Yellownape

Rufous Woodpecker

BUFF-RUMPED WOODPECKER *Meiglyptes tristis*

A small, short-tailed woodpecker with dense buff-and-black barring all over, except for a plain buff rump. The bars on the wings are more widely spaced. The male has a crimson malar stripe. The juvenile is duller and more broadly barred overall, with darker underparts. The similar Buff-necked Woodpecker, with which it often associates, is larger, has a prominent buffish neck patch, and lacks the plain rump. Found in primary and secondary evergreen forests and plantations up to 800 meters; favors forest edges, clearings, and gaps. Often encountered in mixed feeding flocks; feeds mainly on ants and other insects in dense foliage in the mid-story. A common resident in the southern part of the region. Length: 17–18 cm

GREATER FLAMEBACK *Chrysocolaptes lucidus*

A very large woodpecker, similar in appearance to Buff-rumped Woodpecker. Differs from similar Common Flameback in having a longer and larger bill, a split black malar stripe enclosing a white patch, black lores, and white on the hind neck. The female has a black crown and crest with white spots. The juvenile is duller, with more olive upperparts. Usually in pairs; feeds on caterpillars, wood-boring larvae, and ants; obtains these by hammering and pecking on the wood of large trees and snags. The voice is a rapid, staccato, 5- to 10-note *kikikikikiki* … A common resident in deciduous and evergreen forests, mangroves, and plantations. Length: 29–32 cm

MAROON WOODPECKER *Blythipicus rubiginosus*

A common resident of the southern part of the region. A medium-sized, purplish-brown woodpecker with a distinctive long, yellow bill. The head and underparts are olive-brown; the sides of the neck, the nape, and the malar stripe (sometimes lacking) are red; the upperparts are purplish-brown with indistinct brown-and-buff barring on the flight feathers. The female lacks any red on the head. An inhabitant of primary and secondary rain forests and hill forests, mangroves, plantations, and gardens up to 1,500 meters. Found singly or in pairs; feeds mainly on beetles and larvae, foraging in the lower mid-story by hammering and pecking. The voice is a short, sharp, and squeaky *kik* that sounds a bit like the squeak of a child's toy. Length: 23 cm

BAY WOODPECKER *Blythipicus pyrrhotis*

Very similar to Maroon Woodpecker, but found only at high elevations in the southern part of the region. It is larger, with more and blacker barring on the wings and back, and no malar stripe. The female lacks red on the neck. The juvenile is darker, with pale streaks on the head and more prominent barring above. Found in evergreen and deciduous forests up to 2,700 meters. The voice is a maniacal-sounding, descending laugh *keeek-keek-keek-keek-keek*. A common resident, except in central Burma, central to south Thailand, and Singapore. Length: 27–29 cm

Buff-rumped Woodpecker

Greater Flameback

Maroon Woodpecker

Bay Woodpecker

ORANGE-BACKED WOODPECKER *Reinwardtipicus validus*

A rather large woodpecker found in the southern part of the region. The adult male has a short, dark-red crest and an orange-brown face; the nape to lower back is white, blending into an orange rump. The wings and tail are blackish-brown with 3–5 broad, reddish-brown bars on the flight feathers. The underparts are dark red. The long, straight bill is gray with a yellow lower mandible. The female is similar to the male, but the crest is dark brown, the face and underparts grayish-brown, and the rump white. Found in lowland rain forests up to 700 meters. Nearly always in pairs; a deadwood specialist foraging mostly in the mid-story for beetle larvae, termites, ants, and other insects. An uncommon resident. Length: 30 cm

GREAT SLATY WOODPECKER *Mulleripicus pulverulentus*

The largest woodpecker in the region (and, with the probable extinction of Ivory-billed and Imperial Woodpeckers in the Americas, in the world), this species is unmistakable. It is all-gray with a long, thin neck, and a very long, gray-and-yellow bill and buffish throat. The male has a prominent red cheek patch. An inhabitant of primary evergreen, deciduous, and mangrove forests up to 1,000 meters. Often encountered in noisy family groups of up to 7 or 8 birds. The voice is a loud, far-carrying whinny *wit-wit-wit-wee*. Forages in emergent trees, gleaning prey from bark in the upper story; requires large live trees for foraging on bee, ant, and termite nests. A locally uncommon to common resident throughout. Length: 45–51 cm

FALCONIDAE FALCONS AND CARACARAS

COLLARED FALCONET *Microhierax caerulescens*

One of the world's smallest raptors, this tiny falcon is about the same size as a House Sparrow. The upperparts are all-black, with a prominent white collar at the nape and a white face with a black mask. The throat is rufous; the upper breast is white fading into rufous on the lower breast and belly. The sexes are alike. The juvenile bird has a rufous wash on the forehead and supercilium. Found in deciduous forests and clearings in evergreen and mixed forests, where it feeds on large insects, small birds, and lizards by darting out from exposed perches. It frequently returns to the same perch over prolonged periods; has a distinctive habit of bobbing the head when perched. A common resident in Burma, Thailand, Cambodia, Laos, and southern Vietnam. Length: 15–17 cm

EURASIAN KESTREL *Falco tinnunculus*

A fairly common winter visitor throughout the region, this falcon is a familiar sight in all types of open habitats. It flies relatively low on long, pointed wings with shallow wing beats; often hovers when looking for its prey—small mammals, lizards, and large insects. The adult male has a gray head and tail with a black terminal band; the upperparts are rufous spotted with black. The underparts are buffish with black streaks. The female is larger than the male, with a pale-brown head streaked blackish. Both have a distinctive black moustachial stripe. The juvenile is similar to the female but more boldly marked. Length: 32–39 cm

Orange-backed Woodpecker

Great Slaty Woodpecker

Collared Falconet

Eurasian Kestrel

ROSE-RINGED PARAKEET *Psittacula krameri*

An all-green parrot with a narrow, rose-colored ring around the neck and a black throat. There is a pale-blue wash on the back of the head and a short black line on the lores. The bill is red with a blackish lower mandible. The female is also bright green, but lacks the neck ring and black lores. The tail is also shorter. Usually found in open forests and cultivated areas, such as gardens, parks, and plantations. Usually seen in large, fast-moving flocks; is easily detected by its loud, raucous calls. A locally common resident in Burma, introduced in central Thailand and Singapore. Length: 40–42 cm

BLOSSOM-HEADED PARAKEET *Psittacula roseate*

The male is predominantly bright green with a pink head, and a narrow, black collar and throat; there is a small maroon patch on the shoulder, and the long, pointed tail is blue. The bill is orange with a black lower mandible. The female has a gray head and lacks the black collar. Found in deciduous forests, open broad-leaved forests, secondary growth, and parks up to 900 meters. A locally common resident throughout, except in the Malay Peninsula. Gregarious; feeds in the treetops on fruits, buds, and nectar. Length: 30–36 cm

RED-BREASTED PARAKEET *Psittacula alexandri*

A large, bright-green parrot with a blue-gray head and rose-colored breast. The head pattern consists of a thin black line from the cere to the eye, and a broad black band from the chin to the sides of the neck. In the male the upperparts are bright green with a yellowish wash on the wing coverts. The long tail is blue with green outer feathers. The female has a paler-gray head; the underparts are duller pink; the tail is shorter; the large bill is bright red, and the legs and iris gray. Found in all types of lowland forest, where it is often noisy and conspicuous. A highly gregarious species; feeds on fruits, seeds, and flowers; nests in tree hollows. The call is a loud and raucous *kak … kak … kak*, often given in flight. A locally common resident except in south Thailand, Malaysia, and Singapore. Length: 33–38 cm

VERNAL HANGING PARROT *Loriculus vernalis*

A tiny, bright-green parrot with a bright-red back and uppertail. The male shows turquoise on the throat, while the female lacks this feature. The bill and legs are bright red; in flight the underwing is turquoise with green coverts. It is found in broad-leaved forests up to 1,500 meters. Usually solitary or in pairs; has a very fast, direct flight. Gives a distinctive, high-pitched squeak in flight. Feeds on nectar or small fruits; often hangs upside down. Nests in small tree hollows. A locally common resident throughout most of the region. Length: 13–15 cm

Rose-ringed Parakeet

Blossom-headed Parakeet

Red -breasted Parakeet

Vernal Hanging Parrot

BLACK-AND-RED BROADBILL *Cymbirhynchus macrorhynchos*

A striking black-and-red broadbill with a remarkable blue-and-yellow bill. The forehead and chin to upperparts are black, with a prominent white bar on the wings. The underparts and rump are deep red, with a black band across the breast. The iris and legs are dark blue. The sexes are alike. The juvenile is duller, with a maroon wash on the throat and rump and reduced white on the wings. Found in primary and secondary lowland rain forests, usually near moving water, up to 300 meters. Usually in pairs; unobtrusive; feeds on insects and other small invertebrates as well as small fruits. A locally uncommon to common resident in the southern part of the region as well as Cambodia and southern Vietnam. Length: 21–23 cm

LONG-TAILED BROADBILL *Psarisomus dalhousiae*

A remarkable bright-green bird with a long tail and unusual head markings. The adult has a black, helmet-like head pattern with a blue patch on top of the crown and a yellow spot on the sides of the nape; face and throat bright yellow. The back, wings, and underparts are bright green with bright-blue primary feathers and tail. In flight shows white patches at the base of the primary feathers. The sexes are alike. Usually in flocks; inhabits broad-leaved evergreen forests up to 2,000 meters. Rather inconspicuous and usually detected by its unusual call, which is a high, piercing series of *puiii* whistles. Forages in the mid-story for insects. A locally uncommon to common resident, except in Central Thailand, southern Vietnam, and Singapore. Length: 23–26 cm

BLACK-AND-YELLOW BROADBILL *Eurylaimus ochromalus*

A small, colorful broadbill. A common resident in the southern part of the region, including southern Burma. The head and upperparts are black, with a conspicuous white collar and prominent bright-yellow markings on the wings and rump. A narrow black breast band divides the collar and pink underparts. The iris is yellow, the bill bright blue with black edges, and the legs pink. The female is largely like the male, but the breast band is incomplete in the middle. The juvenile is browner, with less-distinct yellow markings, and it lacks the breast band. Inhabits primary and secondary lowland forests up to 900 meters. Sometimes in small groups; feeds predominantly on insects; sits quietly in the mid-story, flying out to glean prey from nearby foliage. The song is a remarkable, frantic, cicada-like trill. Length: 13–15 cm

DUSKY BROADBILL *Corydon sumatranus*

The largest broadbill. The adult has dark-brown plumage with a buffish throat and upper breast, and a small white patch at the base of the primaries, markings that are prominent in flight. Bare pink skin surrounds the eyes and lores; the huge, wide bill is pink with a gray tip. The sexes are alike. The juvenile is brown all over, except for a reduced white patch on the wings. Inhabits evergreen and semi-evergreen forests up to 1,200 meters. Gregarious and noisy; usually in groups of up to 10 in the mid-story and canopy. The voice is a penetrating, harsh, and squeaky *kweer kweer kweer* … An uncommon resident throughout, except for central and northern Burma, central Thailand, and northern Vietnam. Length: 24–28 cm

Black-and-red Broadbill

Long-tailed Broadbill

Black-and-yellow Broadbill

Dusky Broadbill

MALAYAN BANDED PITTA *Pitta irena*

A medium-sized pitta with distinctive yellow, black, blue, and brown markings. The adult male has a black crown with a broad, bright-yellow supercilium extending to bright orange on the nape, and a broad black mask bordered below by a white throat and yellow sides of neck. The rest of the underparts and tail are deep blue with narrow black bars on the breast, and narrow black-and-rufous markings on the sides of the chest. The back is brown; the wing coverts are black with broad white markings. The female is similar, but with narrow black-and-buff barring on the underparts and not as bright orange on the nape. The juvenile is duller, with buff spots and streaks on the breast and supercilium. An inhabitant of primary and secondary rain forests up to 600 meters. Very elusive and usually detected by its call—a short, loud *pwow*. An uncommon resident in south Thailand and Peninsular Malaysia. Length: 21–24 cm

BAR-BELLIED PITTA *Pitta elliotii*

A locally common resident in suitable habitat of Vietnam, Laos, and Cambodia; just extends into neighboring parts of Thailand. Inhabits broadleaf evergreen, semi-evergreen, and mixed deciduous forests up to 800 meters. Plump, with a short bill, a short tail, and longish legs. The male has a very bright green crown and upperparts with a bluish wash on the wings and blue tail; a broad black mask extends to the sides of the neck. The throat and upper breast are a washed-out green; the rest of the underparts are boldly barred bright yellow and black, with a deep-blue patch on the belly. The legs are pinkish. The female is similar, but the crown and throat are warm buffish-brown, and there is no blue on the underparts. The song is a loud, whistled *hwee-hwu*. As is typical of the genus, it hops on the ground with an upright posture, feeding in leaf litter on insects, earthworms, and other small invertebrates. Length: 19–21 cm

HOODED PITTA *Pitta sordida*

A small, green pitta with a distinctive black hood and a chestnut-brown crown. The upperparts are bright emerald green with a turquoise-blue patch on the wings. The underparts are paler green, with a bright-red patch on the belly and undertail. The tail is black. In flight shows large white patches on the wings and a blue rump. The sexes are alike. The juvenile is duller with brownish underparts. Found in primary and secondary forests, mangroves, and plantations. A locally common resident and breeding visitor over much of the region. Length: 16–19 cm

VANGIDAE VANGAS, HELMETSHRIKES, AND ALLIES

LARGE WOODSHRIKE *Tephrodornis virgatus*

A bulky, grayish bird with a large, hooked bill and a prominent black face mask. The upperparts are dark gray with a white rump; the underparts are white with a grayish wash on the breast. The female is duller, with a browner mask and a buffish wash on the breast. The juvenile is heavily spotted and barred buff. A common resident throughout in all types of primary and secondary forested habitats. Usually in pairs or small groups; feeds on large insects, hawking from exposed perches or gleaning foliage; often joins mixed feeding flocks. Length: 18–22 cm

Malayan Banded Pitta, female

Malayan Banded Pitta, male

Bar-bellied Pitta, female

Bar-bellied Pitta, male

Hooded Pitta

Large Woodshrike

COMMON WOODSHRIKE *Tephrodornis pondicerianus*

Similar to Large Woodshrike, but smaller, with a whitish supercilium above the mask and a darker tail with white outer feathers. The sexes are alike. A common resident of drier woodlands and open country in Burma, Thailand, Cambodia, Laos, and central and southern Vietnam. Often in small flocks. Feeds on insects and small fruits in the mid-story, sometimes descending to the ground. The song is an accelerating trill *whi whi whi whi whee*. Length: 14–17 cm

BAR-WINGED FLYCATCHER-SHRIKE *Hemipus picatus*

A small black-and-white insectivorous bird, common in all types of primary and secondary forests throughout the region. The adult male is glossy black on the upperparts, with a white rump and a prominent long white bar on the wings; the underparts are smoky gray; paler whitish on the cheeks. In the very similar female, the male's black parts are replaced with brown. The juvenile has buffish fringing on the feathers, giving it a scaled appearance. Often joins mixed feeding flocks. Sallies and gleans for insects in the mid-story. The call is a high-pitched, staccato *sittitititi* … Length: 12–15 cm

ARTAMIDAE WOODSWALLOWS

ASHY WOODSWALLOW *Artamus fuscus*

An aerial insectivore with a broad-based, pointed bill, large head, and triangular pointed wings. Overall ashy gray with brownish-washed underparts from breast to undertail coverts and a grayish-blue bill. In flight the underwings are paler. The sexes are alike. The juvenile is browner, with buffish tips on the feathers, and has paler underparts with indistinct barring. Found in open and cultivated areas with scattered trees up to 2,000 meters. A common resident throughout. Gregarious; catches insects in flight with its feet and eats them on the wing. Often wags its fanned tail from side to side when perched. Length: 16–18 cm

AEGITHINIDAE IORAS

COMMON IORA *Aegithina tiphia*

A familiar and widespread resident of parks and gardens, plantations, open woodlands, and mangroves. A small, arboreal, leaf-gleaning insectivore with a slender, pointed bill. The adult male has a yellow forehead, face, and underparts, and a greenish head and back; the wings are black with 2 broad white wing bars. The iris is brown with a yellow eye ring. In breeding plumage the male may become blacker on the back and rump, and the underparts become brighter yellow. The female is duller, with less-distinct wing bars. Usually solitary or in pairs. Length: 12–14 cm

GREEN IORA *Aegithina viridissima*

Similar to Common Iora, but the head, back, and breast are green with a yellow vent. Dark lores, with a distinct, broken, yellow eye ring. This female has yellow lores and narrow yellow wing bars; underparts all yellow. An inhabitant of disturbed areas of primary and secondary forests, forest edges, and mangroves. Often joins mixed feedings flocks. A locally common resident in southern Burma, Thailand and the Malay Peninsula. Length: 12–14 cm

Common Woodshrike

Ashy Woodswallow

Bar-winged Flycatcher Shrike

Common Iora

Green Iora

SMALL MINIVET *Pericrocotus cinnamomeus*

A common and widespread resident of deciduous forests, open woodlands, parks, and gardens, except in the southern part of the region. The adult male has a gray head and black face; the breast is burnt orange fading into pale orange underneath. On the upperparts the back is gray with a burnt-orange rump; wings and tail are black with an orange wing patch and orange outer tail feathers. The female is pale gray on the upperparts, with a yellow patch on the wings, a grayish-white throat, and pale-yellow underparts. An arboreal insectivore; usually seen in active flocks flitting from treetop to treetop. Length: 14–16 cm

SCARLET MINIVET *Pericrocotus speciosus*

A common and widespread resident of all types of closed forests up to 1,700 meters. The male is strikingly crimson and black—a black head and upperparts with a large, trapezoid-shaped red patch on the wings and a mostly scarlet tail with central black feathers. The rest of the underparts are scarlet. The female has an olive-gray crown and back, with a yellow forehead, face, and underparts, a broad yellow rump, and yellow patches on dark-gray wings. The juvenile is like the female, but the head and back are grayish with yellow fringing. Usually in active flocks in the upper story. Length: 17–21 cm

LARGE CUCKOOSHRIKE *Coracina macei*

A common and widespread resident of all types of forested habitats up to 2,700 meters. A large, all-gray bird with dark-gray lores and ear coverts, white vent, and dark-gray wing feathers. The female is paler; the underparts and rump are whitish with pale-gray barring. The juvenile is heavily barred and scaled buffish. The flight is strong and undulating; usually seen high in trees or flying over forests. Feeds in the upper story on fruit, large invertebrates, and small vertebrates. The call is a far-carrying, squeaky *kweeep*. Length: 27–30 cm

PIED TRILLER *Lalage nigra*

A locally common resident in the southern part of the region. The male is black on the upperparts, with a broad white supercilium, a large white patch on the wing coverts, white fringes on the flight feathers, and a gray patch on the lower back. The underparts are white, with a gray wash on the breast. The female is like the male, but the upperparts are brownish, and the underparts and rump are finely barred grayish. The juvenile is brown on the upperparts with buff fringing and brown streaks on the underparts. An inhabitant of coastal woodlands, plantations, mangroves, and gardens in the lowlands. Usually solitary or in pairs; generally forages in the foliage of the upper story for insects. Length: 16 cm

BLACK-WINGED CUCKOOSHRIKE *Coracina melaschistos*

A medium-sized cuckooshrike. The adult male is all dark gray with blackish wings and tail, fading into paler gray on vent. The tail is graduated with white tips underneath. The female is plainer, with dark-grayish wings and tail and buffish-white scaling on the underparts. The juvenile is heavily scaled buffish above and below. Mostly occurs in broad-leaved evergreen forests, sometimes in gardens and deciduous forests. A locally common resident and winter visitor throughout. Length: 22–25 cm

Small Minivet, male

Scarlet Minivet

Large Cuckooshrike

Pied Triller

Pied Triller, female

Black-winged Cuckooshrike

BROWN SHRIKE *Lanius cristatus*

Shrikes are active predators with a large head, a black face mask, and a hooked bill. They hunt by dropping from a low perch and swooping down to catch large insects or small vertebrates on or near the ground. The adult male Brown Shrike has a gray or brown head (depending on the race), brown upperparts, with darker flight feathers and rump, and a tail that's tinged rufous. The throat is white and the rest of the underparts pale buffish-brown. The female is duller, with faint barring on the sides of the breast and flanks. The juvenile has narrow brown-and-buffish scaling on the upperparts. A common winter visitor to cultivated areas, secondary growth, gardens, plantations, and forest edges throughout. Length: 17–19 cm

LONG-TAILED SHRIKE *Lanius schach*

A large shrike with a long tail and a black head with a white throat. Some races have a gray head with a black mask. The rest of the upperparts of the adult are pale rufous with black wings and tail, and a white patch at the base of the primaries. The underparts are white with a rufous wash on the flanks. The sexes are alike. The juvenile is duller, with scaly dark markings on the back and underparts. Found in open country, cultivated areas, grasslands, plantations, and gardens. Usually solitary; often perches on a stump or a fence, from which it pounces on prey. A common resident almost throughout. Length: 23–27cm

ORIOLIDAE OLD WORLD ORIOLES

BLACK-NAPED ORIOLE *Oriolus chinensis*

A large, striking, bright-yellow bird with black markings and a strong pinkish bill. The adult male has a broad black band from the lores through the eye, broadening across the nape; the flight feathers are black with yellow fringes. The black tail is tipped yellow. The iris is dark red, the legs bluish-gray. The female is similar to the male, but the back and wing coverts are washed olive-green. The juvenile is all olive-green on the upperparts; the underparts are whitish with blackish streaks. A common and very familiar resident and winter visitor throughout; found in all types of wooded habitats. Length: 24–28 cm

BLACK-HOODED ORIOLE *Oriolus xanthornus*

Similar to the previously described species, but the head to the nape and the breast are black, creating a hooded appearance. The female has an olive wash on the upperparts and paler yellow on the underparts. The juvenile is duller, with yellow streaks on the forehead, and black streaks on the white throat and yellow underparts. The song is a rich, fluty *phu phi-woo*. A common and widespread resident found in all types of forested habitats, including secondary growth up to 900 meters. Length: 22–25 cm

Brown Shrike

Brown Shrike

Long-tailed Shrike

Long-tailed Shrike

Long-tailed Shrike

Black-naped Oriole

Black-hooded Oriole

BLYTH'S SHRIKE-BABBLER *Pteruthius aeralatus*

A widespread and common resident found in evergreen and pine forests. A stocky bird that has a heavy, pointed bill with a small, hooked tip. The male has a black head with a long, white supercilium; the back is gray; the wings and tail are black with chestnut tertials and white tips on the primaries. The throat and underparts are pale gray, with a pinkish wash on the flanks. The female is similar, but with grayish head and upperparts; wings and tail olive-brown; and buffish underparts. A foliage-gleaning insectivore, active in the upper story. Usually encountered in pairs; often joins mixed feeding flocks. Length: 14–15 cm

DICRURIDAE DRONGOS

BLACK DRONGO *Dicrurus macrocercus*

A large, all-black bird with a robust, hook-tipped bill and a long, forked tail. The adult is entirely glossy black, often with a small white spot in front of the eye. The long tail is deeply forked and slightly curled up at the outer tips. The sexes are alike. The immature bird is duller, with a brownish tinge; its underparts are grayish and fringed whitish. This bird of open areas, roadsides, and cultivation often perches on low posts and fences as well as power lines, hawking disturbed insects close to the ground. A common resident and winter visitor throughout. Length: 28 cm

ASHY DRONGO *Dicrurus leucophaeus*

A widespread and common resident and winter visitor to open areas and clearings in all types of forest. Similar to Black Drongo, with all glossy-black plumage, but somewhat paler below; the tail is less deeply forked. Some races are more distinctive, with all-pale ashy-gray plumage and white around the eye. The iris is red. The sexes are alike. The juvenile is like the adult, but lacks any gloss in the plumage. Hawks insects from a prominent high perch. Length: 25–29 cm

GREATER RACKET-TAILED DRONGO *Dicrurus paradiseus*

An unmistakable large drongo with a tall forehead tuft and a spectacular tail. The plumage is all glossy bluish-black; the tail has a shallow fork with 2 highly elongated outer feathers up to 30 cm long, with bare shafts and twisted terminal rackets (elongated tail feathers shaped like rackets). The iris is dark red. The sexes are similar in appearance. The juvenile is duller and lacks the tail rackets. A noisy and conspicuous bird, often found in mixed feeding flocks. Easily detected by its loud, varied vocalizations, which include rasping, squeaking, and churring notes, with some mimicry. Inhabits primary and secondary evergreen and deciduous forests, mangroves, and plantations, mainly in the lowlands. A common resident throughout. Length: 33–36 cm (excluding the elongated tail feathers).

Blyth's Shrike-babbler

Black Drongo

Ashy Drongo

Greater Racket-tailed Drongo

MALAYSIAN PIED-FANTAIL *Rhipidura javanica*

A noisy and active insectivore that forages in thick foliage in the mid-story with jerky movements, wagging and fanning its tail to disturb insects. The adult is dark gray with a short white supercilium and broad white tips on the tail; the underparts are white with a dark-gray breast band. The sexes are alike. The juvenile is duller and browner, with an indistinct breast band. A familiar bird of parks and gardens, plantations, secondary growth, and mangroves up to 450 meters. A common resident of the southern part of the region, including Cambodia and southern Vietnam. Length: 17–20 cm

WHITE-THROATED FANTAIL *Rhipidura albicollis*

A bold, active, and mostly montane black-and-white fantail. The plumage is all brownish-black with an all-white supercilium, white tail tips, and white throat. The sexes are alike. The juvenile is dusky brown on the pale areas. A very active bird that catches insects on the wing, generally in the mid-story. Fans the tail frequently; joins feeding flocks. Inhabits evergreen hill and montane forests, wooded parks, and gardens, generally at higher elevations. The voice is a series of 4–6 high-pitched notes *dee-dee-dee-dit-dooo* rising then descending in scale. A common resident throughout. Length: 17–20 cm

WHITE-BROWED FANTAIL *Rhipidura aureola*

Similar in appearance to other fantails, but with a long, broad, white supercilium and all-whitish underparts. The sexes are alike. The juvenile has a darkish throat and pale-brown scaling on the upperparts. A locally common resident in Burma, northern and western Thailand, Cambodia, southern Laos, and southern Vietnam. Found in drier dipterocarp and deciduous forests up to 1,000 meters. Behavior is typical of the genus. The voice is a series of 6 or 7 melodious whistles, ascending the scale, then descending. Length: 16–19 cm

MONARCHIDAE MONARCH FLYCATCHERS

ASIAN PARADISE-FLYCATCHER *Terpsiphone paradisi*

An exceptionally striking bird of the monarch flycatcher family, with a glossy-black hood and short crest, and an exceptionally long tail in the male. The male can occur in two forms: The rufous morph is rufous-brown on the upperparts and tail, with white underparts washed gray on the chest. The remarkable white morph is all-white except for a black hood and black edging on the wing and tail feathers. In both a bright-blue eye wattle surrounds the brown iris, and the bill is blue with a black tip. Usually solitary or in pairs; sometimes joins mixed feeding flocks. Hawks for insects from an inconspicuous perch. Call is a wheezy, 2- or 3-note *shweet shweet*. A common and widespread resident in primary and secondary broad-leaved evergreen forests, sometimes parks and gardens. Length: 19–24 cm (excluding the male's elongated tail feathers).

Malaysian Pied-Fantail

White-throated Fantail

White-browed Fantail   *Asian Paradise-flycatcher*

COMMON GREEN MAGPIE *Cissa chinensis*

Common and widespread resident of broad-leaved evergreen and deciduous forests up to 2,000 meters. The plumage is bright green with a prominent black mask; dark-red wings have black-and-white markings on the tertials, and a graduated tail has black-and-white tips on the feathers. The dark-red iris is surrounded by a fleshy, bright-red eye ring; the stout bill and legs are bright red. The sexes are alike. The juvenile is duller, with a duller eye ring and a brownish bill. Forages for small vertebrates and insects in dense vegetation in small parties; sometimes joins mixed feeding flocks. Noisy but often elusive. Length: 31–35 cm

LARGE-BILLED CROW *Corvus macrorhynchos*

A bird of open forests and woodlands, open areas, cultivation, and urban areas up to 3,700 meters. A common resident throughout. The plumage is entirely glossy black with longish throat hackles. The long, large bill is strongly arched. The sexes are alike. The juvenile is duller and less glossy. A gregarious, social, and intelligent bird with noisy vocalizations. The voice is a deep, throaty *kaaa-kaaa-kaaa*. Length: 45–60 cm

ALAUDIDAE LARKS

INDOCHINESE BUSHLARK *Mirafra erythrocephala*

A rather plain, ground-dwelling bird with a heavy conical bill and a short crest. The upperparts are pale brown with dark streaking, the underparts pale buffish-brown with dark streaking on the breast. The sexes are alike. Eats small invertebrates and seeds taken from the ground. Often perches on low bushes, fence posts, trees, and power lines. Sings as it flies up from the ground in undulating flight, then flutters down. An endemic resident restricted to eastern and southern Burma, Thailand, Cambodia, Laos, and southern Vietnam. Occurs in dry, open habitats and cultivated areas up to 900 meters. Length: 14–15 cm

HIRUNDINIDAE SWALLOWS

BARN SWALLOW *Hirundo rustica*

An agile, very active aerial insectivore with a slender body, small bill, short legs, and long, pointed wings. The other parts are glossy bluish-black; the dark-red crown and throat are bordered below by a blackish breast band. The rest of the underparts are creamy white. In breeding plumage the forked tail has a row of small subterminal white spots and elongated outer streamers. The sexes are alike. The juvenile is duller and paler, with a short tail. Highly gregarious; congregates in large roosts. Found in open areas, often near water, cities, and towns. A common winter visitor and resident throughout. Length: 14–17 cm

STRIATED SWALLOW *Cecropis striolata*

The adult has a glossy blackish-blue crown and upperparts, with a broad, dark-streaked, orange-red rump. The face and underparts are white with bold, heavy, black streaking. The long tail is deeply forked. The sexes are alike. The juvenile is duller with buffish tips on wing coverts. A common and widespread resident, usually found in open areas, often near water. Hunts for insects on the wing. Length: 18–19 cm

Common Green Magpie

Large-billed Crow

Indochinese Bushlark

Barn Swallow

Striated Swallow

CINEREOUS TIT *Parus cinereus*

A small insectivore with a large head, short, round wings, and a short, stubby tail. Energetic and inquisitive. Gleans insects in the treetops, foraging actively and acrobatically. The adult male has a black head with a large white patch on the cheek and ear coverts; upperparts dark gray with white wing bar. Some races have a greenish wash on the back. The underparts are grayish-white, with a black throat and a broad black ventral band. The female is duller with a narrower ventral stripe. The juvenile is duller and brownish. A locally common and widespread resident found in deciduous and pine forests, mangroves, cultivated areas, parks, and gardens. Length: 12–14 cm

SULTAN TIT *Melanochlora sultanea*

The adult male is glossy black with a floppy, bright-yellow crest and lower breast to vent. The female is similar but less glossy and brownish. A locally common resident except in central Thailand, Cambodia, southern Vietnam, and Singapore. Inhabits broad-leaved evergreen and deciduous forests up to 1,700 meters. Usually encountered in noisy small flocks as they forage actively for insects in the upper story. Length: 20 cm

SITTIDAE NUTHATCHES

CHESTNUT-VENTED NUTHATCH *Sitta nagaensis*

A short-tailed, small bird with a large head and chisel-shaped bill specialized for gleaning small invertebrates from the bark of tree trunks and larger branches. The upperparts are grayish-blue, with a black face mask. The underparts are buffy gray, with deep-chestnut lower flanks and vent. The female is very similar, with slightly more chestnut on the flanks and duller on the underparts. An inhabitant of all types of evergreen forests above 1,000 meters and often found in mixed feeding flocks. A common resident in Burma (except the south), northwest Thailand, Laos, and parts of Vietnam. Length: 13 cm

VELVET-FRONTED NUTHATCH *Sitta frontalis*

A highly distinctive nuthatch with violet-blue upperparts, black forehead and lores, a thin black line extending behind the eye, and black primaries. The underparts are lilac-gray with a whitish throat. The bill is coral-pink and the iris yellow. The female is similar but lacks the post-ocular stripe and has duller underparts. A common resident throughout (except Singapore) in all forested habitats up to 1,800 meters. Often in mixed feeding flocks, usually seen creeping on tree trunks and large branches. Length: 12 cm

BLUE NUTHATCH *Sitta azurea*

Unmistakable, with black crown and blue-tinged black upperparts contrasting with bright-white throat to lower breast. The wings are fringed black with silvery-blue centers; the rest of the underparts are blackish-blue with a pale-blue vent. The pale-blue iris is surrounded by a broad, fleshy white eye ring. The bill is pale. The sexes are alike. An uncommon resident of broad-leaved evergreen forests above 800 meters in the Malay Peninsula. Length: 13 cm

Cinereous Tit

Sultan Tit

Blue Nuthatch

Chestnut-vented Nuthatch

Velvet-fronted Nuthatch

GRAY-HEADED CANARY FLYCATCHER *Culicicapa ceylonensis*

The adult is distinctive, with a gray head and breast, olive upperparts, and bright-yellow underparts. The olive tail and flight feathers have narrow black edging. The black iris is surrounded by a narrow, whitish eye ring. The sexes are alike. The juvenile is similar, but with a brownish head and duller underparts. An active arboreal insectivore, usually seen in the mid-story of all types of wooded habitats. Often joins mixed feeding flocks. Usually solitary; often flicks tail when perched. The song is a squeaky, loud, and characteristic *sil-ly-bil-ly-me*. A common and widespread resident throughout. Length: 12–13 cm

PYCNONOTIDAE BULBULS

PUFF-BACKED BULBUL *Pycnonotus eutilotus*

A large, bulky bulbul with a short crest, and contrasting brown upperparts with whitish underparts. The underparts show a gray wash on the breast and pale-yellow undertail coverts. The long feathers on the rump (the "puff-back") are usually not visible in the field. The iris is dark red. The sexes are alike. An inhabitant of primary lowland rain forests and swamp forests up to 210 meters. Usually seen singly or in pairs, but quite inconspicuous, generally in the mid-story. Joins mixed feeding flocks. A locally common resident in the southern part of the region. Length: 23 cm

BLACK-HEADED BULBUL *Pycnonotus atriceps*

A medium-sized olive-green bulbul with a black head and a pale blue iris. The adult has a black throat; the back is yellowish-green fading to bright yellow on the lower back and uppertail; the tail is tipped yellow with a broad black subterminal band. The wings are olive-green with black primaries. The underparts are bright yellow with an olive-green wash on the breast and flanks. The sexes are alike. The juvenile is duller with a brownish head and iris. Nomadic in response to fruiting; feeds on figs and other fruits and insects; usually in pairs or small groups. Inhabits primary and secondary evergreen and deciduous forests up to 1,600 meters, but more common in the lowlands. An uncommon to common resident throughout. Length: 18 cm

STRIATED BULBUL *Pycnonotus striatus*

A large bulbul with heavy yellow streaking on the head and an olive-green body; the throat and undertail coverts are bright yellow. Has a short, shaggy, upright crest and prominent yellow eye ring. The sexes are alike. An uncommon resident in Burma, Thailand, and parts of Laos and northern Vietnam. Found in primary and secondary evergreen rain forests above 1,200 meters. Length: 23 cm

BLACK-CRESTED BULBUL *Pycnonotus melanicterus*

A distinctive bulbul with bright-yellow underparts, olive-green upperparts, a glossy-black head with a tall, upright crest, and a contrasting pale-yellow iris. Some races may show some red on the throat. The sexes are alike. The juvenile is duller, with a brownish head and some olive-yellow on the throat. An inhabitant of primary and secondary evergreen and deciduous forests. Feeds mostly on small fruits, but occasionally takes insects. Often in small flocks at fruiting trees. A common resident throughout. Length: 18–20 cm

Gray-headed Canary Flycatcher

Puff-backed Bulbul

Black-headed Bulbul

Striated Bulbul

Black-crested Bulbul

RED-WHISKERED BULBUL *Pycnonotus jocosus*

A common but declining resident, except in Peninsular Malaysia and Singapore, where there is a feral population. The adult is unmistakable, with a tall, erect, black crest and a black head, a red spot behind the eye, and prominent white ear coverts bordered with a thin, black moustachial stripe. The throat and underparts are white with a bright-red vent. The upperparts are dull brown. The sexes are alike. The juvenile is brownish with a short crest, no ear patch, and an orange-red vent. Favors secondary growth, scrub, cultivation, and gardens. Length: 18–20 cm

SOOTY-HEADED BULBUL *Pycnonotus aurigaster*

An opportunistic feeder, favoring disturbed habitat near human habitation. Found in secondary forests, scrub, plantations, cultivated areas, and gardens. A common resident except in Peninsular Malaysia and in Singapore, where there is a small feral population. The adult has a short, dull-black crest and distinctive yellow undertail coverts. The upperparts are dull brown except for the pale-gray rump and hind neck; underparts grayish-white. The sexes are alike. The juvenile is brownish on the head with paler undertail coverts. The song is a cheerful, bubbling *witti-wii-it*. Length: 19–21 cm

STRIPE-THROATED BULBUL *Pycnonotus finlaysoni*

The plumage is dull brown overall, but with prominent yellow stripes on the throat to the upper breast, ear coverts, and forehead. The underparts are paler, with whitish streaks on the breast and a yellow vent. The sexes are alike. The juvenile is browner with reduced yellow streaks. A common resident found in secondary growth, scrub, forest clearings, and gardens up to 1,300 meters. Length: 19–20 cm

FLAVESCENT BULBUL *Pycnonotus flavescens*

A relatively large, nondescript bulbul with a grayish head and throat, a short crest, and a pale-whitish area in front of the eye. The upperparts are dull olive-brown; warm-pale-brown underparts show a yellow wash on the vent. The sexes are alike. The juvenile is brownish overall and lacks white on the face. An inhabitant of forest clearings and edges, secondary-growth forests, and scrub above 900 meters. Conspicuous, usually in small groups, feeding mainly on small fruits. A common resident in Burma, Thailand (except the south), Laos, and all but central Vietnam. Length: 22 cm

YELLOW-VENTED BULBUL *Pycnonotus goiavier*

A common and widespread resident except in the northern and central parts of Burma and Vietnam. The plumage is generally a dull brown, but is distinguished by a distinctive head pattern of a dark-brown crown with a short narrow crest, a whitish face and broad supercilium, and dull-brown ear coverts; blackish iris and black eye ring. Underparts paler, with brownish smudges on the breast and yellow undertail coverts. The sexes are alike. The juvenile is paler with less-distinct head markings. A noisy and conspicuous bulbul, often found in small flocks. The voice is a bubbly *pirit pirit prrrt* … Feeds on small fruits and invertebrates, usually foraging near the ground. Inhabits secondary forests, mangroves, plantations, cultivated areas, and gardens, mostly in the lowlands. Length: 19–21 cm

Red-whiskered Bulbul

Stripe-throated Bulbul

Flavescent Bulbul

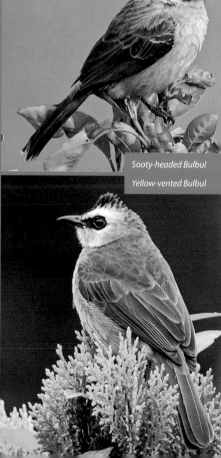

Sooty-headed Bulbul

Yellow-vented Bulbul

STREAK-EARED BULBUL *Pycnonotus blanfordi*

Very plain. An all olive-brown bird with prominent whitish streaks on the ear coverts. The underparts are paler with a yellowish wash on the vent. The sexes are alike. The juvenile is paler, with less-distinct streaks on the ear coverts. Inhabits deciduous forests, scrubland, cultivated areas, parks, and gardens up to 900 meters. A common endemic resident except in northern Vietnam and Peninsular Malaysia. Length: 17–20 cm

CREAM-VENTED BULBUL *Pycnonotus simplex*

A very nondescript, all-brown bulbul, best distinguished from other similar species by the prominent white iris. The upperparts are brown with paler grayish-brown underparts. The sexes are alike. The juvenile has pale-brown eyes. A locally common resident in the southern part of the region. Found in primary and secondary rain forests, hill forests, and plantations. Length: 18 cm

RED-EYED BULBUL *Pycnonotus brunneus*

A nondescript bird with olive-brown upperparts, and pale brown underparts with a buffish vent. The iris is orange-red. The sexes are alike. The juvenile is paler with a pale-gray eye. A foliage-gleaning insectivore and frugivore; usually seen in pairs or small groups. A locally common resident of primary and secondary forests up to 1,000 meters in the southern part of the region. Length: 19 cm

PUFF-THROATED BULBUL *Alophoixus pallidus*

Very similar to Ochraceous Bulbul, but with a greenish-olive tinge on the upperparts, and darker underparts with a yellowish wash. Also slightly larger and with a longer crest. The sexes are alike. The range also differs; this species mostly replaces Ochraceous Bulbul in the northern parts of the region. Inhabits broad-leaved evergreen forests up to 1,400 meters. Length: 22–25 cm

BLACK BULBUL *Hypsipetes leucocephalus*

A locally common and conspicuous resident throughout, often in large, active flocks. Found in evergreen and deciduous forests mostly above 500 meters. The adult is all dark grayish-black, with a prominent long red bill and a short, shaggy crown. The iris is red, and the legs pinkish-red. One race (a winter visitor to northern Thailand and Vietnam) has a distinctive all-white head. The sexes are alike. The juvenile is brownish overall. Length: 23–27 cm

OCHRACEOUS BULBUL *Alophoixus ochraceus*

A large, chunky bulbul with an upright, shaggy crest and a prominent white, puffy throat; the rest of the underparts are pale brown, the head and upperparts warm brown. In some races the underparts are tinged yellow, making it very difficult to separate from the very similar Puff-throated Bulbul. The sexes are alike. The juvenile has a rufous wash on the wings and tail. A bird of broad-leaved evergreen forests; a common resident mostly in the southern part of the region, including parts of Cambodia and southern Vietnam. Length: 19–22 cm

Streak-eared Bulbul

Cream-vented Bulbul

Red-eyed Bulbul

Puff-throated Bulbul

Black Bulbul

Ochraceous Bulbul

ASHY BULBUL *Hemixos flavala*

In the adult the shaggy crown and face are black, with brown ear coverts. The rest of the upperparts are gray, with a broad olive patch on the wings. The throat is white, and the rest of the underparts paler gray. The race in Peninsular Malaysia is all grayish-brown on the upperparts, with a blackish patch on the cheeks and pale-grayish underneath; it is sometimes treated as a separate species, Cinereous Bulbul. The sexes are alike. Found in broad-leaved evergreen forests mostly above 600 meters. A locally common and widespread resident throughout. Length: 19–22 cm

MOUNTAIN BULBUL *Ixos mcclellandii*

A large, olive-green bulbul with a shaggy brownish crown with paler streaks. The pale-gray streaky throat fades into pale-streaked rufous breast and flanks; unstreaked grayish belly and yellow vent. The dark bill is relatively long; often puffs out the shaggy throat feathers. The sexes are alike. A bird of broad-leaved montane forests above 800 meters. A common and widespread resident almost throughout. Length: 21–24 cm

PNOEPYGIDAE CUPWINGS

PYGMY CUPWING *Pnoepyga pusilla*

A tiny, almost tail-less, ground-dwelling babbler; the warm-brown upperparts have buff spots on the wing coverts. The underparts are brown, with prominent buff scaling. The sexes are alike. Usually found on or near the ground in primary and secondary broad-leaved evergreen forests up to 2,700 meters. Very vocal; song a distinctive, high-pitched *ti-ti-tu*, often transcribed as "three blind mice." Generally solitary. A locally common and widespread resident throughout. Length: 8 cm

CETTIIDAE BUSH-WARBLERS AND ALLIES

BROWNISH-FLANKED BUSH WARBLER *Horornis fortipes*

A long-tailed, brownish warbler with paler underparts and a long, buffish supercilium. The crown and upperparts are chestnut brown, the underparts grayish-white with darker streaks. The sexes are alike. Found in scrubby grassy areas in clearings and forest edges above 1,200 meters. A skulking insectivore. A locally common resident and winter visitor in Burma, northern Laos, northern Vietnam, and northwestern Thailand. The voice is the best means of identification; the song is short and explosive, introduced with a long whistle *wheeeeeeee wi-chow* … Length: 12–13 cm

MOUNTAIN TAILORBIRD *Phyllergates cucullatus*

A small, active insectivore with a stubby body and a fine, pointed bill. The head and mantle are dark gray, with a bright orange-rufous forehead and crown, and a narrow, pale-gray supercilium. The rest of the upperparts are olive-green. The throat and breast are whitish, with gray on the sides of the breast; the rest of the underparts are bright yellow. The sexes are alike. This rather skulking bird gleans tiny invertebrates from foliage in thickets, bamboo stands, and dense vegetation. The song is a distinctive, sweet, whistled *dee dee-dee-dee-di'di'di*. A common and widespread resident throughout above 1,000 meters. Length: 10–12 cm

Ashy Bulbul

Pygmy Cupwing

Mountain Tailorbird

Mountain Bulbul

Brownish-flanked Bush Warbler

YELLOW-BROWED WARBLER *Phylloscopus inornatus*

The plumage is olive-green, paler on the underparts, with a board yellowish supercilium and 2 broad yellowish wing bars. The crown and rump are plain. The gray bill is pink at the base, the legs pinkish. The sexes are alike. Smaller than the similar Two-barred Warbler, with a shorter tail and broader, more contrasting wing bars and with pale tips on the tertial feathers. Hume's Warbler is almost identical, but has a gray wash on the upperparts and darker bill and legs. Inhabits all types of forests up to 2,400 meters. A common winter visitor throughout. Length: 11 cm

ARCTIC WARBLER *Phylloscopus borealis*

A large leaf warbler with a conspicuous pale supercilium and dark-olive eye stripe on an olive-green head; the ear coverts are mottled olive. The upperparts are olive-green with a single, buffish-white wing bar and sometimes an indistinct second wing bar. The underparts are whitish, with indistinct grayish streaking on the breast and flanks. The legs are pink. The sexes are alike. An arboreal insectivore, usually seen foraging in the mid to upper story, often in mixed feeding flocks. Less active than many other leaf warblers. Found in all types of forested habitats. An uncommon to common winter visitor throughout. Length: 13 cm

TWO-BARRED WARBLER *Phylloscopus plumbeitarsus*

In general the plumage is similar to that of other leaf warblers—the upperparts are olive-green with a pale supercilium and paler underparts. In similar Greenish Warbler the greater coverts show a single, narrow, yellowish-white wing bar; there is an olive wash on the flanks, and no white in the tail. The sexes are alike. Similar Arctic and Two-barred Warblers have a second wing bar; Arctic is also larger, with a heavier bill. Care needs to be taken with the identification of all *Phylloscopus* warblers. Two-barred Warbler is a common winter visitor to the northern parts of the region, where it is found in broad-leaved evergreen forests and secondary growth generally at higher elevations up to 2,600 meters. Length: 12 cm

LOCUSTELLIDAE GRASSBIRDS AND ALLIES

LANCEOLATED WARBLER *Locustella lanceolata*

A very skulking small bird of thick grass and scrub, usually on or near the ground. Difficult to observe. The plumage is brown on the upperparts; heavy, dark streaking and buffish-brown underneath, with finer streaks on the breast and flanks. The sexes are alike. Usually detected by its trilling *zizizizizizizi* … song or soft *chk chk* call. A common winter visitor almost throughout. Length: 12–14 cm

STRIATED GRASSBIRD *Megalurus palustris*

A large, streaky warbler with a long, graduated tail. The upperparts are buffish-brown, with fine darker streaks on the crown, a long buffish supercilium, and broad blackish-brown streaks on the back and wings. A dark line runs through the eye. The legs are pinkish. The sexes are alike. The largest warbler in the region. A bird of marshes, grasslands, and paddy fields up to 1,500 meters. Forages in reeds and long grass for small invertebrates. Often sings loudly from a conspicuous perch, such as a power line or fence post. A locally common resident, except in Peninsular Malaysia and Singapore. Length: 25–28 cm

Yellow-browed Warbler

Arctic Warbler

Two-barred Warbler

Lanceolated Warbler

Striated Grassbird

GOLDEN-HEADED CISTICOLA *Cisticola exilis*

The adult breeding male is orange-rufous on the head, with heavily streaked, buffish-brown upperparts. The underparts are whitish, with an orange wash on the breast. The legs are pink. In non-breeding plumage the upperparts, including the head, are more heavily streaked, with a warm-buffish supercilium. The female is like the non-breeding male but duller and paler. Very similar Zitting Cisticola has a whitish supercilium. A skulking inhabitant of grasslands and crops. Often gives short song flights or calls from a low perch; one call is a distinctive, buzzing *zzzt zzzt zzt-zzt*. A locally common resident except in the Malay Peninsula and northern Vietnam. Length: 9–12 cm

COMMON TAILORBIRD *Orthotomus sutorius*

A small, active bird with a long, usually cocked, tail and a long, thin bill. In breeding plumage the male has a rufous crown, olive-green upperparts, and pale-whitish underparts, often with a blackish mark on the sides of the neck. The race in the southern part of the region is darker, with dark streaks on the breast. The tail is shorter in the female and the non-breeding male. The juvenile has less rufous on the head. The song is an explosive *chee-up chee-up*. A common resident throughout. Found in scrub, mangroves, gardens, and bamboo stands up to 1,500 meters. Length: 11–12 cm

ASHY TAILORBIRD *Orthotomus ruficeps*

An ashy-gray tailorbird with a distinctive rufous hood. The upperparts are gray, with a brownish tinge on the wings and tail; the throat and breast are ashy-gray, fading to grayish-white on the lower belly. The iris is deep red, and the legs are pink; the bill is pink with a grayish wash. The female is similar, but paler on the underparts, with a gray wash on the flanks and breast. The juvenile is all olive-brown with paler underparts. An inhabitant of dense vegetation in primary and secondary forests, mangroves, plantations, and gardens. Forages for insects in dense vegetation. Very vocal; the song is a rather slow, upwardly inflected *choowit choowit*. A common resident in the southern part of the region and southern Vietnam. Length: 11–12 cm

HILL PRINIA *Prinia superciliaris*

A common but skulking inhabitant of grassy or scrubby slopes and overgrown clearings above 900 meters. A widespread resident. A small insectivorous bird with a very long tail. In non-breeding plumage the upperparts are plain warm brown with a white supercilium, whitish underparts with dark spots on the breast, and a rufous wash on the flanks. In breeding plumage the breast streaks are longer and more extensive. The sexes are alike. Length: 15–21 cm

YELLOW-BELLIED PRINIA *Prinia flaviventris*

A common resident throughout in long grass and reeds near water, mainly around wetlands, paddy fields, and grasslands. Skulking; feeds on small invertebrates in thick vegetation close to the ground. Sings from low bushes and the tops of tall grass stems. The head is gray, with a short white supercilium and red iris; the upperparts are olive-brown. The white throat grades into buffish-white underparts, with a yellow wash on the belly and flanks. The sexes are alike. Length: 12–14 cm

Golden-headed Cisticola

Common Tailorbird

Yellow-bellied Prinia

Ashy Tailorbird

Hill Prinia

WHITE-BROWED FULVETTA *Fulvetta vinipectus*

A common resident in northern Burma and Vietnam, this small, active babbler is distinguished by its prominent head pattern—a brown crown, narrow black crown stripe, broad white supercilium, and black sides of the head with white eye ring. The throat is white fading into grayish underparts. The rest of the upperparts are warm-brown; more reddish on the wings, with contrasting black inner and white outer primaries. The sexes are alike. Inhabits dense stands of vegetation in primary forests above 1,800 meters. Active and noisy, usually in mobile, fast-moving flocks. Length: 12 cm

ZOSTEROPIDAE YUHINAS, WHITE-EYES, AND ALLIES

WHISKERED YUHINA *Yuhina flavicollis*

A small, highly mobile, tit-like babbler with a prominent, erect forward-facing crest. The head and crest are gray with a black moustachial stripe and a rufous hind collar. There is a broken white eye ring. The rest of the upperparts are dark gray. The throat and underparts are white with brownish streaks on the flanks. The sexes are alike. The juvenile is duller, with a narrower moustachial stripe. An active and gregarious insectivore, often in mixed feeding flocks, above 1,000 meters. Sometimes feeds on nectar from the fruits of flowering trees. Favors broad-leaved evergreen forests and secondary growth. A common resident in Burma (except the south), northwestern Thailand, Laos, and northern Vietnam. Length: 13 cm

ORIENTAL WHITE-EYE *Zosterops palpebrosus*

A small, yellowish-green bird. The adult is lime green on the crown and upperparts, with black lores, a prominent white, fleshy eye ring, and a yellow forehead. There are black fringes on the wing feathers. The throat is yellow; the grayish-white underparts have a yellow central stripe. There is a yellow morph in which the underparts are completely yellow. The sexes are alike. The juvenile is similar, but lacks the white eye ring and central stripe on the underparts. Usually seen in active, noisy flocks, gleaning foliage for insects in treetops. Inhabits all types of wooded habitats, including parks and gardens up to 1,800 meters, but is restricted to coastal habitats in the Malay Peninsula. A common resident throughout, except in northeastern and central Vietnam and Singapore. Length: 11 cm

TIMALIIDAE TREE-BABBLERS, SCIMITAR BABBLERS, AND ALLIES

PIN-STRIPED TIT BABBLER *Mixornis gularis*

A common resident in thick vegetation in all types of forested habitats up to 1,500 meters throughout. A noisy and active arboreal insectivore, usually in small parties; not shy, but rather skulking and often difficult to see. Favors dense foliage in disturbed primary and secondary forests, mangroves, scrub, gardens, and plantations. The adult is warm-brown on the upperparts, with a rufous crown. The face and underparts are yellow, with fine streaks on the throat and breast. The sexes are alike. The juvenile is paler below, with more uniform brown upperparts. The song is a slow-paced, mellow *chonk chonk chonk* … Length: 13 cm

White-browed Fulvetta

Whiskered Yuhinia

Oriental White-eye

Pin-striped Tit Babbler

FLUFFY-BACKED TIT BABBLER *Macronus ptilosus*

A large, rich chestnut-brown babbler with a rufous crown, black throat, and conspicuous blue eye ring. The long plumes on the rump and flanks for which the bird is named are usually not visible in the field. When singing, inflated blue skin sometimes shows on the neck sides. The sexes are alike. The juvenile is duller, with paler facial skin. Favors disturbed areas of primary and secondary lowland rain forests, swamp forests, and mangroves up to 200 meters. Typically found in small parties foraging for insects in thick vegetation in the lower story. The song is a mellow *poop* (pause) *poop-poop-poop*. A common resident in the southern parts of the region. Length: 16 cm

CHESTNUT-WINGED BABBLER *Cyanoderma erythropterum*

A common resident in primary and secondary rain forests in the southern parts of the region. An active and noisy, foliage-gleaning insectivore, usually encountered in small flocks in the mid-story. The song is a distinctive mellow and slow-paced *hu-hu-hu-hu-hu* … The adult is brown with chestnut wings and a gray forehead to breast fading into buffish underparts. The iris is dark red with a blue eye ring. When singing, inflated blue skin often shows on the sides of the neck. The sexes are alike. The juvenile has duller facial skin and paler underparts. Length: 13 cm

GOLDEN BABBLER *Cyanoderma chrysaeum*

A highly distinctive, small, golden-yellow babbler. The head and underparts are bright yellow, with black lores and dark streaks on the crown. The rest of the upperparts are olive-yellow. The iris is deep red, and the legs yellowish-pink. The sexes are alike. The voice is very similar to that of Rufous-fronted Babbler, but the notes are slightly clearer and the cadence faster. Inhabits broad-leaved evergreen forests generally above 750 meters, often in mixed feeding flocks. A common and widespread resident. Length: 10–12 cm

RUFOUS-FRONTED BABBLER *Cyanoderma rufifrons*

A very small arboreal babbler, active and rather nondescript. The plumage is olive-brown with a chestnut crown, pale-grayish supercilium, and buffish underparts. The sexes are alike. Very similar Rufous-capped Babbler, in parts of Laos and Vietnam, is paler on the upperparts, with a yellowish wash on the face and underparts; lacks the grayish supercilium. Inhabits dense undergrowth and forest edges in broad-leaved forests, secondary growth, and bamboo stands up to 2,000 meters. Usually seen in small groups, a foliage-gleaning insectivore in the mid to lower story. The song is a simple, rapid series of 8–10 mellow monotone notes. A common resident with a patchy distribution from Burma and northern and western Thailand to the Malay Peninsula and northern Vietnam and Laos. Length: 12 cm

Fluffy-backed Tit Babbler

Chestnut-winged Babbler

Golden Babbler

Rufous-fronted Babbler

WHITE-BROWED SCIMITAR BABBLER *Pomatorhinus schisticeps*

An inhabitant of thick vegetation in a variety of habitats from forests to scrub and grasslands. The head pattern is distinctive, with a prominent yellow bill, a brown crown with a broad white supercilium, a black face mask grading into a chestnut neck patch, and an orange iris. The throat and underparts are white, with a brown wash on the flanks and vent; the upperparts are a warm brown. The sexes are alike. A common and widespread resident in Burma, Thailand, Cambodia, Laos, and central and southern Vietnam. Length: 21–23 cm

LARGE SCIMITAR BABBLER *Megapomatorhinus hypoleucos*

A large babbler and the largest scimitar babbler, with a long, powerful decurved bill. The upperparts are warm brown, with a scaly brown-and-white supercilium extending to the sides of the neck; the ear coverts are brown with a chestnut neck patch below. The underparts are white, with heavy dark streaks on the sides of the breast and flanks. The sexes are alike. The juvenile has less-defined markings on the underparts. An inhabitant of dense vegetation, usually close to the ground, in broad-leaved evergreen and mixed deciduous forests. A common resident throughout. Length: 25–28 cm

GRAY-THROATED BABBLER *Stachyris nigriceps*

A small, active, and noisy babbler with a distinctive head pattern consisting of a black crown with paler streaking, a short gray supercilium behind the eye, gray lores and moustachial stripe, and a white submoustachial stripe. The throat is gray and the iris yellow. The legs are pale pinkish-gray. The rest of the underparts are rufous brown, and the upperparts brown. The sexes are alike. Often in mixed feeding flocks in dense vegetation in broad-leaved evergreen forests and secondary growth. A common resident, but absent from Cambodia, central Thailand, and Singapore. Length: 13 cm

PELLORNEIDAE GROUND BABBLERS AND ALLIES

SOOTY-CAPPED BABBLER *Malacopteron affine*

A medium-sized arboreal babbler with plain brown upperparts, warmer brown on the wings and tail, and a blackish-gray crown. The underparts are dull grayish-white with gray smudges on the breast. The sexes are alike. The juvenile has a duller cap and plain underparts. Forages for insects in the mid-story in lowland rain forests and swamp forests in the southern part of the region. A locally common resident. Usually encountered in small flocks or in mixed feeding flocks, often near water. The song is a distinctive, rambling, rising-and-falling series of clear whistles *phu-phi-phu-phoo-phi-phoo-phu-phi*. Length: 16 cm

White-browed Scimitar Babbler

Large Scimitar Babbler

Gray-throated Babbler

Sooty-capped Babbler

SCALY-CROWNED BABBLER *Malacopteron cinereum*

The adult is olive-brown on the upperparts with a black-speckled rufous cap. The nape is black, and the supercilium and face gray with buffy streaks on the ear coverts. The race in Vietnam, Laos, and northern Thailand lacks the black nape. The underparts are whitish with a gray wash on the flanks and breast. The sexes are alike. Similar Rufous-crowned Babbler, with an overlapping range in southern parts of the region, is larger, with gray streaking on the throat and breast, and lacks the black speckles on the cap. An active insectivore, often found in small parties in the mid-story of broad-leaved evergreen forests. A common and widespread resident. Length: 14–17 cm

PUFF-THROATED BABBLER *Pellorneum ruficeps*

A common and widespread inhabitant of all types of forests. Usually seen on or close to the ground, where it hops and walks, gleaning leaf litter for small invertebrates. A distinctive babbler with a horizontal posture and distinctive head pattern: a rufous crown, buffish supercilium, and white throat, which it often puffs out. The rest of the upperparts are rich brown. The underparts are whitish, with broad dark-brown streaks on the breast and flanks. The iris is dark red, and the legs pinkish. The sexes are alike. The juvenile is dull brown and lacks the head pattern and streaks. There is a variable amount of streaking on the mantle, depending on the subspecies. The song is a clear, far-carrying whistled *wit-wee-chu*. Resident. Length: 17 cm

BLACK-CAPPED BABBLER *Pellorneum capistratum*

A small, terrestrial babbler with a horizontal posture, an inhabitant of primary and secondary lowland rain forests, swamp forests, and plantations, where it gleans leaf litter on or close to the ground. Usually solitary or in pairs. The adult has a distinctive head pattern, with a black forehead to nape, a long white supercilium, dark-gray sides of the face, a blackish moustachial stripe, and a white throat. The upperparts are chestnut brown, the underparts rufous brown. The sexes are alike. The juvenile is brown on the crown, with a rufous wash on the throat. The voice is a clear, sweet, slurred *wee-ee*. A common resident in the southern part of the region. Length: 16–18 cm

SHORT-TAILED BABBLER *Pellorneum malaccense*

A small, ground-dwelling babbler with a very short tail. The upperparts are warm brown; the gray face is bordered below with a grayish-black moustachial stripe. The throat is white, grading into grayish-white underparts with a rufous wash on the breast and flanks. The iris is dark red and the legs pinkish. The sexes are alike. The juvenile is brownish on the head, with rufous fringes on the wing feathers. Forages for insects on the forest floor singly or in pairs. A locally common resident in southern parts of Burma, Thailand, and the Malay Peninsula, where it favors primary and secondary rain forests up to 900 meters. The song is a rather long series of down-slurred *phwee phwee phwee* … whistles. Length: 13–16 cm

Scaly-crowned Babbler

Puff-throated Babbler

Black-capped Babbler

Short-tailed Babbler

WHITE-CHESTED BABBLER *Pellorneum rostratum*

A small, plain babbler with dull-brown upperparts, gray sides of the head, and whitish underparts, with a gray wash on the sides of the breast. The iris is dark red and the legs pinkish. The bill is long and slender with a hooked tip. The sexes are alike. A locally common resident in the southern part of the region. An inhabitant of lowland primary and secondary riverine forests, swamp forests, and mangroves. Usually found near water, where it forages for small invertebrates on the ground at or near the water's edge. Often encountered in pairs. The voice is a cheerful, ringing *wee-ti-weeit*. Length: 15 cm

FERRUGINOUS BABBLER *Pellorneum bicolor*

The adult is rufous brown on the upperparts, with a pale-buffish face and creamy white underparts with a buffish wash on the breast. The tail is relatively long. The sexes are alike. The juvenile is brighter rufous on the upperparts. Inhabits lowland rain forests and swamp forests up to 200 meters in the southern part of the region. Forages for insects in the lower story. The call is a simple, short, high-pitched *wheet*. Often joins mixed flocks. A common resident in southern Burma, Thailand, and the Malay Peninsula. Length: 16–18 cm

STRIPED WREN BABBLER *Kenopia striata*

A small, boldly patterned, ground-dwelling babbler with a white face and yellow lores. The forehead and nape are black with white streaks. The upperparts are brown with prominent whitish streaking on the mantle and wing coverts. The grayish-white underparts are mottled gray on the sides of the breast. The legs are pink. The sexes are alike. Found in lowland rain forests up to 750 meters; usually close to the ground, where it gleans leaf litter in thick vegetation. Moves by hopping; usually in pairs. An uncommon resident in the southern parts of the region. Length: 15 cm

ABBOTT'S BABBLER *Turdinus abbotti*

A small, rather chunky, short-tailed babbler with a large, hook-tipped bill. The upperparts are brown, with a gray face and dark-red iris. The underparts are pale grayish, with a rufous wash on the flanks and belly. The legs are pink. The sexes are alike. The juvenile is warmer brown on the upperparts. A common resident throughout most of the region, though absent from northern Burma and Vietnam. Found in broad-leaved evergreen forests and dense secondary growth; a foliage-gleaning insectivore usually in the lower story. Rather inconspicuous; best detected by its song, a ringing, cheerful *fwee-fee-wi-fwee*. Length: 16 cm

LIMESTONE WREN BABBLER *Turdinus crispifrons*

A largish, all-brown ground-dwelling babbler specializing in forests on limestone formations. Usually observed in small parties actively searching for insects in rock crevices and thick vegetation. The adult has bold white streaks on the head, mantle, and breast. The wings and relatively long tail are a rich chestnut brown, the rest of the underparts grayish-brown. The sexes are alike. An endemic, locally common resident in southern Burma, northern to western Thailand, and northern Laos to northern and central Vietnam. Similar, more widespread Streaked Wren Babbler is smaller, with a shorter tail and white spots on the wings. Length: 18–20 cm

White-chested Babbler

Ferruginous Babbler

Striped Wren Babbler

Abbot's Babbler

Limestone Wren Babbler

MOUNTAIN FULVETTA *Alcippe peracensis*

This small, active arboreal babbler with brownish upperparts and a gray head
and mantle has a prominent broad, black crown stripe and a white eye ring.
The underparts are grayish-white. The iris is dark red and the legs pinkish. The
sexes are alike. Gregarious and noisy; active and mobile in small groups or mixed
feeding flocks in thick foliage in the lower to mid-story. Found in broad-leaved
evergreen forests and secondary growth usually above 900 meters. A common
endemic resident in the Malay Peninsula, northeast Cambodia, central to
southern Laos, and central Vietnam. Length: 15 cm

HIMALAYAN CUTIA *Cutia nipalensis*

An inconspicuous, slow-moving inhabitant of the upper story in broad-leaved
evergreen and pine forests, generally above 1,200 meters. Often joins mixed
feeding flocks; forages for insects on lichen- and epiphyte-laden branches. The
adult male is boldly patterned with a bluish-gray crown, black face mask, and
chestnut upperparts. The wings and tail are black with silvery primaries. The
underparts are white, with bold black bars on the sides of the breast and flanks.
The female is similar but paler, with a black-streaked olive mantle and a dark-
brown mask. The juvenile is duller, with less-defined markings and a brownish
crown. A locally uncommon resident in Burma (except the south), northwest
Thailand, Peninsular Malaysia, northern and central Laos, and far-northern
Vietnam. Length: 17–19 cm

WHITE-CRESTED LAUGHINGTHRUSH *Garrulax leucolophus*

A large, active, and gregarious bird, always in noisy groups, with a distinctive
erect white crest and black mask. The head and breast are all-white; the gray
nape fades into warm brown on the upperparts. The flanks and undertail coverts
are rufous brown. The sexes are alike. The juvenile is similar to the adult but with
a less-pronounced crest and brownish nape. An inhabitant of all types of primary
and secondary forests up to 1,600 meters. Tends to forage on the ground to the
lower story, gleaning foliage and leaf litter for small insects. A common resident
throughout, except the Malay Peninsula and Singapore. Length: 26–31 cm

WHITE-CHEEKED LAUGHINGTHRUSH *Ianthocincla vassali*

The adult is brown on the upperparts, with a dark-gray head and black mask.
The tail has a broad black subterminal band with white tips. The throat and sides
of the neck are white, with a black stripe in the center of the throat. The rest of
the underparts are a duller and paler brown. The sexes are alike. The behavior
is typical of laughingthrushes—active and noisy in large mobile flocks, but
often difficult to observe in thick vegetation. Found in broad-leaved forests
and secondary growth above 650 meters. An endemic resident, uncommon in
Cambodia, southern Laos, and central Vietnam. Length: 28 cm

Mountain Fulvetta

Himalayan Cutia

White-crested Laughingthrush

White-cheeked Laughingthrush

CHESTNUT-CAPPED LAUGHINGTHRUSH *Ianthocincla mitrata*

A gray laughingthrush with a distinctive chestnut crown, broad white eye ring, and bright-orange bill. The lores are black, and there is prominent white streaking on the forehead. The vent is rufous, and the tail is tipped dark gray. The primaries are tipped white, forming a prominent wing patch. The sexes are alike. The juvenile is duller and browner above. An inhabitant of broad-leaved evergreen forests above 900 meters. Active and noisy in small flocks; forages on the ground to the upper story for small invertebrates and fruits. The voice is a loud, slurred whistle *wee-oo-wee-oo-weet* … in 3–8 notes. A common resident in the southern parts of the region. Length: 21–24 cm

BLACK-HEADED SIBIA *Heterophasia desgodinsi*

A slim, long-tailed babbler with a slender bill. The adult has gray upperparts with a black head, wings, and tail; the tail is tipped gray and white. There is a broken white eye ring in some races. The throat and underparts are white with a grayish wash on the sides of the breast and flanks. The sexes are alike. The juvenile is duller with brownish-tinged upperparts. Usually encountered in small flocks in the canopy in evergreen forests above 800 meters. A common resident in northern Burma, Laos, and northern and central Vietnam. Length: 21–25 cm

SILVER-EARED MESIA *Leiothrix argentauris*

An unmistakable, multi-colored bird with a bright-orange bill, forehead, throat, and nape; the face, crown, and submoustachial stripe are black, and it has a silvery-white cheek patch. The rest of the underparts are yellow. The upperparts are mostly olive-gray with a bright-red wing patch and tail coverts, and orange-fringed primaries and outer tail feathers. The adult female is similar but somewhat duller; more yellow, and with yellow tail coverts. The juvenile is duller, with olive underparts and a pale bill. An inhabitant of broad-leaved evergreen forests and secondary growth mostly above 450 meters. Often in small parties; joins mixed feeding flocks. A common resident throughout, except Singapore and southern Vietnam. Length: 17 cm

SPECTACLED BARWING *Actinodura ramsayi*

A medium-sized brown but very distinctive babbler with extensive fine black barring on the wings and tail. The crown is orangey brown, often raised in a crest, and the sides of the face are gray with a white eye ring. The wings are rufous with very contrasting black barring. The less conspicuously barred tail is tipped white. The sexes are alike. Found in broad-leaved evergreen forests, secondary growth, scrub, and grasslands usually above 1,000 meters. A common resident in the northern parts of Burma, Thailand, Laos, and Vietnam. Length: 24 cm

CHESTNUT-TAILED MINLA *Actinodura strigula*

A locally common resident in broad-leaved evergreen forests at higher elevations, usually above 1,600 meters. Found almost throughout the region. An active arboreal insectivore often seen in mixed feeding flocks. The adult has olive upperparts with a contrasting chestnut head. The underparts are olive-yellow with a barred black-and-white throat. The wings and tails are very distinctively marked with black, white, and chestnut. The sexes are alike. The juvenile is grayish on the head and upperparts, duller overall. Length: 16–19 cm

Chestnut-capped Laughingthrush

Black-headed Sibia

Silver-eared Mesia

Spectacled Barwing

Chestnut-tailed Minla

ASIAN FAIRY BLUEBIRD *Irena puella*

The male is an instantly recognizable, startlingly deep-blue and velvety-black bird with red eyes. The forehead to uppertail coverts are brilliant glossy blue; the square tail and wings are black. The underparts are all black. The female is duller blue all over, darker on the wings and tail. Found in all types of forested habitats; an arboreal frugivore that often congregates at fruiting trees. Generally feeds in the mid-story. The voice is a loud, rollicking, 4- to 10-note *hwit-hwit-hwit-hwit* … A common resident throughout. Length: 24–27 cm

MUSCICAPIDAE OLD WORLD FLYCATCHERS

ASIAN BROWN FLYCATCHER *Muscicapa dauurica*

In the adult the upperparts are grayish-brown with paler lores, a short whitish submoustachial stripe, and an indistinct malar stripe. The underparts are whitish with a brownish wash on the sides of the throat and breast. The iris is brown with a thin pale eye ring. The bill is black with a yellowish base to the lower mandible. The sexes are alike. The juvenile is spotted buffish on the upperparts and has dark scaling on the whiter underparts. Found in all types of wooded habitats, where it forages mostly in the mid-story from a prominent perch, sallying out to catch insects on the wing. Usually solitary. This species can very easily be confused with others in the genus; care is required for identification. The widespread Dark-sided Flycatcher has a more prominent submoustachial stripe and half-collar, with heavy streaking on the underparts. Very similar Brown-streaked Flycatcher is much browner, with brown streaks on the breast and flanks. A common resident and winter visitor throughout. Length: 13 cm

ORIENTAL MAGPIE ROBIN *Copsychus saularis*

A very familiar and common inhabitant of gardens, parks, cultivated areas, and open woodlands throughout. The adult male is glossy black on the upperparts, with a broad white stripe on the center of the wing and white outer tail feathers. The underparts are glossy black from the chin to the breast, and sharply delineated from the white belly and undertail. The female is duller with grayish upperparts and breast. The juvenile has a buffish mottled breast. Very vocal; the powerful, varied song consists of plaintive whistles on different pitches, as well as mimicry. Often sings from a conspicuous perch. Feeds on invertebrates and small vertebrates such as lizards, on which it pounces from a low perch. Usually in pairs. Length: 20 cm

WHITE-RUMPED SHAMA *Copsychus malabaricus*

The adult male is glossy black on the head, breast, and upperparts except for a prominent white rump. The underparts are rufous; the legs are pink. The black tail is very long and graduated, with white feathers on the undertail. The female is duller with a shorter tail. The juvenile is brown, with buffish speckles on the head and breast and whitish underparts. A skulking bird of thickets and dense secondary growth in broad-leaved and deciduous forests. Hops and runs with short flights in the understory, where it gleans foliage for insects. Usually solitary or in pairs. The song is a rich, melodious string of 2- or 3-note phrases with a bubbly quality; often incorporates mimicry. A commonly heard alarm call is a soft, easily overlooked *tchak*, like the sound of a stick breaking. A common resident throughout. Length: 27 cm

Asian Fairy Bluebird

Asian Brown Flycatcher

Oriental Magpie Robin, female

White-rumped Shama

BIRDS | **MUSCICAPIDAE** OLD WORLD FLYCATCHERS

VERDITER FLYCATCHER *Eumyias thalassinus*

An all-blue, relatively large flycatcher. A common resident and winter visitor throughout the region. Inhabits open evergreen forests and clearings, where it is often encountered on high perches from which it sallies out to catch insects on the wing. Usually solitary or in pairs. The male is turquoise blue with black lores and a narrow frontal band over the bill; the underparts are somewhat paler, with whitish tips on the undertail coverts. The female is paler with pale-grayish lores and fine whitish barring on the throat. As is typical of flycatchers, the juvenile is duller, with buffish scaling and speckles. This species can very easily be confused with Pale Blue Flycatcher, which is bluer with a shorter tail, longer bill, and contrasting blue and bluish-gray on the underparts; it lacks the white tips on the undertail coverts. Length: 15–17 cm

BLUE WHISTLING THRUSH *Myophonus caeruleus*

A large, all dark-blue thrush with a rather horizontal posture. Spotted on the head, mantle, and underparts with paler blue; the wings and tail are unmarked glossy dark blue. The stout bill is bright orange-yellow and hooked at the tip. One race, a winter visitor to the region, has an all-black bill. The sexes are alike. The juvenile is brownish, with a duller bill. An inhabitant of broad-leaved evergreen and deciduous forests, usually found near water such as rivers, streams, waterfalls, and caves, where it forages for small invertebrates in rock crevices and leaf litter, up to 3,000 meters. The call, a high-pitched harsh *cheet*, can be heard above the sound of fast-running water. The genus has a characteristic habit of fanning the tail downward, possibly in order to disturb insects. A common resident and uncommon winter visitor throughout. Length: 30–35 cm

WHITE-CROWNED FORKTAIL *Enicurus leschenaultia*

A striking bird with black-and-white plumage and a remarkable long, deeply forked tail; always found near rivers and streams in primary forests up to 2,400 meters. The steep forehead to crown is white, contrasting with the black face and back; the breast is black and sharply delineated from the white belly. The lower back and rump are white; the tail is barred black and white. The legs are pinkish. The sexes are alike. The juvenile is brownish, with no white on the crown and a shorter tail. A shy bird; restless and easily disturbed. Flies low to the ground, usually uttering a shrill, high-pitched whistle. Actively forages for small invertebrates on rocks and riverbanks, constantly spreading the forked tail. A locally common and widespread resident. Length: 25 cm

Verditer Flycatcher

Blue Whistling Thrush

White-crowned Forktail

White-crowned Forktail

LITTLE PIED FLYCATCHER *Ficedula westermanni*

The male is an unmistakable, tiny, black-and-white flycatcher; the upperparts are black with a broad white supercilium that extends to the back of the neck and an extensive white wing stripe. The underparts are white with a black undertail. The female is gray with a rufous-brown rump; the underparts are paler. The juvenile is heavily spotted and speckled buffish. An active arboreal insectivore in the upper story of broad-leaved and pine forests, generally at higher elevations. Usually encountered singly or in pairs. A common resident, though absent from Singapore, central Thailand, and northeastern and southern Vietnam. Length: 10–11 cm

SNOWY-BROWED FLYCATCHER *Ficedula hyperythra*

A small, dumpy flycatcher with a prominent, bright-white supercilium on slaty-blue upperparts. The underparts are deep rufous orange. The legs are pale pink. The female is brown on the upperparts, with an orange forehead and eye ring; the tail is washed rufous, and the underparts are buffish-orange. The juvenile is brown with buffish feather centers, giving a speckled appearance. A rather tame and often inquisitive bird; perches on the sides of trees and low perches near the ground, from which it pounces on small invertebrates. Usually encountered singly or in pairs. Favors primary broad-leaved evergreen forests above 1,000 meters. A common resident throughout, except central and southern Thailand and southern Vietnam. Length: 11–13 cm

WHITE-CAPPED REDSTART *Phoenicurus leucocephalus*

A large redstart with black upperparts and breast, a deep-red rump, and a prominent white cap from the crown to the nape. The rest of the underparts are deep red. The tail is also deep red with a broad black terminal band. The sexes are alike. The juvenile is duller, with buffish scaling, and black scaling on the whitish crown. An active, dumpy bird found almost exclusively above 900 meters near water along fast-moving rivers and streams, where it forages for insects among rocks. Often perches on prominent rocks and outcrops, bobbing the head and cocking the tail. A locally common resident in the northern parts of Burma, Thailand, Laos, and Vietnam. Length: 19 cm

DAURIAN REDSTART *Phoenicurus auroreus*

A medium-sized redstart, black on the back and throat, with silvery-gray crown and nape, a broad white wing patch, and a rufous rump. The rest of the underparts are rufous chestnut. The female is brown, with a duller, less-extensive whitish wing patch and pale-brown underparts. The juvenile is like the female, but with buffish scaling on the plumage. A locally common winter visitor to the northern parts of the region, where it is found in open forests, cultivated areas, parks, and gardens up to 2,500 meters. Has a habit of sitting on prominent perches and shivering the tail. Length: 15 cm

Little Pied Flycatcher

Snowy-browed Flycatcher

White-capped Redstart

Daurian Redstart, male

BLUE ROCK THRUSH *Monticola solitarius*

The non-breeding male is an all dusky-blue thrush with faint, paler scaling and darker on the wings. In one race, a winter visitor throughout the region, the belly is chestnut. In breeding plumage the bird is bluer with no scaling. The female is duller blue, with pale scaling and fringes on the underparts. Uses prominent perches on rocks, cliffs, houses, and dead trees, from which it pounces on prey on the ground. Found in urban areas and all types of rocky habitats up to 1,800 meters. An uncommon resident and winter visitor. Length: 23 cm

SIBERIAN STONECHAT *Saxicola maurus*

A bird of open habitats such as grassland, scrub, and cultivated areas, where it pounces on insects from a prominent perch. The adult breeding male is black on the head and throat; the rest of the upperparts are black with buffy fringes, a white bar on the wings, and a whitish rump. The underparts are rufous, paler on the belly, and with a broad white patch on the sides of the throat and neck. In non-breeding plumage the male has blackish upperparts with buffy fringing, black flecks on the lores and ear coverts, and less-distinct white markings on the wings and neck. The female is similar to the non-breeding male but lacks the black flecks on the head. A common resident and winter visitor throughout. Length: 14 cm

PIED BUSHCHAT *Saxicola caprata*

The breeding male is all-black, with contrasting white wing patches, vent, and rump. In non-breeding plumage the male has buffish fringing, including rufous fringes on the uppertail coverts. The female is streaky brown, with washed-out rufous uppertail coverts. The juvenile is brown, with buffy scaling and fringes on the feathers. Found in open areas, grasslands, scrub, and paddy fields up to 1,600 meters. Often seen perched on prominent low bushes or posts, from which it sallies out to catch flying insects or pounces on prey on the ground. Often cocks tail. A common resident except in the southern parts of the region and in northern Vietnam. Length: 14 cm

GRAY BUSHCHAT *Saxicola ferreus*

The breeding male is distinctive, with mostly gray plumage, a bold white supercilium, and a broad black face mask. The flight feathers are black with narrow gray fringes. The white throat fades into grayish-white underparts. In non-breeding plumage the upperparts show brownish fringing, and the underparts are brownish. The female is brown with a rufous-washed rump and paler underparts. Inhabits pine forests, broad-leaved evergreen forests, parks, and gardens. Perches on prominent branches, often for long periods, from which it sallies out for or pounces on prey. A common resident and winter visitor except in the Malay Peninsula. Length: 15 cm

Blue Rock Thrush, female

Blue Rock Thrush, male

Siberian Stonechat, male

Pied Bushchat

Gray Bushchat, female

Gray Bushchat, male

ORANGE-HEADED THRUSH *Geokichla citrina*

The adult male has a deep-chestnut-orange head, neck, and underparts, with the rest of the upperparts dark gray. The adult female is similar, but more olive-gray on the upperparts. The juvenile is quite different, with dark-brown plumage mottled buff and blackish, and indistinct stripes on the head. A shy and unobtrusive bird of the forest, where it forages on the floor in leaf litter or in the understory for small invertebrates and fruits. Favors broad-leaved evergreen forest and thick secondary growth. An uncommon resident and winter visitor throughout. Length: 20–23cm

STURNIDAE STARLINGS

ASIAN GLOSSY STARLING *Aplonis panayensis*

A highly gregarious, all glossy-black starling with conspicuous, large, bright-red eyes. The sexes are alike. The juvenile is quite different, with brown upperparts, buffish-white underparts heavily streaked brown, and a yellow, orange, or pink iris; the color of the iris increases in intensity with age. Found in lowland forests, mangroves, coastal scrub, parks, and gardens up to 200 meters, it is primarily frugivorous; breeds and roosts communally in very large numbers. Often perches in dead trees and on power lines. The call is a clear, metallic note often uttered in flight and when feeding. A common resident in the southern part of the region. Length: 17–20 cm

COMMON HILL MYNA *Gracula religiosa*

A stocky, glossy-black myna with conspicuous yellow wattles on the head and a white wing patch, conspicuous in flight. The bright-yellow wattle extends from behind the eye around the nape; there is a separate, smaller wattle below the eye. The bill is bright orange with a yellow tip; the legs are yellow. The sexes are alike. The juvenile lacks the gloss in the plumage and has reduced wattles. A forest-dwelling, strictly arboreal frugivore that sometimes takes insects; usually in pairs or small flocks. Has a very diverse range of songs and calls; the commonest call is a ringing, down-slurred *tee-ong*. A locally common and widespread resident. Length: 28–30 cm

CRESTED MYNA *Acridotheres cristatellus*

A largely black myna with a conspicuous short crest, white wing patch, and white tips on the tail. The sexes are alike. The juvenile is browner, with less white and a shorter crest. An inhabitant of paddy fields, cultivated areas, parks, gardens, and urban areas in the lowlands; usually found in small flocks. Forages on the ground for small invertebrates and fruits. A common resident in Laos and Vietnam (except the far south); a locally common feral resident in Peninsular Malaysia and Singapore. Length: 22–27 cm

BLACK-COLLARED STARLING *Gracupica nigricollis*

A large pied starling with a conspicuous yellow eye wattle that extends behind the eye. The head and underparts are white with a broad black collar; the upperparts are black with white wing markings and rump. The sexes are alike. The juvenile is brown on the head and upperparts, and lacks the black collar. Found in open country, grasslands, paddy fields, and cultivated areas up to 1,500 meters. A common resident except in the southern part of the region. Length: 26–30 cm

Orange-headed Thrush

Asian Glossy Starling

Common Hill Myna

Crested Myna

Black-collared Starling

BLUE-WINGED LEAFBIRD *Chloropsis cochinchinensis*

This small, arboreal insectivore is typical of the family, with predominantly green-and-yellow plumage, slender bill and body, and short legs. Forages in the canopy, mostly for insects but also for small fruits and nectar. The male is green (the color, as the name suggests, is similar to that of forest leaves), with a cobalt-blue patch on the flight feathers and tail; the face is black to the upper breast, forming a mask, with a blue malar stripe and bordered by yellow. The female is much plainer, lacking the face mask and with duller-blue wings. The juvenile is similar, but lacks the malar stripe. Found in primary and secondary broad-leaved evergreen and deciduous forests, often in mixed feeding flocks. A common resident throughout the region. Length: 16–18 cm

ORANGE-BELLIED LEAFBIRD *Chloropsis hardwickii*

A highly distinctive leafbird with green upperparts, black face mask and breast, broad blue malar stripe, dark-blue flight feathers and tail, a bright-blue shoulder patch, and bright orange-yellow underparts. The female is much duller, with all-green upperparts, a pale-blue malar stripe, and dull-yellow underparts. A locally common resident of broad-leaved evergreen forests in Burma, northern Thailand, Peninsular Malaysia, northern and central Laos, and Vietnam (except the south). Length: 19–21 cm

DICAEIDAE FLOWERPECKERS

ORANGE-BELLIED FLOWERPECKER *Dicaeum trigonostigma*

Tiny; a distinctively gray-blue and orange plumaged inhabitant of all types of wooded habitats, including cultivated areas and gardens. A common resident in the southern parts of the region from south Burma to Singapore. The male is grayish-blue on the upperparts, with a broad orange stripe on the lower back to uppertail coverts. The throat and breast are paler blue gray, the rest of the underparts bright orange. The female is dull olive-gray, with a yellow wash on the underparts and a yellow vent. Feeds on small fruits, especially mistletoe, as well as small invertebrates and nectar, mostly in the treetops. Length: 8 cm

SCARLET-BACKED FLOWERPECKER *Dicaeum cruentatum*

A tiny, dumpy arboreal bird with a short bill, wings, and tail. The male is mostly black with a bright scarlet crown, back, and rump. The underparts are creamy white; the sides of the breast and flanks are grayish-black. The female is olive-brown, with red lower back and rump; the underparts are pale brown. The juvenile is all dull brown with buffish underparts. Usually encountered in pairs; feeds on small fruits, especially mistletoe, nectar, and small insects. Typical of the family, the call is a short, high-pitched *tsit*. A common resident in the canopy of open forests, secondary growth, and gardens throughout. Often flies very high and direct. Length: 8 cm

Blue-winged Leafbird

Orange-bellied Leafbird

Orange-bellied Flowerpecker

Scarlet-backed Flowerpecker, female

Scarlet-backed Flowerpecker, male

RUBY-CHEEKED SUNBIRD *Chalcoparia singalensis*

A small sunbird with metallic-green upperparts and an orange throat and breast;
the rest of the underparts are yellow. The ear coverts and cheeks are purplish-red.
The bill is relatively short and straight. The female is like the male, but with olive-
brown upperparts and no cheek patch. The juvenile is similarly dull, but lacks the
orange throat. An inhabitant of all types of forested habitats up to 1,400 meters.
Feeds on small invertebrates, fruits, and nectar in the mid- to upper story. The
voice is a shrill, squeaky *tswee*. A common and widespread resident throughout.
Length: 11 cm

PLAIN-THROATED SUNBIRD *Anthreptes malacensis*

A stocky sunbird with a robust bill. The male is metallic green on the upperparts,
with metallic purple on the shoulders and uppertail coverts, and metallic blue
on the wings and tail. The side of the head and throat are purplish-brown with
a metallic-purple malar stripe. The rest of the underparts are bright yellow.
The female is all olive-green above, with yellow around the eye and bright
yellow below. The juvenile is similar to the female, but with a paler bill. Feeds
primarily on insects, but also small fruits and nectar. An inhabitant of all types of
disturbed and more open habitats in the lowlands, including secondary growth,
mangroves, plantations, and gardens. A common resident in the Malay Peninsula,
central Thailand, Cambodia, southern and central Laos, and southern Vietnam.
Length: 14 cm

OLIVE-BACKED SUNBIRD *Cinnyris jugularis*

A very familiar inhabitant of woodlands, mangroves, coastal forests, parks, and
gardens throughout the region. A small sunbird with a long, decurved bill and
olive-green upperparts, a contrasting metallic-blue bib, and yellow underparts.
The female lacks the metallic-blue plumage on the underparts and has a
pale-yellow supercilium; extensive white in the tail differentiates it from other
female sunbirds. A common resident. Feeds mostly on nectar as well as small
invertebrates; an aggressive, active bird usually encountered at lower levels. The
call is a short, rising *tsweet*. Length: 10 cm

MRS. GOULD'S SUNBIRD *Aethopyga gouldiae*

A spectacular red-and-yellow sunbird with long tail streamers. The male has
crimson upperparts with a metallic purple-blue crown, ear coverts, throat,
and tail. The wings are brown. The underparts and rump are bright yellow. The
female is very similar to other female sunbirds, with a grayish hood, olive-green
upperparts, and dull-yellow underparts; best distinguished by the prominent
yellow rump. Found in broad-leaved evergreen forests above 1,000 meters, where
it actively feeds on nectar, of rhododendrons in particular. A common resident
and winter visitor in Burma, northern Thailand, Laos, and northern and central
Vietnam. Length: 11–16 cm

Ruby-cheeked Sunbird

Plain-throated Sunbird

Olive-backed Sunbird, female

Olive-backed Sunbird, male

Mrs. Gould's Sunbird

CRIMSON SUNBIRD *Aethopyga siparaja*

A relatively small, bright-red sunbird with a bright metallic-blue forehead and a metallic-purple malar stripe, a bright-yellow rump, and a gray belly. The female is dull olive-brown with paler underparts that have a yellow wash. A common inhabitant of broad-leaved evergreen forests, deciduous forests, secondary growth, parks, and gardens throughout the region. Generally only in the lowlands in the southern parts of the region. Feeds at flowering trees at all levels. Resident. Length: 11–13 cm

LITTLE SPIDERHUNTER *Arachnothera longirostra*

A small, very long-billed bird with brownish-green upperparts and darker on the wings and tail; has a blackish-gray moustachial stripe and pale-whitish lores and cheeks. The throat is whitish fading into bright-yellow underparts. The male may show an orange pectoral tuft. The juvenile is similar but browner. A very active bird, usually seen flying rapidly through the lower story, where it feeds on small invertebrates and nectar, especially from banana and ginger flowers; pierces the base of flowers to extract nectar. The call is a distinctive, harsh *chit chit*, usually uttered in flight. Inhabits primary rain forests, secondary growth, plantations, and gardens. A common resident throughout. Length: 16 cm

SPECTACLED SPIDERHUNTER *Arachnothera flavigaster*

A large spiderhunter with a large triangular ear patch, wide yellow eye ring, and long, thickish bill. The upperparts are olive-green, darker on the wings and tail; the underparts are yellow, duller on the throat and breast. The legs are pinkish. The sexes are alike. An aggressive bird that feeds on small invertebrates, fruit, and nectar. Found in disturbed areas and forest edges in primary and secondary lowland rain forests. A locally common resident in the southern parts of the region, although now absent from Singapore. Length: 22 cm

STREAKED SPIDERHUNTER *Arachnothera magna*

A large, heavily streaked spiderhunter with yellowish-olive upperparts and paler underparts. The legs are bright orange. The sexes are alike. The juvenile is less heavily streaked. An arboreal inhabitant of broad-leaved evergreen and deciduous forests; feeds on nectar, especially favoring bananas and ginger, and small invertebrates in the lower to mid-story, generally at higher elevations. Very territorial and quite aggressive. A common and widespread resident throughout, except for Cambodia. Length: 17–20 cm

Crimson Sunbird

Little Spiderhunter

Spectacled Spiderhunter

Streaked Spiderhunter

EASTERN YELLOW WAGTAIL *Motacilla tschutschensis*

A slender, terrestrial insectivore with a long tail and long legs; wags the tail up and down as it walks on the ground. In breeding plumage the male has a gray head with a long, narrow, white or yellow supercilium, greenish upperparts with paler fringing on the darker wings, and white outer tail feathers. The underparts are yellow. There is considerable racial variation; mostly the head pattern varies—some lack the supercilium, with more or less gray on the head. The female is duller with a grayish-brown head and paler underparts. Found in all types of open habitats, often near water. A common winter visitor throughout. Length: 16–18 cm

GRAY WAGTAIL *Motacilla cinerea*

Similar to Eastern Yellow Wagtail, but all-gray upperparts contrast with thin white supercilium and yellow rump; white underparts have a bright-yellow wash on the breast and undertail coverts. In breeding plumage the male has a prominent black throat. The female is paler, with a buffish throat; may show some black speckling on the throat in breeding plumage. Found in a variety of open and forested habitats, often near streams. Actively forages on the ground, darting and running for small invertebrates. Pumps tail up and down. The flight is strongly undulating, often very close to the ground. A common and widespread winter visitor throughout. Length: 19 cm

WHITE WAGTAIL *Motacilla alba*

A typical wagtail with distinctive white, black, and gray plumage. There is much racial variation, but all have some white on the face and black on the head and throat or breast. The underparts are white, the upperparts black. The female is gray on the back. In non-breeding plumage the black plumage on the throat is mottled. Usually solitary or in pairs. Behavior is typical of the wagtails described previously. A common to rare resident or winter visitor throughout. Length: 19 cm

Eastern Yellow Wagtail, first winter

Eastern Yellow Wagtail, male breeding

Gray Wagtail

White Wagtail

ORIENTAL PIPIT *Anthus rufulus*

A bird of open grasslands, fields, and plantations, and a common resident throughout. In the adult the crown and upperparts are buffish-brown with fine dark-brown streaking, dark-brown flight feathers with buffy fringing, an unmarked buffy supercilium, and a moustachial stripe along with a darker malar stripe. The underparts are buffy, with short dark streaks on the breast and a rufous wash on the flanks. The bill is pink with a gray culmen; the legs are pink. The sexes are alike. Forages for insects on open ground, usually singly or in pairs. Length: 15–16 cm

OLIVE-BACKED PIPIT *Anthus hodgsoni*

A pipit of forest habitats, found in open forests, woodlands, and plantations up to 3,000 meters. Often in small flocks; forages unobtrusively for small insects on the ground in thick leaf litter and undergrowth. Flushes as a group into nearby trees when disturbed. An uncommon resident and common winter visitor throughout, though rarer in the Malay Peninsula. The plumage is olive-green on the upperparts, with fine black streaks on the crown and faint darker streaking on the back. The head pattern consists of a buffish supercilium, whiter behind the eye, a narrow black eye stripe, a buffish moustachial area, and a black malar stripe. There is an indistinct black spot on the ear coverts. The throat is buffy white; the rest of the underparts are white with broad black streaks on the breast and flanks. The sexes are alike. Length: 16 cm

EMBERIZIDAE BUNTINGS AND NEW WORLD SPARROWS

LITTLE BUNTING *Emberiza pusilla*

A small, streaked bunting; the chestnut head has dark-brown stripes and a thin, pale eye ring. The upperparts are dark brown with broad chestnut fringing. The underparts are buffish, with narrow darker streaks on the breast and flanks. The tail is long and notched. The sexes are alike. Inhabits secondary scrub, open meadows, grassland, cultivated areas, and parks; often encountered in large active flocks. A common winter visitor to Burma, northern Thailand, northern and central Laos, and northern Vietnam. Length: 12 cm

FRINGILLIDAE FINCHES, EUPHONIAS, AND ALLIES

BLACK-HEADED GREENFINCH *Carduelis ambigua*

A small finch with yellow-green plumage and a prominent pink, conical bill. In the male the head is black, the underparts yellowish. The flight feathers are blackish-brown, with a prominent bright-yellow wing patch. The bases of the outer tail feathers are also yellow. The female is duller overall. Found in open woodlands, pine forests, parks, and gardens above 1,200 meters; often in flocks perched in treetops. A locally common resident in northern Southeast Asia. Length: 13–14 cm

Oriental Pipit

Olive-backed Pipit

Little Bunting

Black-headed Greenfinch

BAYA WEAVER *Ploceus philippinus*

A finch-like bird with a short, thick, conical bill. The group is known for its construction of remarkable ball-shaped woven nests. In breeding plumage the male is dark grayish-brown on the upperparts, with buffish fringing, and has a golden crown with brown cheeks. The underparts are unstreaked buffish-brown. The female lacks the yellow on the head and has a tawny supercilium. The non-breeding male is similar to the female. Gregarious; feeds predominantly on grass seeds but also small invertebrates. Inhabits grasslands, reeds, paddy fields. Often considered an agricultural pest. Locally common and widespread throughout. Length: 15 cm

ESTRILDIDAE WAXBILLS AND ALLIES

SCALY-BREASTED MUNIA *Lonchura punctulata*

A small, brown munia with a distinctive scaly breast. The upperparts are rich brown, with yellowish-brown on the uppertail and rump. The underparts are whitish, with dark-brown feather edges. The sexes are alike. The juvenile is buffish-brown, and paler on the underparts with a paler-gray bill. Usually encountered in small flocks among grasses in cultivation, paddy fields, secondary growth, and gardens, often with other species of munia. A common resident throughout the region. Length: 10 cm

WHITE-RUMPED MUNIA *Lonchura striata*

A gregarious, finch-like seed-eater with a short, strong, conical bill and short wings and tail. The upperparts are dark brown with thin white streaks on the back, a white rump, and a pointed black tail. The breast is brown with whitish edging, the rest of the underparts whitish. The sexes are alike. The juvenile is duller, lacks the whitish streaking, and is all buffish on the underparts. Found in small, noisy flocks in grasslands, scrub, paddy fields, and open areas. A common resident throughout. Length: 11 cm

Baya Weaver

Baya Weaver, juvenile

Scaly-breasted Munia

White-rumped Munia

MAMMALS

SUNDA PANGOLIN *Manis javanica*

An unusual-looking, small, ant-eating mammal with an elongated and streamlined body covered with thick, tough, overlapping keratin scales. When it senses danger it rolls up into an impenetrable ball, protecting the vulnerable face and underbelly. The name Pangolin comes from the Malaysian word *penggulung*, which means "roll." It has a small head with small eyes, a very small mouth with no teeth, and a very long tongue up to 40 cm. The male is larger than the female. It is highly specialized for its diet of ants and termites—hence the alternative name Scaly Anteater. Has long, powerful claws for digging out ant and termite nests; scoops up its prey with the long, sticky tongue. Predominantly nocturnal; sleeps in a burrow during the day. Generally solitary. A creature of the forest floor, although it climbs trees fairly regularly. Found in a wide range of habitats, including primary and secondary forests, bamboo, grasslands, and cultivation. Heavily hunted throughout its range for its meat, which is considered a delicacy, and for the scales, used in Chinese medicine. A probably declining resident throughout, except in northern Burma, Thailand, and Vietnam, where it is replaced by the very similar Chinese Pangolin. Length: body to 65 cm, tail to 55 cm

COMMON TREESHREW *Tupaia glis*

A small, squirrel-like creature; differs from squirrels in its long, pointed snout and very different teeth—small and pointed, all of a similar size and adapted for eating insects. The fur is rufous brown on the upperparts and buffy brown underneath, with a pale band on the shoulder. The male and the female are similar in appearance. Very agile and active during the day, mostly on or near the forest floor. Mostly insectivorous, but will also eat small fruits, seeds, and leaves. The genus name comes from *tupai* , the Malaysian word for "squirrel". Preyed upon by birds of prey, snakes, and small carnivores. A common inhabitant of tropical rain forests and plantations in the Malay Peninsula to Singapore. Length: body 17–24 cm, with the tail a similar length

SUNDA COLUGO *Galeopterus variegatus*

The secretive and cryptic forest-dwelling colugo is one of only 2 species in the order Dermoptera, meaning "skin wing." Sometimes referred to as a "flying lemur," it is neither a lemur nor is it capable of flight. Huge gliding membranes stretch between neck, limbs, and tail, enabling it to make long glides of up to 100 meters from tree to tree. Has the most extensive membrane (patagium) of any mammal. The pelage is also remarkable—strongly mottled gray, greenish, buff, and brown, it resembles the bark of a tree to the extent that when still the animal is almost invisible. The female is larger than the male and lighter in color. During the day it clings, head up and motionless, high on tree trunks. Becomes active at dusk when it starts to glide from tree to tree in search of places to feed. Strictly arboreal, it is unable to walk on the ground; feeds on leaves, shoots, fruits, flower buds, and sap. Young born very underdeveloped, like marsupials; spend the first part of their life in a quasi-pouch made by the female's upturned tail and the membrane between the legs and tail. Inhabits primary and secondary forests and plantations in parts of Vietnam, Laos, and Cambodia, and from southern Thailand and Burma to Singapore. Length: to 70 cm, including tail

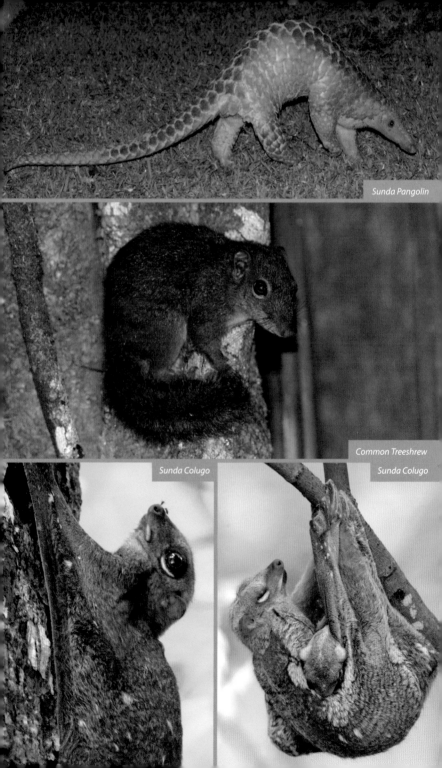

Sunda Pangolin

Common Treeshrew

Sunda Colugo

Sunda Colugo

MAMMALS

LARGE FRUIT BAT *Pteropus vampyrus*

A huge fruit-eating bat found in southern Vietnam and Cambodia through southern Thailand and Burma to Peninsular Malaysia and Singapore. One of the world's largest bats. Has a fox-like face with mostly black pelage and a paler mantle, although this varies with sex and age. The young are paler, and the female may lack the pale mantle. The male often protects a small harem. Inhabits all types of forests, including plantations. Roosts in huge colonies, often comprising thousands of individuals, where it hangs head down from tree branches. Very vocal at roosts and when feeding; often restless and fans itself with outspread wings during the hottest parts of the day. Roosting sites are used for many years, and the trees become stripped of their leaves and bark, and often eventually die. These bats fly out in streams from the roost at night to find fruiting trees; may fly up to 50 kilometers in one night. Feeds on fruits as well as nectar and flowers. An important dispenser of seeds and pollinator of rain-forest trees. Often considered an agricultural pest as it will consume mangoes, bananas, and rambutans. Hunted for food in some areas. A declining resident. Length: 40 cm; wingspan to 1.5 m

GREATER FALSE-VAMPIRE *Megaderma lyra*

A relatively large insectivorous bat with very large ears and a large, erect nose leaf (a fleshy, leaf-shaped structure on the nose) adapted for echolocation. The pelage is grayish, and there is no tail. As in all bats, the wings are modified hands with an extensive patagium (membrane) enabling flight. The sexes are similar. The wings of the Megadermatids are short and broad; their large surface area allows good maneuverability; a hook on the first digit enables grasping. This bat hunts by gleaning prey close to the ground and from pond surfaces in a variety of habitats. Will fly out from a nighttime roost to catch prey, returning to the roost to eat. Feeds on small vertebrates and large invertebrates, even taking small birds and other bats; does not feed on blood. Nocturnal; roosts in small groups in caves, buildings, or tree hollows during the day. A fairly common resident throughout the region. Length: 6–10 cm

FAWN LEAFNOSED BAT *Hipposideros cervinus*

In the alternative name Fawn Roundleaf Bat, *roundleaf* refers to the shape of the elaborate nose leaf, which functions in echolocation; this fleshy protrusion focuses and modifies the signals emitted by the bat. It produces clicking sounds for echolocation with the larynx and emits the sound through the nostrils (rather than the mouth as in other insectivorous bats). The pelage is fawn brown; the eyes are very small, with bare pink skin around the nose and mouth. The ears are triangular, with very pointy tips and dense, fine fur inside. The male has a small gland on the forehead; the female has only a small depression in the area. The female is larger than the male. Roosts in caves, hollows, and buildings. These gregarious bats congregate in groups of up to several thousand individuals; they do not touch each other and fold their wings around themselves when roosting. An agile, insectivorous flyer, it catches most of its prey on the wing as it flies a few meters above the ground. Highly territorial. Common throughout the Malay Peninsula from sea level to 1,400 meters in primary and secondary rain forests and open forests. Length: 50–55 mm

Large Fruit Bat

Greater False-Vampire

Fawn Leafnosed Bat

MAMMALS

ASIAN WRINKLE-LIPPED BAT *Chaerophon plicatus*

A locally common and widespread bat belonging to the family Molissidae (the free-tailed bats), so called for the tail that extends beyond the membrane connecting the hind legs and tail. A strong flyer with relatively long, narrow wings. Found in Burma, Thailand, western Cambodia, and Peninsular Malaysia. Small and chocolate brown, with paler underparts, relatively small, rounded ears, and a wrinkled upper lip. The small nose is somewhat pig-like. The sexes are similar. Forms large to huge colonies of thousands of individuals; roosts in caves and sometimes abandoned buildings. Generally forages close to the roost site in forested areas and over rice paddies. A high and fast flyer that feeds on small arboreal invertebrates. Probably declining due to forest loss, destruction of caves for limestone mining, and harvesting for food. Length: 40–50 mm

LESSER SHEATH-TAILED BAT *Emballonura monticola*

The name derives from the short tail that protrudes from a sheath-like membrane. Has rufous-brown fur, triangular ears, and a simple, unleafed nose. The sexes are similar. This tiny bat roosts in groups in caves, crevices, and tree hollows. The female gives birth to a single pup twice a year. Nocturnal, it captures its small insect prey on the wing using echolocation. Found throughout the Malay Peninsula to Singapore. Length: 43–45 mm; weight: 5–7 g

BENGAL SLOW LORIS *Nycticebus bengalensis*

A slow-moving primate with a light-brown, thick, woolly pelage and a dark stripe running down the back. A whitish stripe between the eyes runs down the nose; there are dark eye patches, the head is rounded, and the small ears are hidden by fur. The tail is reduced to a stump. The sexes are alike. Has large, forward-facing eyes adapted for its strictly nocturnal habits. Mostly solitary and strictly arboreal; the movement is typically slow and deliberate. Found in primary rain forests and deciduous forests, where it feeds on sap, nectar, flowers, fruit, and invertebrates. Sleeps during the day, rolled up in a ball in the middle of thick vegetation. Predators include pythons, birds of prey, and Orangutan. It is thought to be quite common, but this is difficult to gauge. Occurs throughout the region except in the Malay Peninsula, where it is replaced by the similar Sunda Slow Loris. In both species a gland on the arm produces a toxin that is activated by the animal's saliva; thus it is able to deliver a poisonous bite. Length: to 38 cm; weight: to 2 kg

Asian Wrinkle-lipped Bat

Asian Wrinkle-lipped Bat

Lesser Sheath-tailed Bat

Bengal Slow Loris

MAMMALS

BANDED SURILI *Presbytis femoralis*

This small, slender species of leaf monkey comprises many subspecies; the pelage ranges from black to light brown or gray, paler on the underside, with whitish long whiskers on the cheeks and black skin on the face. The tail is long, straight, and dark. Males average somewhat larger than females. Usually has a single offspring, but sometimes twins, every 2 years; the newborn is white, with a dark mark on the back. Diurnal and primarily frugivorous, but also feeds on young leaves. Spends more time foraging in the understory than other leaf monkeys. When not foraging, spends much of its time resting quietly. Mostly occurs in small groups of 5 or 6 individuals—usually a male, several females, and juveniles and young; the group forages together, traveling around in a core territory in search of food. Adult males maintain territorial boundaries by loud calling and displaying. Group cohesiveness is maintained with mutual grooming. Found in mangroves, swamp and riverine forests, and primary and secondary rain forests, generally in areas with taller trees. Probably declining due to habitat loss. Occurs from southern Burma and Thailand to far-northern Peninsular Malaysia and in far-southern Peninsular Malaysia to Singapore. Resident. Length: body 43–61 cm, tail 61–84 cm

SUNDAIC SILVERED LANGUR *Trachypithecus cristatus*

This medium-sized, rather shy monkey has a gray pelage with paler tips giving a silvered appearance; the face is black; there is a pointed crest of hair on the head, and long cheek whiskers. Males are on average larger, but otherwise the sexes are alike. Females give birth to a single offspring once a year. The newborn is orange, with white face, hands, and feet. Predominantly favors young leaves, but also eats fruits, seeds, and flowers. Occurs in groups of 9–48 individuals, usually consisting of a single male, many females, juveniles, and young. Communication within the group consists of a variety of vocalizations, as well as visual communications such as yawning, branch shaking, head shaking, and chasing; social grooming is equally important to the cohesiveness of the group. Highly territorial; aggressive behavior between males is not unusual. Diurnal and arboreal; hesitant to come to the ground. Found in all types of forests, but usually close to the rivers or the coast; resident in western Peninsular Malaysia and Singapore. Very similar Indochinese Silvered Langur is found in southern Burma and Thailand, southern Laos, Cambodia, and central Vietnam. Length: body M 52–56 cm, F 46–50; tail 63–84 cm

DUSKY LEAF MONKEY *Trachypithecus obscurus*

This smallish leaf money is variable in color; may be brown, gray, or black with paler underparts, legs, and tail. The face is gray, with white around the mouth and spectacle-like patches around the eyes; another name for the species is Spectacled Leaf Monkey. Males average slightly larger than females. The female gives birth to 1 offspring every 2 years. The newborn is orange with a pink face. Favors dense primary forests with tall trees, but also found in secondary forests, parks, and gardens. Arboreal and active in the tree canopy, where it moves by climbing, jumping, and leaping, using all four feet. Occurs in groups of 5–20 individuals with 1 male, many females, and juveniles. Plucks leaves and shoots; may feed from as many as 87 different types of plant. Less aggressive than related species. Hunting and habitat loss are the major threats; its numbers are probably declining. Resident in the far south of Burma and Thailand to Singapore. Length: 42–61 cm

Banded Surili

Sundaic Silvered Langur

Dusky Leaf Monkey

Dusky Leaf Monkey

MAMMALS

STUMP-TAILED MACAQUE *Macaca arctoides*

Also known as the Bear Macaque, this large monkey has thick, shaggy, dark-brown fur and a bright-pink or red face whose color fades with age. The tail is so short that the animal may appear tailless. Relatively docile and often kept as a pet. The newborn is white and fluffy; usually the female gives birth to 1 infant every 2 years. The male is much larger than the female, with longer canine teeth. Some older males go bald with age. Mostly vegetarian, with a diet of fruit, seeds, shoots, and young leaves, but also small vertebrates, eggs, and insects. Typically terrestrial, but will climb in search of fruit or when fleeing from danger. Lives in groups of 20–50 individuals of both sexes with a strong social hierarchy. All females remain within the group and thus are all related in some way. Young males leave and join other groups. An uncommon resident in Cambodia, Laos, northwestern Peninsular Malaysia, northern Burma, Thailand, and Vietnam. Favors primary tropical and subtropical rain forests. The home range is thought to be several square kilometers; during the day it travels on average 2–3 kilometers in search of food, resting in shade in the heat of the day. Habitat destruction and hunting are the major threats; declining through much of its range. Length: M 52–65 cm, F 48–58 cm

NORTHERN PIG-TAILED MACAQUE *Macaca leonine*

A large, mostly terrestrial monkey, patchily distributed in Burma, Thailand, Cambodia, Laos, and Vietnam. Fairly common, but declining due to habitat loss, hunting, and the pet trade. Although predominantly terrestrial, it does climb vegetation in search of food. Walks with four feet on the ground. Diurnal and frugivorous; about 75% of the diet is fruit, but also eats insects, fruits, shoots, and seeds; known to raid plantations and orchards. Found in all types of primary and secondary forests, but prefers undisturbed forest. The fur is golden brown with whitish underparts; the fur on the face is pale and long, with a dark-brown area of shorter fur on the head extending down onto the forehead in a peak, giving the appearance of a depression. The face is bare pink with reddish, upward-pointing streaks starting at the outer corners of the eyes and slanting upward. The short tail is less than half the body length and carried half erect. The female is smaller; the male has larger canine teeth. The newborn is black. Very similar Southern Pig-tailed Macaque occurs in the Malay Peninsula; has more olive-brown pelage than Northern, and lacks the red streaks at the external rim of the eyes. Length: M 49–57 cm, F 46–54 cm; weight: M to 14.5 kg, F to 11 kg

LONG-TAILED MACAQUE *Macaca fascicularis*

This small monkey varies in color from light brown to grayish-brown; paler underneath; has a pinkish face with white around the eyes. The male has a moustache and whiskers; the female has whiskers and a beard. Both have a tail that is longer than the body. The male is taller and heavier, and has larger canine teeth. The newborn is black. Like other macaques, has cheek pouches in which it stores food, carrying it away to eat at a different location. Primarily arboreal, it walks and leaps on four feet in the canopy, but comes down to the ground often to feed. Found in primary and secondary riverine, coastal, and swamp forests and mangroves; prefers to be near water, often near human habitation, where it raids plantations and crops. Predominantly frugivorous; when fruit is not available, eats a variety of other things, including insects, eggs, leaves, flowers, seeds, and grass.

continued overleaf

Stump-tailed Macaque

Stump-tailed Macaque

Northern Pig-tailed Macaque

Long-tailed Macaque

MAMMALS

LONG-TAILED MACAQUE *continued*

When it lives near water will hunt for crabs, shrimps, or frogs; also known as the Crab-eating Macaque. Lives in hierarchical troops of up to 60 individuals with many males and females. Large groups are thought to be protective because of a higher likelihood of detecting predators. The female remains within the group she was born into; rank is passed from mother to daughter. The female gives birth to a single newborn on average every 18 months. Has an extensive range of vocal communications and is quite noisy. At night the troop roosts in a single tree along a riverbank, choosing branches overhanging the river, probably in order to escape potential predators. Common and widespread in southern Burma, central Thailand through the Malay Peninsula to Singapore, southern Laos, Cambodia, and central to southern Vietnam. Length: M 41–65 cm, F 38–50 cm

SIAMANG *Symphalangus syndactylus*

A large, all-glossy-black gibbon; tailless and with very long arms; the largest of the lesser apes. The most characteristic feature is a large, sparsely haired throat pouch, almost as large as the animal's head when inflated, allowing it to make very loud, resonating calls and songs. The male is somewhat larger than the female. Lives in family groups usually of 4–6 individuals including a monogamous adult pair, juveniles, and an infant. The female gives birth to 1 young on average every 3 years. Diurnal; spends the day feeding and grooming, resting around midday. Strictly arboreal; moves through the canopy by brachiation—swinging by the arms from hold to hold. Very territorial, it lets other groups know its territory with loud, far-carrying calls; calls from very tall emergent trees so that neighboring groups can be seen; calling starts early in the morning and peaks in the mid-morning; will call later in the day if it encounters other groups. Vegetarian; has been recorded eating up to 160 different species of plant; favors ripe fruit, especially figs, and young leaves, but will also eat flowers and insects. Occurs in the Malay Peninsula, where it favors tropical hill forests generally up to 1,500 meters. An important disperser of seeds in the forest. Threatened by the illegal pet trade and habitat loss. Length: M to 1 m; weight: M 14 kg

WHITE-HANDED GIBBON *Hylobates lar*

A smaller gibbon with variable pelage ranging from light brown to black, with white hands and feet, and a ring of white fur around the bare black face. Tailless, with very long arms and short legs, especially adapted to its mode of brachiating locomotion (swinging by the arms from hold to hold) in the treetops; very agile and acrobatic, traveling from limb to limb in an apparently effortless manner. The sexes are similar, but males average somewhat heavier. Strictly arboreal; may spend a lifetime without ever descending to the ground. Habits are similar to those of the Siamang and other gibbons; lives in family groups and defends a territory with loud calls and songs. An elaborate duet between the male and the female is thought to maintain the pair bond. About 75% of the diet is fruit, especially figs. Found in primary lowland to submontane rain forests and mixed deciduous forests in eastern and southern Burma, Thailand (except the west), and the Malay Peninsula. Hunted for its meat and for the pet trade; also threatened by habitat destruction. Length: 42–58 cm

Siamang
White-handed Gibbon

MAMMALS

GOLDEN JACKAL *Canis aureus*

A bit like a small wolf, this dog has golden-brown fur; the back is mottled black, brown, and white; the tail is long and fluffy. About the size of a tall dog, with long, pointed ears and a long muzzle. The sexes are alike. Common and widespread in Burma, north and central Thailand, Laos, north Cambodia, and west-central Vietnam; can occur in high densities in areas with sufficient food and habitat. Favors dry areas, but can occur in a wide variety of habitats due to its omnivorous and opportunistic feeding habits—grasslands, dry forests, deserts, and agricultural areas. Will eat garbage near human habitation, but mainly eats small mammals, eggs, frogs, insects, and berries. Monogamous; breeding pairs defend territories and are very vocal with a variety of barks, growls, howls, and cackling calls for defense of territories and social bonding. The female gives birth to up to 9 pups in an underground den. Travels long distances in search of food, consuming it on the spot and returning to the den to regurgitate it for the young. The young typically remain with the adults for up to 2 years, and then help to raise the next litter. Length: body 70–85 cm, tail 25 cm

DHOLE *Cuon alpinus*

Otherwise known as Asiatic Wild Dog, this beautiful canid is about the size of a German Shepherd, with reddish fur and whitish on the throat and underparts. Has a luxuriant fluffy tail with a dark tip and rounded ears. The sexes are alike. Highly social, living and hunting in large clans, breaking off into smaller packs to hunt. Feeds on medium-sized ungulates such as Sambar, Common Barking Deer, and Lesser Mousedeer, as well as Eurasian Wild Pig, rabbits and hares, and rodents; also consumes insects and berries. Chases prey on long hunts and kills by disemboweling; lets the pups eat first at the kill. The female typically has a litter of 4–6 pups, which stay at the den site for 60–70 days, during which time members of the clan bring food to the mother at the den and regurgitate food for the young once they are weaned. Very vocal; communicates with eerie whistles as well as a variety of clucks, yelps, and screams. Lives in all types of forested habitats throughout the region. Length: body 90 cm, tail 40–45 cm

SUN BEAR *Helarctos malayanus*

A small bear found in lowland tropical rain forests, it is the smallest member of the bear family. It is brownish-black with short and sleek fur, a yellow, crescent-shaped mark on the chest, yellow fur around the face, small rounded ears, and a short tail. The male is larger than the female by 10–20%. The name comes from the pattern on the chest. Has long, sickle-shaped claws that it uses to break into tree trunks, fallen logs, and termite mounds. An excellent climber, with a long, slender tongue it uses to extract honey from beehives; another name for this species is Honey Bear. Omnivorous; feeds on small vertebrates, invertebrates, eggs, fruit, berries, and roots; especially favors termites and figs. Has poor eyesight but a strong sense of smell. Does not hibernate. The female produces 1 or 2 cubs a year. Primarily nocturnal and generally solitary. Endangered and threatened by hunting (it is thought to be a pest), habitat destruction, and poaching for the pet trade and for body parts used in traditional Asian medicine. Occurs throughout the region. Length: 1.2–1.5 m; height: 70 cm at shoulder

Golden Jackal

Dhole

Sun Bear

MAMMALS

YELLOW-THROATED MARTEN *Martes flavigula*

A slender, agile small carnivore in the mustelid family along with minks, badgers, otters, ferrets and weasels. Has a long body, a long bushy tail, and large paws. The pelage is brightly colored, with mostly rusty brown on the body and a yellow throat; a dark-chocolate-brown face, hind legs, and tail; and reddish cheeks. The female is somewhat smaller than the male. Hunts in pairs or, less commonly, in groups of up to 6 individuals, usually during the day. Omnivorous; feeds on rodents, eggs, small birds, insects, berries, fruits, and nuts. Primarily hunts on the ground, but is an excellent tree climber. The female gives birth to litters of up to 5 kits, which are born blind and hairless. Has an unpleasant odor and is quite fearless. Maintains a large territory and is known to travel 10–20 kilometers in a single 24-hour period. Not considered to be endangered due to its widespread distribution and stable population, and it occurs in many protected areas. Found in all types of wooded habitats over a wide altitudinal range throughout the region. Primarily diurnal, but may be active at night, especially when there is a full moon. Length: M 50–72 cm, F 50–62 cm; tail is about two-thirds of body length

LARGE INDIAN CIVET *Viverra zibetha*

This small, cat-like animal belongs to the viverrid family, a small group of medium-sized carnivores found in the Old World tropics; characterized by a long body and snout, and short legs; most have stripes or spots; most have perianal glands that produce a strong odor with which they mark their territories. This species has a grizzled brown pelage with broad black-and-white bands on the chest, a white muzzle, and a banded tail. The male is larger than the female. This relatively large, mostly carnivorous civet eats rodents, frogs, snakes, eggs, insects, and crustaceans as well as berries, roots, and garbage. Spends most of its time on the ground, but is an agile tree climber in search of birds and eggs. Nocturnal and generally solitary. Sleeps in abandoned burrows in the ground; very territorial, with territories up to 5 square kilometers. The female has 2 litters of 2–4 pups annually. Found throughout the region in primary and secondary evergreen and deciduous forests as well as plantations. Remains common throughout, but is heavily hunted with dogs and traps for its meat. Length: body 86 cm, tail 33 cm

ASIAN PALM CIVET *Paradoxurus hermaphrodites*

This small civet has a grayish-brown pelage with black stripes on the back and black spots on the sides of the body, a black mask on the paler face, and black ears and paws. The body and tail are long, the tail almost the same length as the body; there are no rings on the tail. The sexes are alike. Emits a very unpleasant odor; the scientific name comes from the scent glands at the base of the tail, found in both male and female, that resemble testicles. Found throughout the region, mostly in primary forests, but occurs at lower densities in secondary forests and plantations. A very adept climber; omnivorous, but the main bulk of the diet is fruit. Spends equal amounts of time on the ground and in trees. As a fruit eater it is an important disperser of seeds in the forest, contributing to its regeneration. Generally common throughout. Length: body 50 cm, tail 48 cm

Yellow-throated Marten

Large Indian Civet

Asian Palm Civet

MAMMALS

SMOOTH-COATED OTTER *Lutrogale perspicillata*

This small carnivore occurs throughout the region except for northern Vietnam. The largest otter in Asia, it is found in forests near water in wetlands, swamps, rivers, lakes, and rice paddies. Spends much of the time in the water, but is also comfortable on land. Sometimes found near salt water, but always requires a source of freshwater. Declining throughout its range due to habitat loss and contamination of waterways with pesticides, as well as poaching. This relatively large otter has a more rounded head than other otters, small, low-set ears, a hairless nose, thick whiskers on the muzzle, a flattened tail, and short, strong legs with large webbed feet bearing strong, sharp claws. The dark-reddish-brown and thick, velvety fur is short and sleek, paler on the underparts, with a yellowish throat. The male is larger than the female. Up to 70% of the diet is made up of fish, but also consumes eggs, frogs, crustaceans, and insects. A highly social animal that hunts in groups of up to a dozen individuals, including a breeding pair and juveniles. Forms strong monogamous pairs and has litters of up to 5 pups, which are blind and helpless at birth. Hunts during the day in a territory of 7–12 square kilometers. As with many small carnivores, uses scent to communicate; vocalizations consist of chirps and whistles. Spends the nights in hidden dens built under dense vegetation, in trees, or among boulders. Length: to 1.3 m; weight: 7–11 kg

SMALL ASIAN MONGOOSE *Herpestes javanicus*

This small mongoose, also known as the Javan Mongoose, has a long, slender body; the head is long, with a pointed snout and short ears. The fur is grizzled gray to rufous brown all over. The male is bigger, with a wider head. Occurs commonly throughout Southeast Asia and is highly adaptable, able to live in and near human habitation. Can live in a variety of habitats, but prefers deciduous forests, shrublands, and grasslands; generally avoids closed forests. Mostly solitary; is an opportunistic feeder, taking insects, eggs, birds, frogs, and snakes. Famed for its ability to kill snakes, in particular, by delivering a deadly bite to the back of the head. Terrestrial and reluctant to climb trees; active by day and by night. Has been introduced to many islands and countries throughout the world; is considered one of the world's worst invasive species; initially introduced to many places to control rat populations in cane plantations, a tactic that proved to be ineffective as the mongoose turned to easier picking and has now been implicated in the extinctions or steep declines of dozens of small vertebrates on islands throughout the world. Length: body 25–41 cm, tail 23–39 cm

CRAB-EATING MONGOOSE *Herpestes urva*

This mongoose is found throughout Burma, Laos, Cambodia, Vietnam, and Peninsular Malaysia, and in northwestern and southern Thailand. Grizzled gray, with a conspicuous white stripe on the sides of the neck. The face is pinkish, with a bright-pink nose, paler throat, black limbs, and a long, shaggy, whitish tail. The sexes are similar. Eats crabs but also eggs, birds, frogs, snails, small mammals, and snakes. Solitary and mostly diurnal, occurs in a variety of habitats in both open and closed forests from the lowlands to 1,000 meters. Most often found near water; the preferred habitat of this semi-aquatic, strong swimmer is near water in edge biomes. Thought to still be fairly common throughout, but possibly impacted by habitat loss. Length: body 45–50 cm, tail 25–30 cm

Smooth-coated Otter

Small Asian Mongoose

Crab-eating Mongoose

MAMMALS

BINTURONG *Arctictis binturong*

Also known as the Bearcat, this is neither a bear nor a cat, but superficially resembles a cross between the two. Binturong is the Malay name for the animal. About the size of a small dog; the body is covered in long, shaggy gray fur, often with silvery tips, with a lighter mane around the face. The long bushy tail is fully prehensile; this is one of the few Old World mammals with a prehensile tail and one of only 2 members of the carnivora to possess one. The female is 20% larger than the male. Primarily frugivorous, but also eats eggs, insects, and small animals. Found in the forest canopy of lowland primary and, to a lesser extent, secondary rain forests, but declining due to habitat loss; other threats include hunting for food and for the pet trade. The female typically gives birth to 2 young. Solitary and nocturnal; sleeps during the day on branches; shy, but notoriously aggressive when cornered, defending itself with powerful jaws and teeth. Emits a scent from its anal glands sometimes described as resembling the smell of buttered popcorn. Not highly territorial; home ranges often overlap. Uncommon to rare throughout the region. Length: body 61–96 cm, tail 56–89 cm

TIGER *Panthera tigris*

One of the largest and most spectacular carnivores in the world, this huge cat, the largest of the felids, is unmistakable. Its reddish-orange pelage with black stripes makes it immediately recognizable. The backs of the ears are black, with a large, conspicuous white spot. No two individuals have the same stripe patterns. The male is considerably larger than the female. A strong swimmer, it likes to spend the hotter parts of the day half-submerged in cool water in streams and lakes. Predominantly terrestrial but a strong tree climber. Very territorial and generally solitary, maintaining a large territory whose size is dictated by the availability of prey. The male has a larger territory that usually overlaps those of a number of females. Due to its need for large areas of intact habitat that support its prey animals, the range of the Tiger has become seriously fragmented; hunting and poaching have also led to a rapid decline in populations, and it is now extinct from many parts of Southeast Asia. Found in a variety of habitats, but requires intact forest, favoring dense vegetation with secluded locations suitable for dens, with abundant prey and access to water. Preferred prey animals are medium-sized to large mammals such as Gaur, Sambar, Common Barking Deer, and Eurasian Wild Pig. This stalk-and-ambush predator kills by latching on to the prey animal's throat with its powerful jaws, which leads to strangulation. Tends to hunt more at night. Typically the female gives birth to 2 or 3 young every 2 years and cares for them without assistance from the male. In Southeast Asia this species is now generally rare and, also because of its secretive nature, difficult to observe. Length: body 1.4–2.8 m, tail 60–110 cm; weight: to 300 kg

Binturong

Tiger

MAMMALS

LEOPARD *Panthera pardus*

A large cat (although much smaller than Tiger) with relatively short legs, a broad head, a long body and tail, and a very distinctive yellowish pelage with black spots. As with Tiger, no two individuals have the same pattern. Male larger than the female. A rare all-black form is known as a "black panther." The male is much larger than the female. An opportunistic hunter that can occupy a variety of habitats, it is a very fast runner and an excellent tree climber. Able to thrive in grasslands, woodlands, and deciduous and evergreen forests. The diet is broad, consisting mostly of small to medium-sized ungulates, but also monkeys, rodents, birds, frogs, and insects. Typically nocturnal and shy; difficult to detect due to its excellent camouflage and secretive nature. Hunts by stalking its prey, relying on stealth and camouflage to evade detection until it is close enough to outrun the quarry, usually with a great burst of speed. Tends to kill by breaking the prey's neck. The male's home range is large, dependent on the density of prey species, and usually overlaps those of several females. Found throughout Southeast Asia, where it is locally uncommon and declining in fragmented populations. Threats within the region include habitat destruction and fragmentation, and hunting for the trade in body parts. Length: 1.6–2.3 m

ASIAN GOLDEN CAT *Catopuma temminckii*

Found in Burma, the Malay Peninsula, Thailand, and Vietnam, this medium-sized, heavily built felid occurs in tropical and subtropical deciduous and evergreen forests. The tail, which is tipped black, is about half as long as the body; the coat color is usually golden brown but can be brown, black, or gray with white and black lines on the cheeks and forehead, and spots on the paler underparts. The male is larger than the female. Mostly diurnal and crepuscular; generally solitary except during mating. As with other felids, the male's territory is larger and overlaps those of several females. Appears to be an opportunistic feeder, although little is known of its behavior due to its secretive habits. Known to consume small prey items, such as rodents, birds, reptiles, and sometimes Common Barking Deer. It is hunted for its meat, pelt, and body parts used in Asian traditional medicine; populations are considered to be declining. Length: 116–160 cm; weight: to 15 kg

LEOPARD CAT *Prionailurus bengalensis*

This small felid is the most commonly encountered cat in the region. Its name comes from its superficial resemblance to a Leopard; the pelage is golden yellow, with black spots and white-and-black lines on the cheeks and forehead. About the size of a domestic cat, with large eyes and a large pink nose. The sexes are alike. Found in all types of forested habitats, including plantations, throughout the region up to 3,000 meters. Solitary outside of the breeding season; active day and night, but mostly nocturnal. Equal parts terrestrial and arboreal, and an agile climber. Feeds on a wide variety of prey, from small mammals and birds to frogs, fish and insects. Hunts by pouncing and biting. Although relatively common, it is threatened by hunting for its pelt, body parts, and the pet trade. Has been hybridized with the domestic cat to produce the increasingly popular Bengal breed. Length: body 44–100 cm, tail 23–44 cm

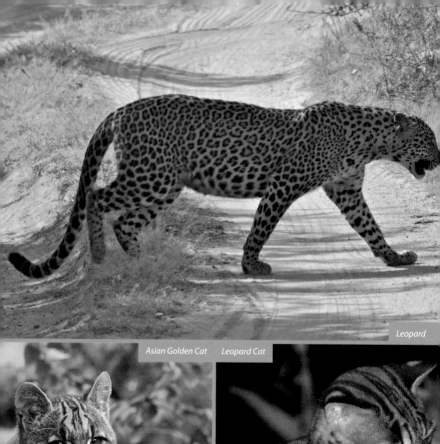
Leopard

Asian Golden Cat   Leopard Cat

MAMMALS

ASIAN ELEPHANT *Elephas maximus*

One of the best-loved animals in the world, the Asian Elephant is an iconic creature that features heavily in the mythology, religion, and history of the region. Elephants have been domesticated since perhaps 2000 BC for use in warfare and agriculture. The largest land animal in Asia, it is instantly recognizable with its long trunk and huge ears. The female is smaller than the male and lacks tusks; some males also lack them. The tusks are used in feeding and communication, especially in agonistic behavior. Long-lived, up to 60–70 years, and highly intelligent. In Southeast Asia it is uncommon in fragmented populations in grasslands and all types of forests. Needs to drink daily, so never occurs far from a permanent water source. Uses the highly dexterous trunk to pluck grass, bamboo, and leaves and pass them to its mouth, consuming up to 150 kilograms of food a day; consequently it defecates 16–18 times a day, producing about 100 kilograms of dung. Due to its requirements for large amounts of food, it has a huge home range and is thus considered an "umbrella species," meaning that its conservation will protect innumerable other species that occupy the same habitats. Lives in groups of 6–7 related animals, with a dominant older female; the younger males disperse upon reaching sexual maturity. The female gives birth to a single newborn on average once every 4 years; the gestation period is 22 months. Threatened by habitat loss and hunting; it is thought that the overall population has been reduced by at least 50% over the last three generations. Length: 5.5–6.5 m; weight: M to 5 tons, F to 3 tons

EURASIAN WILD PIG *Sus scrofa*

This species, the ancestor of the domestic pig, occupies a very wide range of habitats and is common to abundant throughout the region. It is omnivorous, mainly feeding on fruits, seeds, and roots, but also earthworms and other invertebrates. Generally crepuscular and nocturnal; highly gregarious, in herds of up to 20 individuals. The basic social unit is one or more females with offspring from previous litters and adult males during the breeding season. Has a large home range and typically travels quite long distances in search of food. The male is larger than the female. Has a stocky body, a long, pointed head and rounded back, a short tail with a tuft, and a typical, flattened pig nose. The fur is brownish, sparse, and coarse, with grizzled whitish bristles on the face, and sometimes short tusks. The male is larger than the female. The young are warm brown with pale horizontal stripes. The female gives birth, once a year, to a litter of 4–8 piglets in a nest constructed of grass. The life span in the wild is about 10 years. Length: 1.5–2.4 m; weight: to 350 kg

BEARDED PIG *Sus barbatus*

Very similar to the far more widespread and well-known Eurasian Wild Pig, but larger and distinguished by prominent whitish bristles on the nose and cheeks, giving it a bearded appearance; the beard is more pronounced in the slightly larger male, with hairs up to 15 cm long. Both sexes have sharp tusks, longer in the male at up to 25 cm. Breeding tends to occur during fruiting events in the rain forest when there is plentiful food for the young. Mainly active at dawn and dusk; spends the middle of the day resting or wallowing in mud. Known to follow gibbons and monkeys in order to feed on fruit dropped from the treetops. Usually occurs in small groups, which at times may congregate in large migratory gatherings of 100 or more; during this time, may cover

continued overleaf

Asian Elephant

Eurasian Wild Pig

Bearded Pig

BEARDED PIG *continued*

distances of 600 kilometers or more in response to mass fruiting events in the rain forest—a behavior not seen as often these days due to the high degree of forest fragmentation within its range. Found in tropical lowland rain forests in Peninsular Malaysia. Length: 1.0–1.7 m

LESSER MOUSEDEER *Tragulus kanchil*

This tiny animal is one of the smallest of the hoofed mammals and, strictly speaking, is not a deer. The pelage is orange brown with grizzled black hindquarters and white underparts. The triangular head has a dark line between the eyes and the nose; the nose is pointed and black, the eyes large. About the size of a rabbit, with long, very slender legs and a rounded body. The male has elongated canines (tusks) that protrude from the sides of the mouth. The female breeds year-round and can become pregnant again within hours of giving birth; produces 1 offspring, which is fully active with 30 minutes of birth. Solitary and generally nocturnal, though it may be seen during the day. A shy but quite common denizen of the forest floor, feeding on fallen fruit, leaves, and buds. Threatened by habitat loss and hunting. Occurs in dense evergreen forests in the Malay Peninsula to central Thailand, Laos, and Cambodia, and south to central Vietnam. Length: 46–56 cm; weight: 2–3 kg

SAMBAR *Rusa unicolor*

This very large deer has a coarse, shaggy, brown pelage with whitish underparts and a short tail that it raises when alarmed to show a flash of white. The male grows 3-tined antlers annually that are shed annually, is larger than the female, and has a shaggy mane. The rutting male and the lactating female have an unusual gland, sometimes known as the "sore spot," on the lower neck that looks like an open wound; its function is still somewhat unclear, but it appears to be a scent gland. The male is generally solitary, while the female occurs in groups of 6–8 individuals. Mostly nocturnal and crepuscular, probably in response to hunting pressures; rests during the day in shady secluded areas. Herbivorous, it feeds on leaves, buds, fruit, grasses, and bark. Occurs in all types of forested habitats, including secondary and logged forests. An important prey animal for Tiger, Leopard, and Dhole. Found throughout the region; populations declining due to habitat destruction and, especially, hunting. Length: 2.5 m; weight: to 240 kg

COMMON BARKING DEER *Muntiacus muntjak*

Also known as Indian Muntjac, this small deer is found in tropical and subtropical forests, woodlands, and grasslands throughout the region. Has a short, soft, orange-brown coat with white underparts; there is a black line over the eyes from the forehead to the muzzle. The male has short, backswept antlers; the female has corresponding small, knobby protuberances with tufts of fur. The male also has short tusks that are elongated canine teeth. The larger territory of the male overlaps those of several females. Omnivorous; feeds on all types of vegetation, including leaves, buds, grass, and fruit, as well as eggs and small mammals. Both male and female are solitary outside the breeding season, and very territorial; mark the territory with scent from the glands below the eyes and scrapes on the ground. When it senses danger it makes a barking call in order to let the predator know it has been detected. Length: 89–135 cm

Lesser Mousedeer

Sambar

Common Barking Deer

GAUR *Bos frontalis*

This huge and spectacular animal is related to cows and buffalos; the largest species of wild cattle, it is massive in stature with relatively small hindquarters. The overall color is dark brown to black, with a paler muzzle, a huge dewlap, and long white socks. Both sexes have horns, which are flattened and grow from the sides of the head in an upward sweep. The male is about 25% larger than the female and has a more pronounced shoulder hump. This species is mostly diurnal. Feeds in the mornings and evenings, resting in the middle of the day. That said, it has adopted nocturnal habits in areas where there is high hunting pressure. Females and juveniles form small maternal herds of 8–10 individuals; the male tends to be solitary or to form bachelor herds outside the breeding season. In some areas, may have a home range of up to 130 square kilometers. The female gives birth to a single 23-kilogram offspring on average once a year. Grazes and browses, favoring young grass but also consuming leaves, fruits, and twigs. Shy and often surprisingly hard to detect in its favored forest habitat. This magnificent animal has declined markedly in Southeast Asia due to habitat loss and hunting as well as diseases spread by cattle. Length: 2.5–3.3 m; height: 2.2 m; weight: to 1,500 kg

BLACK GIANT SQUIRREL *Ratufa bicolor*

This spectacular squirrel is one of the largest in the world. The thick pelage is black with buffy underparts and face; the black tail is long and fluffy. The sexes are alike. Inhabits the canopy of primary tropical and subtropical forests; not tolerant of disturbed habitats. The remarkable vocalizations include very loud, bubbly, staccato grunts and squeaks. Diurnal and in general arboreal, although occasionally comes to the ground to feed for short periods. Eats seeds, fruits, and leaves as well as eggs and insects. Solitary; the female raises 1 or 2 young in a drey (a squirrel's nest typically in the form of a ball of leaves and twigs), often in a tree hollow. Thought to live 8–9 years, quite long for a squirrel. Found in low densities throughout the region up to 1,400 meters. Threatened by habitat loss and hunting. Length: to 58 cm, with a tail of roughly equal length (up to 80 cm head to tail)

CREAM-COLOURED GIANT SQUIRREL *Ratufa affinis*

Slightly smaller than the Black Giant Squirrel, this species is identified by its colorful markings and slightly smaller size. The back and head are dark gray to brown, and the belly is buff; the ears are short and rounded. The sexes are alike. Diurnal; most active at dawn and dusk, when it forages for seeds, leaves, and bark, plus eggs and insects, primarily in the forest canopy. Occurs in primary forest and not tolerant of disturbed habitats. Its loud, far-carrying vocalizations are similar to those of Black Giant Squirrel. Builds a globular nest in thick vegetation in the treetop in which it roosts and raises young. When resting often lies horizontally on large branches; when feeding sits crosswise on a branch with the tail hanging down, holding the food item with the front paws. Found in the Malay Peninsula, but extinct in Singapore; in widespread decline due to habitat loss and hunting. Occurs at low densities in the forest probably due to competition for food from the great variety of arboreal vertebrates in its preferred habitat. Very sensitive to logging due its requirements for habitats with closed canopy. Usually solitary. Length: to 78 cm, including tail

Gaur

Black Giant Squirrel

Cream-coloured Giant Squirrel

PREVOST'S SQUIRREL *Callosciurus prevostii*

This colorful squirrel is common in the Malay Peninsula, where it inhabits the mid- to upper story of primary and secondary rain forests. A medium-sized squirrel with a bushy tail and a short, blunt snout. The sexes are alike. Another name is Asian Tricolored Squirrel. There are a number of subspecies, most colorful, with black upperparts and tail, white flanks and thighs, and red face, shoulder, and underparts; some other subspecies are duller. The diet is typical of the family—seeds, fruits, buds, flowers, eggs, and insects. As with other species of squirrel, it is an important disperser of plant species within the forest due to its habit of carrying fruits and often dropping the seeds. The largest squirrel in this genus, which contains at least 15 species. Predominantly diurnal and arboreal, it occasionally comes to the ground to feed. At a year old, the female begins to produce up to 3 litters a year with 2–4 pups per litter. Roosts and nests in tree hollows or in dreys constructed of leaves and twigs in the canopy. The newborns are relatively undeveloped at birth, with closed eyes and no fur. Length: 25 cm, including tail

PLANTAIN SQUIRREL *Callosciurus notatus*

This very adaptable, medium-sized squirrel is found in a wide range of habitats, including forests, mangroves, urban parks, plantations, and gardens, but is less common in primary habitats. The pelage is predominantly olive brown with chestnut underparts and a conspicuous black-and-white stripe along the flanks. The sexes are alike. Feeds on leaves, nuts, and shoots supplemented with eggs and insects; considered a pest in orchards. Quick and agile, it is able to leap distances of up to 2 meters between branches. Mostly arboreal and active in the mid to lower story. Litters of 1–4 pups are born blind and hairless; leaves the nest after approximately 6 weeks. The life span is thought to be 3–7 years. Usually solitary, although sometimes in small groups in the breeding season, when up to 7 males may pursue a single female. Has a number of predators, including birds of prey, snakes, and carnivores. Common and widespread in the Malay Peninsula. Length: to 40 cm, including tail

IRRAWADDY SQUIRREL *Callosciurus pygerythrus*

Common in western Southeast Asia, this squirrel has a name that comes from its range close to the Ayeyarwady (Irrawaddy) River in Burma. Diurnal and arboreal, it occurs in the mid-story of temperate, subtropical, and tropical forests as well as plantations, parks, and gardens. It is a rather dull, medium-sized squirrel with olive-brown pelage, paler on the underparts. The sexes are alike. Active and agile, it forages in vegetation and on the ground. The habits are otherwise typical of the genus. Length: body 18–23 cm, tail 17–19 cm

SUNDA BLACK-BANDED SQUIRREL *Callosciurus nigrovittatus*

Very similar to Plantain Squirrel but with a gray belly. The sexes are alike. The habits are also similar, but it is not tolerant of overly disturbed areas; found mainly in primary and selectively logged forests. A lowland specialist found in the Malay Peninsula, where it is locally common, but declining. Near-threatened due to habitat degradation and fragmentation. Diurnal and usually solitary. Length: body 17–22 cm, tail 16–21 cm

Plantain Squirrel

Prevost's Squirrel

Irrawaddy Squirrel

Sunda Black-banded Squirrel

MAMMALS

PALLAS'S SQUIRREL *Callosciurus erythraeus*

Another name for this widespread squirrel is Red-bellied Squirrel; but there are as many as 26 subspecies, some of which do not have red on the belly. The pelage is olive brown, with underparts varying from red to brown; has a thick, bushy tail. The sexes are alike. Its habits are similar to those of others in the genus. The common name commemorates Peter Simon Pallas, a German naturalist who first described many Asian species in the late 1700s. This squirrel is common in all forest types in Burma, northern and western Thailand, Laos, Cambodia, and the central Malay Peninsula. Length: body to 20 cm, tail 20 cm

VARIABLE SQUIRREL *Callosciurus finlaysonii*

This common squirrel occurs in any type of primary or secondary forest, from rain forests to open woodlands and plantations, and is tolerant of degraded habitats. Found from eastern Burma through Thailand, Cambodia, and central to southern Laos to far-southern Vietnam. Variable in color and patterning; the upperside is usually darker than the belly; the pelage varies from black and brown to red or cream. The sexes are alike. There are 16 subspecies; one found in Cambodia is bright red with a cream-colored ring at the base of the tail; in Thailand an all-white form occurs. Able to exploit a very wide variety of food resources and able to change its food habits according to availability, which accounts for its relative abundance. Arboreal and diurnal; spends over 50% of its active time foraging for buds, flowers, fruit, seeds, bark, and sap; also eats bird eggs and insects. When not foraging, spends its time traveling, grooming, nest building, and resting, and in social interactions. As with many species of squirrel, known to hoard food. Length: body 20 cm, tail to 24 cm

CAMBODIAN STRIPED SQUIRREL *Tamiops rodolphii*

This tiny squirrel is found in evergreen and semi-evergreen forests, but is less common in deciduous forests and plantations. Common to abundant in eastern Thailand, Cambodia, southern Laos, and Vietnam. The body is small, with characteristic pale-yellow stripes on the cheeks and a black-and-buffy stripe from the neck along the length of the back to the base of the tail; the tips of the ears have white tufts. The female is slightly larger than the male. The tail is slender and tapered. Diurnal and arboreal; very agile in the canopy, where it feeds on seeds, nuts, nectar, buds, and sap. Known to keep food caches. Movements appear frantic; uses tree hollows for nesting and roosting. Preyed upon by carnivores, snakes, and birds of prey. Length: body 10 cm, tail 10 cm

HORSE-TAILED SQUIRREL *Sundasciurus hippurus*

A medium-sized squirrel named for its very thick, bushy tail. The head, shoulders, and front legs are dark gray, the body reddish-brown to chestnut; the belly is brown to dark gray, and the tail is darker, usually glossy black. The sexes are alike. Found in lowland primary and, less commonly, secondary rain forest in the Malay Peninsula, but absent from Singapore. Mainly arboreal; most active in the mid- to lower story; nests in the canopy. Diet is typical of squirrels. Usually solitary or in pairs. The call is a loud *chek chek* … As in all squirrels, the vision is excellent, and it is an agile climber. May be threatened by habitat loss. Length: body to 29 cm, tail to 29 cm

Pallas's Squirrel

Variable Squirrel

Variable Squirrel

Variable Squirrel

Cambodian Striped Squirrel

Horse-tailed Squirrel

MAMMALS

THREE-STRIPED GROUND SQUIRREL *Lariscus insignis*

This medium-sized squirrel is terrestrial, never observed more than a meter from the ground when it travels over fallen trees. Known to burrow into soil in search of food; feeds on roots, fallen fruits, and insects. Nests in fallen trees on the ground. Mainly found in lowland primary rain forests below 500 meters, but can tolerate secondary habitats. The pelage is rich orange brown on the upperparts, with 3 broad dark stripes on the back from the shoulders to the base of the tail; the underparts are pale grayish. The sexes are alike. Shy; utters a *chi-it* alarm call when disturbed, accompanied by flicking of the tail. Uncommon in the Malay Peninsula, extinct in Singapore. Length: body 23 cm, tail 14 cm

LOW'S SQUIRREL *Sundasciurus lowii*

A very common small squirrel in the Malay Peninsula; in fact, one of the most common squirrels where it occurs, with densities of up to 14 animals per square kilometer in suitable habitat. Favors secondary and disturbed forests; found at a lower density in unlogged forests. Named after Hugh Low, a British naturalist in Malaysia in the mid-1800s. The upperparts are brown and the underparts cream or buff. The nose is relatively straight and pointed, and there is a distinctive pale eye ring. The sexes are alike. Feeds on fruit and insects, and is diurnal and arboreal. Length: to 25 cm, including tail

RED GIANT FLYING SQUIRREL *Petaurista petaurista*

This very large, nocturnal squirrel possesses a huge membrane between the fore and hind limbs that enables it to glide long distances (up to 75 meters) between trees in the forest; the membrane is composed of sheets of muscle that can be flexed and relaxed in order to control the direction of the glide. In order to glide, it climbs to a high point on a tree and jumps with a downward trajectory. A good climber with strong, curved, sharp claws. The pelage is dark rich red all over, with black tips on the nose, ears, feet and hands, and tail. Sometimes shows black eye rings; the eyes are large, adapted for its nocturnal habits. The sexes are alike. Found in all types of forested habitats; quite common through Burma and western Thailand to the Malay Peninsula. Feeds on pinecones, seeds, leaves, fruit, nuts, and insects; nests and roosts in tree hollows, producing litters of 2 or 3 young twice a year. The estimated home range is 3 hectares, but it is nomadic, moving around in response to food availability. Length: body to 40 cm, tail to 43 cm

Three-striped Ground Squirrel

Red Giant Flying Squirrel

Low's Squirrel

Low's Squirrel

MAMMALS

ASIAN HOUSE RAT *Rattus tanezumi*

This familiar rodent is abundant near human habitation throughout the region. It is a medium-sized rat with grizzled brown pelage, paler on the underparts. The tail is dark gray, long, and naked. The sexes are alike. Lives in large groups of males and females with a dominant male. This pest species breeds prolifically and can produce litters of 10–12 pups with a gestation period of 3 weeks; it can thus produce 3 litters in the time it takes to plant and harvest a crop. Omnivorous; feeds on scraps, insects, snails, seeds, grains, and fruits. Nocturnal; inhabits urban and cultivated areas, grasslands, and plantations; builds burrows under rocks and in soil and logs. Terrestrial. Closely related to the European House Rat, but recent studies suggest it is a separate species. The major rodent pest in Southeast Asia, it can significantly reduce crop production. Length: body 30–40 cm, tail 14–20 cm

MALAYAN PORCUPINE *Hystrix brachyura*

Porcupines are large rodents with coats of sharp quills they use for defense against predators. The quills, modified hairs composed of keratin, are embedded in the skin musculature that can relax or erect the quills. Quills are striped black and yellowish, are interspersed with brown, and are concentrated on the rear of the body. The legs are short and stocky. The sexes are alike. Nocturnal and terrestrial. Quite common throughout the region in all types of forest habitats up to 1,500 meters, but needs rocky outcrops for its burrow, which is occupied by a family group. Digs for food in the ground; feeds on roots, tubers, seeds, bark, and fruits. The female produces litters of 2 or 3 pups twice a year. Hunted for food but not considered threatened due to its relative abundance and tolerance of a wide range of habitats. Length: body 72 cm, tail 11 cm

BURMESE HARE *Lepus peguensis*

A typical rabbit with long ears and large, powerful hind legs. The pelage is warm brown. The sexes are alike. Common and widespread from central to southern Burma, Thailand, Cambodia, southern Laos, and Vietnam into the upper Malay Peninsula. Found in dry lowland forests, grass and shrublands, and rice paddies, but avoids wet habitats; has possibly spread with forest loss. The female produces several litters of 3 or 4 a year. Crepuscular and nocturnal, feeding on grass, bark, and twigs. Heavily preyed upon, it is constantly alert. As is typical of the family, lives in groups and digs burrows for sleeping and nesting. Length: 36 cm

Asian House Rat

Asian House Rat

Malayan Porcupine

Burmese Hare

REPTILES

BURMESE PYTHON *Python bivittatus*

This huge, beautifully patterned snake is found throughout Southeast Asia, in all types of habitats, usually near water. The base color is light brown, with dark-brown blotches bordered with black; there is a large arrow-shaped marking on the top of the head. The female is slightly longer and much heavier than the male. An excellent swimmer and climber, but spends most of the day hidden in thick vegetation. When young, will spend much of its time in trees; as it matures its size and weight makes this increasingly difficult, and it reverts to a more terrestrial lifestyle. The female lays clutches of 12–36 eggs and remains with them until they hatch; wraps her body around the nest and continually quivers to produce warmth, but provides no maternal care after hatching. Solitary and nocturnal; feeds mainly on birds and mammals. Stalks prey using chemical receptors on the tongue and heat-sensing pits on the lips. Kills by constriction, first seizing the prey with the sharp, rear-facing teeth, then wrapping around the prey to suffocate it. Stretchy ligaments allow the jaw to be dislocated so the prey can be swallowed whole. Often preys on domestic animals near human habitation, so is often regarded as a pest. Length: average 4 m, but to 6 m; weight: to 90 kg

RETICULATED PYTHON *Python reticulatus*

A huge, nonvenomous constrictor snake; the longest snake in the world. Has a complex geometric pattern of many colors, with diamond shapes on the back, and an unmarked head with a line running from the eye to the gape. Sexually dimorphic; the female is larger. The pattern employs disruptive colors to allow camouflage, assisting the ambush-hunting technique in which it drops from trees onto prey. Feeds on small to medium-sized mammals such as deer and pigs, as well as rats, dogs, and cats in urban areas; kills by constricting and suffocating, then swallowing the prey item whole. Has heat sensitive-pits in the lips that help in locating prey. This solitary species can go for very long periods without food. The female lays clutches of up to 100 eggs. Usually breeds between September and March; the female broods the eggs but provides no care after hatching. Found in rain forests, woodlands, mangroves, grasslands, and plantations throughout Southeast Asia. Heavily dependent on water, so often found near ponds and streams. Heavily hunted for its skins and meat, the populations are declining throughout the region. Attacks on humans are very rare. Length: to 8 m

DOG-FACED WATER SNAKE *Cerberus rynchops*

A very common snake found mostly in coastal habitats but sometimes inland. It favors slow-moving, brackish or fresh waters in mangroves, streams, ponds, tidal pools, and other wetlands. Feeds on fish, crabs, and amphibians at night with a sit-and-wait method of hunting; may also pursue prey at times. The body is grayish-brown on the back with dark bands or blotches; there is a black line from eye to neck. The ventral surface is brown with cream patches or mottling. It is relatively heavy-bodied, and the head is blunt with a rounded snout and small eyes. The eyes are very close to the snout and located on the top of head so it is able to see when half-submerged in water or mud. The sexes are alike. Very mildly venomous, with small fangs at the rear of the mouth; rarely a threat to humans. The female gives birth to 8–30 live young. Nocturnal. Common throughout the region. Thrives in and near human habitation, especially fishing villages. Length: to over 1 m

Burmese Python

Reticulated Python

Dog-Faced Water Snake

REPTILES

ORIENTAL WHIP SNAKE *Ahaetulla prasina*

Also known as the Asian Vine Snake, this mildly venomous snake is not aggressive and not dangerous to humans. The modified teeth that inject the relatively weak venom are located at the back of the mouth. Feeds mainly on lizards, but also on nestlings and frogs. The head is elongated, like an arrowhead, with a pointed snout. A slim and elegant snake. Varies from brown to yellow or bright green, with a thin pale line along the sides of the body. The sexes are alike. Diurnal and arboreal; lives in shrubs and bushes in all types of treed habitats, including gardens and plantations up to 1,300 meters. When threatened it is known to inflate the neck to display black-and-white blotchy skin between the scales. Viviparous, it gives birth to litters of 4–10 live young that are brownish in color. Common throughout Southeast Asia. Popular in the pet trade; also threatened by hunting for the trade in Asian traditional medicine. Similar Big-eyed Green Whip Snake has large eyes and is not found in disturbed habitats; reaches a maximum length of only 1 meter. Length: to 2 m

JASPER CAT SNAKE *Boiga jaspidea*

This slender snake with very large eyes is an uncommon resident in Vietnam and through the Malay Peninsula. Arboreal and nocturnal, it is found in primary and secondary rain forests, usually favoring thick vegetation in undisturbed forests up to 1,500 meters. Only mildly venomous, with rear fangs and a small mouth. Diet includes small vertebrates, including birds, geckoes, and skinks as well as eggs. The body is reddish-brown with black-and-red flecks and spots on the dorsal side; yellow with black scales on the ventral surface of the throat and front of the body. Has a broad head, large eyes, and a slender neck. The sexes are alike. Docile and known to lay its eggs in termite nests. Length: to 1.5 m

GOLD-RINGED CAT SNAKE *Boiga dendrophila*

Also known as the Mangrove Snake, this serpent is characterized by a striking black-and-yellow pattern. Black above with broad, bright-yellow bands (in some subspecies the yellow markings are reduced and restricted to the flanks or even absent); the scales around the mouth are yellow with black fringes, and the throat is yellow, the lower surface black or dark blue. The elliptical pupils resemble those of a cat. The sexes are alike. Considered mildly venomous, it is rear-fanged. The body is long; the head and eyes are large, reflecting its nocturnal habits. Eats lizards, birds, snakes, and small mammals. Found in lowland rain forests, swamp forests, and mangroves, favoring riverine habitats, in Peninsula Malaysia, southern Thailand, and Singapore. A strong swimmer. Lies motionless among leafy branches during the day and is active among trees or on the ground at night. Very docile during the day, but may be more aggressive at night. Lays clutches of 4–10 eggs. Length: to 2.4 m

Oriental Whip Snake

Jasper Cat Snake

Gold-ringed Cat Snake

REPTILES

PARADISE TREESNAKE *Chrysopelea paradisi*

Member of this genus are known as flying snakes for their ability to glide in the forest. Paradise Treesnake is an agile tree climber that glides by dangling from the end of a branch, then launching from the tree, adopting an S-shaped posture and flattening out the belly to create a concave surface on the underparts. As it glides it undulates the body but holds the head still; it looks like it is slithering in the air. Glides may be up to 25 m; this snake rarely descends from the canopy. Diurnal. Mildly venomous with small rear fangs; preys on small mammals, birds, lizards, and frogs. The body is slender with a long tail. The base color is black, with beautiful rich-green, red, yellow, and orange patterns. The sexes are alike. Occupies a variety of habitats, including mangroves, secondary rain forests, and parks and gardens in southern Burma and Thailand, Peninsular Malaysia, and Singapore. Length: to 1.5 m

PAINTED BRONZEBACK *Dendrelaphis pictus*

This genus is characterized by a large, elongated head, large eyes, and an enlarged row of vertebral scales; the body is long and slender. Painted Bronzeback has a bronze head and upper body; a black stripe begins on the snout, passes through the eye, creating the appearance of a mask, and continues down the length of the flanks, with a yellowish stripe below it on the flanks. The underbody is pale yellow to cream. It has a bright red tongue. The sexes are alike. Diurnal and only mildly venomous. An adaptable snake found in forests, scrubland, parks, and cultivated areas throughout the region, where it is widespread and common. Terrestrial and partially arboreal in shrubs and bushes, it feeds mainly on lizards and frogs, and is preyed upon by larger snakes and birds of prey. This shy snake moves rapidly and, when threatened, rears up and flattens the neck to reveal bright-blue skin in order to shock the would-be aggressor. Length: to 1.4 m

COMMON MOCK VIPER *Psammodynastes pulverulentus*

This small snake is identifiable by its very large head relative to its slender body. The triangular, viper-like head gives this snake its name, but it is only mildly venomous, with rear fangs. That said, it can be aggressive and is capable of causing a painful wound. Occurs in a wide range of colors, from light brown to dark brown, grayish, yellow, red, or almost black, but always has a bifurcating pattern on the top of the head. There are light- and dark-brown stripes along the length of the body with scattered small black spots. The underside is pale, speckled brown. The eye has an orange-brown iris and a vertical pupil. The female is larger than the male; gives birth to a litter of 3–10 live young. Can be active by day and night; preys on frogs and small lizards. Commonly found in all types of habitats throughout the region. Length: to 60 cm

Paradise Treesnake

Painted Bronzeback

Common Mock Viper

REPTILES

KING COBRA *Ophiophagus hannah*

The world's largest venomous snake. Found throughout Southeast Asian forests and plantations up to 2,000 meters. Although usually not aggressive, it can be very fierce when cornered and should never be approached, particularly when the female is defending eggs. Feeds mainly on snakes—*Ophiophagus* means "snake eater." As with many snakes, it senses its prey using chemical receptors on the forked tongue that pick up scent particles that are then transmitted to an organ on the roof of the mouth. After eating a large meal it may not eat again for many months. The venom is highly toxic and fatal to humans. The color of this snake may vary from various shades of brown to black; the belly is cream to yellowish; the large, black-edged, shield-like scale on the top of the head is diagnostic. The sexes are alike. The young are dark with yellow bands. The female lays her eggs concealed in a nest of vegetation. Mostly active at night, often near streams. When threatened, it spreads the sides of the head to create a hooded appearance and can raise up to a third of its body length off the ground while emitting a growling hiss. Length: to 6 m

YELLOW-LIPPED SEA KRAIT *Laticauda colubrine*

This attractive snake is specially adapted for life in the sea but spends approximately 25% of its time on land. Usually found in shallow waters around coral reefs and rocky shores in warm tropical waters; mates, lays eggs, sheds skin, and digests food on coral atolls and rocky outcrops, often in large congregations; often climbs trees. Lays clutches of up to 12 eggs, unlike other sea snakes, which give birth to live young. Grayish-blue above with black bands of uniform width; unbanded yellow below. The head is black with a yellow upper lip, mask, and snout. The body is rounded and the tail laterally compressed in a paddle-like shape; the small head is only slightly distinct from the body, and the tail has a similar pattern to the head—this is thought to be a defense against predators. The female is more robust than the male, but otherwise the sexes are similar. Swims and travels on land with a serpentine motion. The venom is highly toxic, but it is not aggressive. Probes crevices and holes with the head in search of the favorite prey item—eels. Found in all seas of the region; common and widespread. Length: M to 1.2 m, F to 1.6 m

WAGLER'S PIT VIPER *Tropidolaemus wagleri*

This highly venomous snake is named for the German naturalist Johann Georg Wagler, who was the director of the Munich Zoological Museum in the early 1800s. This species is sexually dimorphic. In the female the background body color is black (never green) with yellow crossbands around the body, a black post-ocular stripe, and a banded belly. The male and the juvenile have a vivid green background color with white spots (white crossbars in the juvenile female) and a white-and-red post-ocular stripe, and a uniform belly. The large, triangular-shaped head is characteristic; the body is thin and the tail prehensile, adapted for its arboreal lifestyle. Nocturnal and rather slow-moving; remains motionless for long periods, hunting by waiting and striking out at passing prey—predominantly rodents, birds, and lizards. Uses pits on the side of the nostrils to detect temperature and thus sense prey. Gives birth to live young, which are venomous as soon as they are born. The venom is a strong hemotoxin, potentially fatal to humans. Known to be preyed upon by King Cobras. Occurs in primary and secondary rain forests and mangroves in southern Thailand, Peninsular Malaysia, and Singapore. Length: F to 1 m, M rarely more than 75 cm

King Cobra

Yellow-lipped Sea Krait

Wagler's Sea Viper

REPTILES

COMMON HOUSE GECKO *Hemidactylus frenatus*

This gecko is a native of Southeast Asia but has been introduced throughout the world. A very familiar nocturnal animal that forages for food by climbing walls in houses and buildings in search of insects attracted to lights; also found in forests, plantations, and grasslands. Requires a warm, humid climate. Grayish to pinkish-brown, uniform or marbled; the upper body is covered in small granules. The lower surface is whitish. Has large eyes with vertical pupils and a thick, tapered tail, which it will lose if alarmed, thus distracting the would-be predator; the tail also acts as a fat-storage unit; if lost it eventually regenerates. The male is larger than the female. The female lays 2 hard-shelled eggs that are partially attached to a hard surface. The name *gecko* is onomatopoeic for the call, which is also the case for the names in Malaysian (*chichak*) and in Thai (*jing-jok*). Length: to 15 cm

SPOTTED GECKO *Gekko monarchus*

A medium-sized gecko. Rough-skinned, with a base of gray to light brown and pairs of black spots on the upper body; a black W at the base of the neck is diagnostic. The sexes are alike. Nocturnal and usually found in pairs. Inhabits primary and secondary lowland forests and can often be seen on walls of buildings adjacent to a forest. The female lays 2 round, hard-shelled eggs in leaf litter or rotting wood, or adhered to hard surfaces. The call is a repeated *tok-tok*. Occurs in the Malay Peninsula. Eats insects and is shy by nature. Length: to 10 cm

TOKAY GECKO *Gekko gecko*

A very distinctive large gecko. The base color is blue-gray, with a pattern of red-orange spots. Has soft granular skin. The male is brighter and larger than the female; both have large eyes with thin, vertical pupils; the iris varies in color from yellow to brown. Nocturnal and arboreal; the favored habitat is rain-forest trees and rocky outcrops, but adapts well to human habitation and often found in residences. The second-largest gecko species (the largest is in New Caledonia). Solitary and very territorial. Can move very fast; clings to walls and ceilings with toes covered with fine setae (bristles). The female lays 1 or 2 hard-shelled eggs and guards them until hatching. Feeds on insects and small vertebrates, but specializes in beetles; has a very hard bite. The name is onomatopoeic for the very loud, explosive *tock-kay* call. Widely hunted for traditional medicine and the pet trade throughout the region. Length: M to 51 cm; weight: M to 400 g

ORIENTAL GARDEN LIZARD *Calotes versicolor*

A common species found throughout the region in undergrowth and low bushes in disturbed habitats and urban areas. Feeds on insects, small lizards, and even rodents; swallows the prey whole. Quite a large lizard. Variable in color from uniform brown to olive or yellowish; can change the color of the head from red to black or a mixture of the two. A dorsal crest extends from the back of the head to the upper back; has rows of smaller spines above the ear openings. The body is robust and the tail long, stiff, and pointed. The male has swollen cheeks and in the breeding season develops a bright-red throat. During the breeding season the male becomes very territorial and performs "push-ups" to deflect competing males. The female lays 10–20 spindle-shaped eggs in moist soil. Length: total, with tail, to 37 cm

Common House Gekko

Tokay Gekko

Oriental Garden Lizard

Spotted Gekko

REPTILES

COMMON SUN SKINK *Eutropis multifasciata*

This large skink has a heavy, cylindrical body, a short, blunt snout, and sturdy limbs. The upperside is dark olive brown, sometimes with black lines on the back; the flanks are variable and may be black or bronze with black speckles. There is often a reddish wash on the flanks or the sides of the head; yellowish underneath. The scales on the back are keeled. The sexes are alike. A common lizard throughout the region, diurnal and semi-arboreal. Found in open areas, including forest clearings, riverbanks, parks, and rocky outcrops. Eats insects and worms. Preyed on by larger snakes and birds of prey. Length: including tail, to 36 cm

LONG-TAILED GRASS SKINK *Takydromus sexlineatus*

The tail is extraordinarily long. The body is brown, with a cream line on each side and a thicker dark line that runs through the eye below that; the underparts are paler. Sometimes may show a greenish tinge on the throat. The head is small with a pointed snout; the body is long and slender. The sexes are alike. Diurnal; can often be seen basking in the sun. Feeds on small invertebrates. A grassland specialist, usually found among tall grass that it often climbs. Preyed upon by snakes and birds. The genus name is derived from the Greek for "fast runner." Uncommon throughout the region. Length: body alone about 12 cm; overall length, with tail, to 36 cm

CRESTED GREEN LIZARD *Bronchocela cristatella*

A bright-green, slender lizard, sometimes with a bluish tinge on the head and more yellowish underneath, a distinctive crest on the neck and back, and a small gular sac often absent in the female. When threatened, it often turns browner. The iris varies from brown to bright red. The tail is very long and thin, comprising 75% of the total length. An agile, diurnal lizard that is mostly arboreal; hunts insects in thick vegetation and will run rapidly if it falls to the ground. The female lays up to 4 spindle-shaped eggs, which she buries in soil. Occurs in primary and secondary forests, less commonly in disturbed areas and parks in the Malay Peninsula to Singapore. Length: to 57 cm, including tail

BLANFORD'S GLIDING LIZARD *Draco blanfordi*

The most striking feature of the genus is the ability to glide, sometimes remarkably long distances—glides of up to 60 meters have been recorded. Blanford's Gliding Lizard is the largest *Draco* or flying dragon. It possesses wing-like skin flaps (patagia) along the sides of the abdomen that are attached to extended movable rib bones, enabling it to glide from tree to tree; these wings are brightly colored when extended. The male is gray brown with dark mottling; the throat flag is long and light gray; also has red and black patches under the flaps at the side of the neck; the throat is unmarked pale green. The female has a shorter throat flag and dark banding on the back. The male has a territory of 2 or 3 trees overlapping the territories of a number of females. Waits for insects passing by and pounces with its short, sticky tongue. The female comes down to the forest floor to lay 2–5 eggs, then fills the hole; does not care for the young. Found in lowland and hill rain forests in Burma, eastern Thailand, central Vietnam, and Peninsular Malaysia. Length: M to 13 cm, F to 11 cm, not including tail; total length to 38 cm

Common Sun Skink

Long-tailed Grass Skink

Crested Green Lizard

Blandford's Gliding Lizard

REPTILES

WATER MONITOR *Varanus salvator*

The world's second-largest lizard after the Komodo Dragon. Dark brown or gray with yellow spots, and yellow on the underparts; the yellow markings decrease as the animal ages. The male is much larger than the female. The tail is laterally compressed with a keel, adapted for its semi-aquatic lifestyle. The sexes are alike. A strong swimmer, it lives in all types of habitats but always close to water. Eats almost anything, including fish, frogs, birds, mammals, eggs, crabs, snakes, garbage, and carrion. Builds burrows in riverbanks; lays eggs under fallen logs. An agile tree climber that will readily ascend if pursued. Hunts by pursuing and chasing down the quarry; very fast with strong legs. When hunting in the water, remains submerged and then pounces, much like a crocodile. Typically a lowland species up to 600 meters; found in Burma, western and southern Thailand, coastal Cambodia, and Vietnam (except the northwest). Abundant through most of its range in all types of habitat; also thrives in agricultural areas and some cities. Hunted for trade in traditional medicine and for its meat. Length: to 2 m; weight: 20 kg

HAWKSBILL TURTLE *Eretmochelys imbricata*

This endangered species has a worldwide distribution; it is highly migratory and found mostly in tropical coral reefs. A typical sea turtle with a flattened body and a large protective carapace; its flipper-like arms are adapted for swimming in open seas. The carapace is amber in color, with irregular patterns of light and dark streaks and mottling. The head is elongated with a distinctive sharp, curved beak. The sexes are alike. Omnivorous, feeding mostly on sponges but also on venomous jellyfish and algae. Breeds biannually, nesting on remote beaches; climbs onto the beach at night to lay up to 140 eggs in a hole dug in the sand with the rear flippers, then cover them with sand, a process that can take many hours. Heavily threatened by hunting for its shell and meat. Found in suitable habitat throughout the region. Length: to 1 m; weight: to 80 kg

ASIAN SOFTSHELL TURTLE *Dogania subplana*

This unusual turtle in a monotypic genus has a large head and a flat and fleshy carapace with straight sides. The tubular nose is long and tapered. The carapace is greenish-brown with 2 or 3 pairs of dark spots that fade with age. The plastron, or flat belly part of the shell, is cream in the male and gray in the female. Favors clean running water in rocky highland forest streams with sandy bottoms, where it feeds mainly on snails, but also small fish and crustaceans that it crushes with its strong jaws; also scavenges. Typically lies semi-obscured in the river substrate, with just the nose and eyes exposed, relying on camouflage to escape detection. Found in southern Burma and Thailand through the Malay Peninsula to Singapore. Length: 35 cm

Water Monitor

Hawksbill Turtle

Asian Softshell Turtle

REPTILES

GIANT LEAF TERRAPIN *Heosemys grandis*

This large turtle is found in still water bodies such as ponds, lakes, and swamp forests. Favors shallow water; when out of water remains hidden in vegetation, although it sometimes basks in the sun in open areas. Herbivorous, feeding on all sorts of vegetable matter. The carapace is brown with a paler vertebral keel; scales at the rear of the carapace have pronounced serrated edges. Robust head is pale orange with black spots and streaks. The female is smaller than the male, with a shorter, narrower tail. The scales of the young have yellowish centers. Found in southern Burma, central and southern Vietnam, Cambodia, Laos, central and western Thailand, and Peninsular Malaysia; extinct in Singapore. Threatened by hunting and trade for food and traditional medicine. Length: to 48 cm; weight: to 12 kg

ASIAN GIANT TORTOISE *Manouria emys*

The largest tortoise in the region and the fourth-largest in the world. The light- or dark-brown carapace is broad and flattened. There are 5 large claws on the fore limbs, which are covered with heavy, overlapping scales. The hind limbs have 4 pointed claws and prominent tubular scales on the thighs. The male has a longer, thicker tail than the female. This species has a preference for cool, moist habitats; is found in moist temperate and tropical evergreen forests, never far from water. The female builds a nest on the ground that protects her for 3 or 4 days after she lays up to 50 eggs. Herbivorous, but occasionally takes invertebrates or frogs. Severely threatened by hunting for food and the pet trade. Uncommon to rare throughout the region. Length: 50 cm; weight: to 25 kg

ESTUARINE CROCODILE *Crocodylus porosus*

The largest of all living reptiles, this huge predator was historically found throughout Southeast Asia but is extinct in most of the region and now found only in Peninsular Malaysia. Threatened by hunting for the leather trade and its meat and eggs, and by habitat loss. Occurs in river estuaries, coastal regions, and mangroves. The male is larger than the female. Unmistakable, with a large triangular head and heavy jaws; has prominent eye sockets and nostrils. An opportunistic predator that feeds on fish, waterbirds, mammals, and carrion. Hunts by overpowering the prey, then drowning it and dismembering it in swallow-size chunks. A strong swimmer that propels itself with its powerful broad, laterally flattened tail. The female lays 40–60 eggs in nests in mounds of mud and vegetation, and protects them until they hatch. When the nestlings hatch and start calling she excavates the nest and carries them to the water, where she remains with them for several months. Known to live to over 60 years. Very dangerous and known to attack humans. Length: to 9 m; weight: to 500 kg

Giant Leaf Terrapin

Asian Giant Tortoise

Estuarine Crocodile

FROGS

ASIAN TOAD *Duttaphrynus melanostictus*

A common and widespread, stocky toad that occurs in all types of habitats, but favors disturbed habitats, including rural and urban areas up to 1,800 meters throughout the region and is able to tolerate brackish water. Terrestrial; can be found among rocks and leaf litter as well as on lawns, paths, and roads. Color varies widely, from pale gray and olive green to brown, sometimes with black and red spots on the many warts and ridges on the back and sides; the underside is paler plain or spotted. A prominent parotoid gland behind the eye secretes a predator-deterring toxin; bony ridges travel along the top of the head and the short, blunt snout. There is a very distinct tympanum (ear hole), and the male has a large vocal sac. The female is slightly larger than the male. Feeds on a wide range of invertebrates. Generally solitary and nocturnal. Breeds during periods of heavy rain; the tadpoles are small and black, usually found in still water such as puddles and ponds. The call is a rather high-pitched *kwa kwa kwa*. Length: to 20 cm

WALLACE'S FLYING FROG *Rhacophorus nigropalmatus*

This remarkable frog, named after the great 19th-century naturalist Alfred Russel Wallace, is distinguished by its large size and the black webbing on its very large feet. An inhabitant of the mid-canopy in primary lowland tropical rain forests, it has the ability to make long glides between trees from high perches by spreading the toes to use their webbing as a parachute; can glide up to 15 meters from a launching point, and its specially adapted toe pads enable it to land safely on smooth tree trunks. The upperside is bright green with yellow sides; has large eyes with a horizontal slit-shaped pupil; the underparts are whitish. There is a prominent tympanum, and it has a rounded snout and smooth skin. The very large feet have bulbous discs on the toes. The male is smaller than the female. Feeds on small invertebrates. Descends to the ground only to mate, often in large aggregations in vegetation near forest ponds. The female produces a fluid that she whips up by beating her hind legs to form a foam nest; she then lays the eggs in the foam above the water; when the tadpoles hatch they fall into the water. Occurs throughout the Malay Peninsula; while it is generally rarely seen, it is not endangered. However, it faces threats from habitat loss and degradation. Length: to 10 cm

HARLEQUIN FLYING FROG *Rhacophorus pardalis*

Another gliding frog of the canopy, found in tall primary and secondary rain forests. Its yellow flanks, spotted with black, and the red webbing between its toes make it easily identifiable. The upperside is mottled brown, sometimes with scattered white spots. The underside is pale pink; it has a short rounded snout and large yellow or orange eyes with a horizontal pupil. The female is larger than the male. As with other shrub frogs, this species comes to the ground only to breed; it builds a foam nest in the same manner as Wallace's Flying Frog. Extensive webbing between the toes allows it to glide between branches and trees in dense forest. Found in the Malay Peninsula, it is believed to be relatively common but is not often seen, as it is usually high in the canopy. The male calls with a series of chuckles. Length: to 7 cm

Asian Toad

Wallace's Flying Frog

Harlequin Flying Frog

FROGS

GREEN PADDY FROG *Hylarana erythraea*

A common frog, found throughout the region in subtropical and tropical lowland and montane forests, freshwater lakes, marshes, rural gardens and rice paddies, and roadside ditches up to 1,200 meters. Easily identified by the black-bordered white bands along the side of the body; the back is usually green, sometimes brown. The ventral surface is whitish. Has white lips, a reddish tympanum, with large eyes and a pointed snout. The hind legs are very long, and it is a strong jumper. Nocturnal, shy, and agile. Sexually dimorphic; the female is considerably larger. The call is a squeaky warble, given by the male from shallow water usually late at night. The female lays her eggs in still water with abundant vegetation. The tadpole is about 40–50 mm in length, mottled dark and light gray and with a red iris. Length: M to 4 cm, F to 7 cm

FOUR-LINED TREEFROG *Polypedates leucomystax*

A very familiar small to medium-sized frog found throughout Southeast Asia in wetlands, forests, and especially around human habitation; not in primary forests. Usually encountered close to the ground. A sexually dimorphic species; the female is larger. The base color is a shade of brown that varies from light brown to yellowish-, reddish-, or grayish-brown to dark brown, with variable patterns of spots and stripes, but usually with 4 darker lines on the back. Breeds year-round in wetter habitats and during the wet season in drier areas. Males congregate at stagnant bodies of water, calling from the edges; after mating the female lays 100–400 eggs in foam nests that are attached to vegetation above or at the edge of the water. The repetitive, monosyllabic call is a familiar sound throughout the region. Length: M 5 cm, F 8 cm

ASIAN GRASS FROG *Fejervarya limnocharis*

This very common and widespread small frog is found throughout Southeast Asia. It occurs in all types of open, wet habitats, including rice paddies, forest clearings, parks, and gardens; usually found in vegetation at water's edge. Gray brown to olive, with raised ridges on the back and a white belly. The snout is pointed, and there is a V-shaped dark mark between the eyes, usually with a yellow vertebral stripe. The throat of the male is mottled brown. Sexually dimorphic, the female a little larger. Nocturnal. The call is a loud *kraa-kraa-kraa* …
Length: F to 6 cm, M to 5 cm

Green Paddy Frog

Four-lined Treefrog

Asian Grass Frog

COMMON ROSE *Atrophaneura aristolochiae*

This beautiful swallowtail butterfly is common and widespread throughout Southeast Asia in forested habitat. The female is velvety black, with a large whitish patch with black veins on the fore wing; the hind wings are black with a long tail, a chain of bright-red spots on the ridged margins, and a white patch in middle of the wing. The underside is similar but not as bright. The body and head are crimson. The male has narrower fore wings, with no white on the wings, and lacks the red spots on the upperside. The flight is slow and high as it flutters from flower to flower in search of nectar. This inedible butterfly is commonly mimicked by the edible Common Mormon (see following page). Common Rose sequesters poisons from the food plants it consumes while a caterpillar, making it poisonous to potential predators. When handled, it emits a foul odor. Caterpillar is short and fat; brown with red tubercles and a white patch on a segment of the thorax. Wingspan: 9–10 cm

GOLDEN BIRDWING *Troides aeacus*

This large and spectacular butterfly is found throughout the region. The male has black fore wings with white-bordered veins and bright-yellow hind wings; the underside is similar to the upperside. The female is larger, with dark-brown wings and with a different, more intricate yellow pattern on the hind wing. Birdwings have club-like antennae; the body is black with yellow strips and yellow on the underside of the abdomen. Tends to glide at higher levels; a strong flyer found in tropical and semi-tropical evergreen forests. Often seen basking in sunlit areas. The adult feeds on nectar-bearing flowers and is an important pollinator. The female lays spherical eggs under the leaves of climbing vines, one under each leaf; when an egg hatches the caterpillar feeds on the leaves; it is poisonous due to its ingestion of compounds from the vines' leaves that become concentrated in the tissues. Caterpillar is brownish; spine-line tubercles projecting from the upper body are black with red tips. The chrysalis is camouflaged to look like a dead leaf. Wingspan: 16 cm

RAJAH BROOKE'S BIRDWING *Trogonoptera brookiana*

A dramatically beautiful butterfly found in the Malay Peninsula near rivers and hot springs in tropical rain forests. Named after James Brooke, a 19th-century ruler of Sarawak in Borneo known as the White Rajah. The male has elongated black wings with a chain of triangular bright metallic-green spots on the fore wings and a green patch near the body on the hind wing; the underside is dark brown; the body and antennae are black, the head bright red. The female is quite different, with brown wings and white patches at the tips of the fore wings and base of the hind wings. Often gathers in large spectacular groups at puddles and salt licks. Drinks water containing salts and minerals from puddles and feeds on nectar from flowers, particularly that of the *Bauhinia* genus. The male is seen much more often as the female is very secretive; she lays up to 50 small, round white eggs on the leaves of a suitable food plant. Caterpillar is brown and green, with pale brown spikes. Wingspan: 15–17 cm

Common Rose

Golden Birdwing

Rajah Brooke's Birdwing

INVERTEBRATES

COMMON MORMON *Papilio polytes*

This large swallowtail is common and widespread in Southeast Asia, where it is typically seen in forest clearings. The name refers to the practice of polygamy in the Mormon religious sect; the male of this species is often found with 3 or more females. The male is distinctive: all blackish-blue on the upperside, sometimes with a small red streak at the base of the fore wing; lacks tails on the hind wing. Entirely black on the fore wing; the hind wing is black with prominent bright-crimson markings. The polymorphic females display mimicry of inedible species, with up to 26 different forms recorded. There are tailed and tailless female forms; one of the commonest is generally similar to the male but with a white patch at the apex on the fore wing. Another female form has long tails, with red at the base of the fore wings and the edge of hind wings, and with black-bordered white cells on the inner hind wings. One other female form is pale brown with grayish streaks and red at the base of the fore wing and bluish-black at the base of the hind wing; it lacks tails. The caterpillar is bright green with white markings and an eye-like spot on the thorax. Wingspan: to 15 cm

COMMON BLUEBOTTLE *Graphium sarpedon*

The male and female of this species are similar. The upperside is black with a striking broad turquoise medial band; the underside is similar, with a brownish base. There is a small red spot near the body on the base of the wings, and some short red lines on the rear of the hind wings. The head and body are black. Typically found in wet lowland forests; the flight is rapid and busy. The young caterpillar is black, with short branching spines and a short yellow tail; as it grows it changes to green and develops a hump in the thoracic region, sparse short black spikes, and a pair of white spikes in place of the tail. The caterpillar feeds on laurel bushes, including cinnamon trees; the range of the species has expanded due to the expansion of cinnamon plantations. The adult feeds on the nectar of a range of flowering bushes and trees. Congregations of adult males also can often be seen sipping water containing salts and minerals at small puddles, and they are attracted to carcasses and animal droppings. Found throughout Southeast Asia. When resting holds the wings erect; when feeding rapidly quivers the wings. Wingspan: 7 cm

RED-BASE JEZEBEL *Delias pasithoe*

The male of this medium-sized butterfly is black on the underside, with broad white streaks on the fore wing; the hind wing is yellow with a bright-red base. The upperside is plainer, with diffuse white streaks and a yellow wash on the inside hind wing. The head and body are black. The female is brownish, with markings that are similar but less distinct than those of the male. Inhabits forests and meadows. Migratory behavior has been recorded. The caterpillar is reddish-brown, with rows of bristles on each segment; the base of the bristles is yellow and the tips are black; it is about 5 cm in length; feeds on young leaves of the cheesewood tree. Common and widespread throughout the region. Wingspan: 6–9 cm

Common Mormon, female

Common Bluebottle

Red-base Jezebel

BLUE SPOTTED CROW *Euploea midamus*

A locally common butterfly often seen visiting flowers and puddles in forests throughout Southeast Asia. The sexes are similar; the adult is blackish-brown on the underside with a series of white marginal and submarginal spots; the upperside has a sheen of deep metallic blue. The body is black with prominent white spots. The caterpillar is a spectacular bright yellow with jet-black curly tubercles and spots along the sides of the body. The favored host plants are various species of the Apocynaceae (dogbane) family. Wingspan: 8 cm

LARGE TREE NYMPH *Idea leuconoe*

A graceful butterfly with semi-transparent white wings with black veins and numerous black spots. The head and thorax are streaked and spotted black; the white abdomen has a black line across the upperside. The flight is characteristically slow, weak, and fluttery; it glides and looks like it's floating—hence the alternative name Paper Kite. Generally found in the upper story. Thought to be distasteful to potential predators; the body contains toxins derived from the caterpillar's ingestion of poisonous substances from plants. The adult male will rest in patches of sunlight with the wings partly open or outspread. A common species in mangroves and lowland rain forests throughout the region. Another 4 species of *Idea* occur in Southeast Asia—Malayan Tree Nymph, Spotted Tree Nymph, Common Tree Nymph, and Burma Tree Nymph. All are similar in appearance and behavior to Large Tree Nymph. Wingspan: 13–15 cm

CLIPPER *Parthenos sylvia*

Mostly found in primary forest, usually near rivers up to 300 meters, in Burma, Thailand, and Malaysia, this is a familiar, fast-flying butterfly. The upperside has a base color of purple or blue, with a complex pattern of white spots and black stripes and blotches. The underside is pale greenish-gray. The sexes are similar in coloring and pattern, but the female is larger. Flies with shallow, rapid wing beats alternating with short glides. Feeds on nectar, particularly that of lantanas. The caterpillar is black with green or yellow stripes and long-branched, reddish-brown spines. Wingspan: 4–6 cm

COMMON ARCHDUKE *Lexias pardalis*

This species displays extreme sexual dimorphism. The male is black, with bright metallic-blue margins; the underside is brown with white spots. The female is brown with buffy spots; the underside is dark brown on the fore wings with greenish hind wings, both with white spots. The antennae of both are black with orange tips. The very similar Archduke *Lexias dirtea* has entirely black antennae. Common Archduke is a strong, rapid flyer; it is essentially a forest butterfly found in shaded, dense primary forest groves. It is attracted to rotting fruit. The caterpillar is bright leaf green, with complex, long, spinous bristles with orange tips. Fairly common in suitable habitat throughout the region. Wingspan: 10 cm

Blue Spotted Crow

Large Tree Nymph

Clipper

Common Archduke

INVERTEBRATES

BLUE PANSY *Junonia orithya*

The male of this beautiful nymphalid butterfly has velvety black fore wings; the inner half has 2 orange-and-blue bands; the outer half is brown, with 2 orange eyespots with black centers toward the outer edges. The hind wing is bright blue with a small area of velvety back at the base; there is a large orange eyespot and a smaller black spot. The edges of both fore and hind wings show 2 thin black lines. The underside is marbled shades of brown with 2 prominent eyespots. The female is similar to the male but larger and duller. The caterpillar has a shiny black head and a greenish-brown body covered with hairy spines. Found in lowland parks, gardens, and open grassy areas throughout the region. Typically visits tiny flowers in open grassy areas, and bathes in the sun with wings open. Has a rapid, gliding flight. Wingspan: 4–5.5 cm

TROPICAL SWALLOWTAIL MOTH *Lyssa zampa*

This spectacular nocturnal moth is found throughout the region, but is most common in montane forests. Brown with diagonal white bands on the upperside over both the fore and hind wings, with dark stripes on the leading edge of the fore wing and the rear of the hind wing. Conspicuous tails on the hind wing are tipped white. Usually immobile during the day, quite active at night. Some migration behavior has been recorded. The caterpillar is yellowish with a reddish-brown head and legs; there are pale-brown bands over the wrinkled body and white spiracles ringed with black. Wingspan: to 16 cm

CICADA Cicadidae

This familiar family of insects is best known for their loud, buzzing songs; sometimes the combination of thousands of insects creating noise can be overwhelming. Males produce a species-specific noise with specially adapted membranes located on the abdomen. Their songs are among the loudest sounds in the forests. In the Asian forests there is a very high biodiversity, with many species inhabiting the same ecosystem. In this noisy environment, cicadas must compete over the sounds of other insects, frogs, and birds to be heard. Many species of cicada have evolved songs with characteristic rhythmic patterns and, in many cases, even a high degree of frequency modulation. Some also have a fixed time for singing and are acoustically active only during a certain species-specific period each day, often for 30–60 minutes. The life cycle is also unusual: when the young hatch from the eggs the nymphs immediately burrow into the ground to suck on the sap of plant roots; depending on the species, the nymphs spend up to several years underground before surfacing as adults. The cicadas belong to the hemipterans, the true bugs. They have a stout body, with a broad head, transparent wings, and large eyes. Wingspan: from 3 cm to the largest (the Empress Cicada) with a wingspan of 18–20 cm

Blue Pansy

Tropical Swallowtail Moth

Cicada

INVERTEBRATES

LANTERN BUGS *Pyrops* spp.

The lantern bugs are a genus of planthopper in the order Hemiptera, the true bugs, which includes the cicadas, aphids, leafhoppers, and other insects that possess proboscis-like mouthparts designed for piercing plants and sucking out liquids. They are large insects with a remarkable elongated, snout-like projection called a rostrum on the head that they use to suck juices out of fruits and flowers. They do not emit light but are called lantern bugs for their bright colors—the wings are beautiful: brightly colored and patterned. Various species of this genus are found in different locations throughout Southeast Asia. Usually seen sitting head upward on tree trunks. Length: to 8 cm; wingspan: to 6.5 cm

FULVOUS FOREST SKIMMER *Neurothemis fulvia*

The dragonflies are a large order of flying insects with large eyes, 2 pairs of transparent wings, and a long, thin body. Predators, they feed on mosquitoes, flies, bees, and other small insects; usually found near water, where they lay their eggs. The aquatic larva (nymph) uses highly extendable jaws to capture aquatic invertebrates and small fish or tadpoles. This species, a medium-sized dragonfly, is widely distributed and common throughout the region; thrives in disturbed habitats and breeds in weedy ponds, marshes, and paddy fields. The male's body and head are red to rusty, with clear transparent patches on the ends of the wings. The body of the female tends to be paler; the wings transparent amber yellow. Often seen perched on grasses and shrubs. Length: 2–2.5 cm

BLACK-TIPPED PERCHER *Diplacodes nebulosa*

A small dragonfly. The male is blue with dark patches on the tips of the transparent wings. The female is pale yellow, with a broad black line along the top of the abdomen; the wings are all transparent. The male is strongly territorial and aggressive. A locally abundant species in marshes and weedy ponds throughout the region. Length: 2.5 cm

GREEN METALWING *Neurobasis chinensis*

Damselflies differ from dragonflies in being smaller and in holding their wings folded against the body at rest (dragonflies hold their wings apart and perpendicular to the body). One of the most beautiful damselflies in the region, the male of this species has iridescent green hind wings with a black tip; he flashes this color brightly in territorial and courtship behavior by slowing down his wing beats in sunlit spots in the favored streamside habitat. The rounded fore wings are transparent with a greenish tinge; the head is black, the thorax iridescent green with a coppery wash; the abdomen iridescent green with black on the underside. In the female the wings are transparent with creamy opaque spots on the front edges. A common damselfly on fast-flowing streams in primary and secondary tropical rain forest, it can tolerate partially deforested streams. Often perches on logs and rocks in the center of streams. The female lays eggs on submerged logs. Commonly found in the region except possibly in Cambodia; extinct in Singapore, where it was last recorded in 1970. Length: 3 cm

Lantern Bug

Fulvous Forest Skimmer

Black-tipped Percher

Green Metalwing

TROPICAL CARPENTER BEE *Xylocopa latipes*

These very robust bees are some of the largest bees in the world. They are shiny black with blue, green, and purple wings that have a metallic sheen in sunlight. The male and female are alike except that the male has very hairy, light-colored front legs with long hairs extending from the back of the leg. This species is widely distributed across Southeast Asia. A solitary nectar feeder often seen at flowers, it seems to favor purple flowers; an important pollinator, which can be found in all forested habitats and meadows where adequate pollen flowers occur. Constructs nests in dead wood by boring with strong mandibles; the nests are often long tunnels, up to 11 cm, with multiple galleries; the entry to the nest hole is usually about 1 cm in diameter. Although intimidating in appearance, this species is relatively docile, and the sting is said to not be terribly painful; it never attacks. Has a loud, low-pitched buzz. Often returns to the same perches over and over. Length: to 35 mm

GOLDEN ORB-WEB SPIDER *Nephila pilipes*

This group of spiders makes probably the largest and strongest webs in the spider world. The name of this species comes from the color of the silk. The web, designed for catching large flying insects, is wheel-shaped, though not symmetrical; the silk is strong enough to catch small birds (the spider doesn't eat small birds); it often leaves a trail of insect husks to make the web visible for larger creatures. The huge female has shiny black legs with yellow or red joints; the head is yellow on top, black below; and the top of the abdomen is finely spotted or striped yellow and black. The tiny male is only a tenth of the size of the female and often lives on the female's web, stealing food; is known to mate with the female possibly without her noticing. The female digs a shallow hole, then produces an egg sac that she covers with soil. This spider is venomous but not lethal to humans, though the bite causes pain, redness, and sometimes blistering. Common in all types of wooded habitats throughout the region. Length: F to 20 cm across, from leg tip to leg tip

Tropical Carpenter Bee

Golden Orb-web Spider

INVERTEBRATES

LEECHES Haemadipsidae

The haemadipsids (commonly known as the "jawed land leeches") are terrestrial, parasitic, blood-feeding leeches and are most common in Southeast Asia and Australia. There are many different species. They have 5 pairs of eyes and 2 or 3 jaws. Under the microscope the jaws look like tiny, half-circular saw blades; extremely sharp, they have either small teeth or a cutting edge. The 2-jawed species leave a V-shaped bite; the 3-jawed ones leave a Y-shaped bite. These bloodsuckers use their jaws to attach to their temporary hosts. They feed on all types of vertebrates, including humans. The sanguinivorous (i.e., bloodsucking) leeches have a substance called hirudin in their saliva that is an anticoagulant. Leeches tend to be more prevalent after rain; they dry out easily and, once they do, will enter into a torpid state; when it rains they rapidly spring into action. Leeches do not transmit any known disease, though bites in rare cases may cause temporary infection. Leeches are responsive to light and mechanical stimuli; they can detect movement, so if you brush against a tree or tread heavily they will feel rather than hear you coming. They are also outfitted with heat receptors and can detect hosts by their body temperature. Length: 2–3 cm

GIANT PILL MILLIPEDES Sphaerotheriida

These short-bodied millipedes will roll up like a golf ball when disturbed. They resemble wood lice, to which they are unrelated, but are much larger, with 13 segments and large, kidney-shaped eyes. Each body segment has 2 pairs of legs. They possess a pair of large antennae, which are short and thick. While there are many species within a number of families in the order Sphaerotheriida, they superficially all look the same. They feed on dead organic matter on the forest floor. Not venomous. Length: to 10 cm

TARANTULAS *Chilobrachys* spp.

This species belongs to the Theraphosidae family—a group of large, hairy arachnids known as tarantulas. There are about 45 species in mainland Southeast Asia. The tarantulas are long-legged, long-living spiders with bodies covered in short hairs called setae. Old World tarantulas lack urticating (irritating) hairs. The Chilobrachys genus of tarantula is widespread in Southeast Asia but is rarely seen. Mostly nocturnal, they build burrows, several feet deep, where they spend most of their time; the inside of the burrow is insulated with silk. They emerge only to hunt prey, which they kill by injecting a strong venom containing a cardiotoxin through their large fangs; they feed on large insects and small vertebrates, such as cockroaches, crickets, bird nestlings, and mice. Typically the favored habitat is humid tropical rain forest. The female can live to over 12 years. Length: 15 cm

Leeches

Giant Pill Millipede

Tarantula, male on top of female

REFERENCES

Banks, J. *Wonders of the East: The Butterflies of Malaysia. 120 of Asia's finest butterflies.*
(40-minute DVD). Cinebutterflies, 2015. cinebutterflies.com.

Barlow, H. S. *Introduction to the Moths of South East Asia*. Malaysian Nature Society, 1983.

Braack, L.E.O. *Fascinating Insects of Southeast Asia*. Marshall Cavendish, 1996.

Chandler, R. *Shorebirds of North America, Europe, and Asia: A Photographic Guide.*
Princeton University Press, 2009.

Das, I. *Field Guide to the Reptiles of South-East Asia*. New Holland Publishers, 2010.

Francis, C. M. *A Guide to the Mammals of Southeast Asia*. Princeton University Press, 2008.

Robson, C. *Birds of Southeast Asia*. Princeton University Press, 2005.

Sterling, E. J., M. M. Hurley, and L. D. Minh. *Vietnam: A Natural History*. Yale University
Press, 2006.

Strange, M. A. *A Photographic Guide to the Birds of Southeast Asia, including the
Philippines & Borneo*. Princeton University Press, 2002.

Wallace, A. R. *The Malay Archipelago*. Periplus Editions, 2000.

PHOTO CREDITS

Scott Baker: Reticulated Python *Python reticulatus*
Kwan Choo (Associate of the Royal Photographic Society of Great Britain):
Little Grebe *Tachybaptus ruficollis*, Yellow Bittern *Ixobrychus sinensis*, Purple Heron
Ardea purpurea, Black Kite *Milvus migrans*, Lesser Sand-Plover *Charadrius mongolus*,
Bronze-winged Jacana *Metopidius indicus*, Marsh Sandpiper *Tringa stagnatilis*, Wood
Sandpiper *Tringa glareola*, Oriental Pratincole *Glareola maldivarum*, Brown-headed
Gull *Larus brunnicephalus*, Whiskered Tern *Chlidonias hybrid*, Spotted Dove *Streptopelia
chinensis*, Emerald Dove *Chalcophaps indica*, Pink-necked Green-Pigeon *Treron vernans*,
Plaintive Cuckoo *Cacomantis merulinus*, Asian Koel *Eudynamys scolopaceus*, Greater
Coucal *Centropus sinensis*, Dollarbird *Eurystomus orientalis*, Rhinoceros Hornbill *Buceros
rhinoceros*, Speckled Piculet *Picumnus innominatus*, Sunda Woodpecker *Dendrocopos
moluccensis*, Grey-capped Woodpecker *Dendrocopos canicapillus*, Greater Yellownape
Picus avinucha, Vernal Hanging Parrot *Loriculus vernalis*, Long-tailed Broadbill
Psarisomus dalhousiae, Dusky Broadbill *Corydon sumatranus*, Ashy Woodswallow
Artamus fuscus, Long-tailed Shrike *Lanius schach*, Black-naped Oriole *Oriolus chinensis*,
Black-hooded Oriole *Oriolus xanthornus*, Black Drongo *Dicrurus macrocercus*,
White-throated Fantail *Rhipidura albicollis*, Large-billed Crow *Corvus macrorhynchos*,
Indochinese Bushlark *Mirafra erythrocephala*, Cinereous Tit *Parus cinereus*, Black-crested
Bulbul *Pycnonotus melanicterus*, Sooty-headed Bulbul *Pycnonotus aurigaster*, Yellow-
vented Bulbul *Pycnonotus goiavier*, Streak-eared Bulbul *Pycnonotus blanfordi*, Cream-
vented Bulbul *Pycnonotus simplex*, Ochraceous Bulbul *Alophoixus ochraceus*, Pygmy
Cupwing *Pnoepyga pusilla*, Yellow-browed Warbler *Phylloscopus inornatus*, Hill Prinia
Prinia superciliaris, Yellow-bellied Prinia *Prinia aviventris*, Oriental White-eye *Zosterops
palpebrosus*, Fluffy-backed Tit Babbler *Macronus ptilosus*, Golden Babbler *Cyanoderma
chrysaeum*, White-browed Scimitar Babbler *Pomatorhinus schisticeps*, White-browed
Shrike-Babbler *Pteruthius aviscapis*, Grey-throated Babbler *Stachyris nigriceps*, Puff-
throated Babbler *Pellorneum ruficeps*, Mountain Fulvetta *Alcippe peracensis*, White-
crested Laughingthrush *Garrulax leucolophus*, Silver-eared Mesia *Leiothrix argentauris*,
Asian Brown Flycatcher *Muscicapa dauurica*, Verditer Flycatcher *Eumyias thalassinus*,
Blue Rock Thrush *Monticola solitaries*, Daurian Redstart *Phoenicurus auroreus*, Siberian

Stonechat *Saxicola maurus*, Pied Bushchat *Saxicola caprata*, Orange-headed Thrush *Geokichla citrina*, Common Hill Myna *Gracula religiosa*, Black-collared Starling *Gracupica nigricollis*, Blue-winged Leafbird *Chloropsis cochinchinensis*, Plain-throated Sunbird *Anthreptes malacensis*, White Wagtail *Motacilla alba*, Baya Weaver *Ploceus philippinus*, White-rumped Munia *Lonchura striata*, Scaly-breasted Munia *Lonchura punctulata*, Long-tailed Macaque *Macaca fascicularis*, Siamang *Symphalangus syndactylus*, White-handed Gibbon *Hylobates lar*

Choy Wai Mun: Bushy-crested Hornbill *Anorrhinus galeritus*, Black-browed Barbet *Psilopogon oorti*, Golden-whiskered Barbet *Psilopogon chrysopogon*, Large Cuckooshrike *Coracina macei*, Cream-coloured Giant Squirrel *Ratufa affinis*

Jonathon Dashper: Wreathed Hornbill *Aceros undulates*

Irene Dy: Whimbrel *Numenius phaeopus*, Oriental Bay Owl *Phodilus badius*

David Fisher: Blossom-headed Parakeet *Psittacula roseate*, Asian House Rat *Rattus tanezumi*, Archduke *Lexias pardalis*

Con Foley: Lesser Frigatebird *Fregata ariel*, Pacific Reef Heron *Egretta sacra*, Javan Pond-Heron *Ardeola speciosa*, Osprey *Pandion haliaetus*, Black-shouldered Kite *Elanus caeruleus*, Changeable Hawk-Eagle *Nisaetus limnaeetus*, Eastern Marsh Harrier *Circus spilonotus*, Crested Goshawk *Accipiter trivirgatus*, Eurasian Moorhen *Gallinula chloropus*, Eurasian Coot *Fulica atra*, Whimbrel *Numenius phaeopus*, Eurasian Curlew *Numenius arquata*, Black-tailed Godwit *Limosa limosa*, Bar-tailed Godwit *Limosa lapponica*, Curlew Sandpiper *Calidris ferruginea*, Long-toed Stint *Calidris subminuta*, Red-necked Stint *Calidris ruficollis*, Black-headed Gull *Larus ridibundus*, Caspian Tern *Hydroprogne caspia*, Oriental Turtle-Dove *Streptopelia orientalis*, Red Collared-Dove *Streptopelia tranquebarica*, Barred Cuckoo-Dove *Macropygia unchall*, Thick-billed Pigeon *Treron curvirostra*, Green Imperial-Pigeon *Ducula aenea*, Little Bronze Cuckoo *Chrysococcyx minutillus*, Green-billed Malkoha *Phaenicophaeus tristis*, Raffles's Malkoha *Phaenicophaeus chlorophaeus*, Barn Owl *Tyto alba*, Coppersmith Barbet *Psilopogon haemacephala*, Blue-eared Barbet *Psilopogon australis*, White-bellied Woodpecker *Dryocopus javensis*, Banded Woodpecker *Picus miniaceus*, Common Flameback *Dinopium javanense*, Buff-rumped Woodpecker *Meiglyptes tristis*, Greater Flameback *Chrysocolaptes lucidus*, Maroon Woodpecker *Blythipicus rubiginosus*, Bay Wood-pecker *Blythipicus pyrrhotis*, Orange-backed Woodpecker *Reinwardtipicus validus*, Great Slaty Woodpecker *Mulleripicus pulverulentus*, Malayan Banded Pitta *Pitta irena*, Large Woodshrike *Tephrodornis virgatus*, Common Iora *Aegithina tiphia*, Pied Triller *Lalage nigra*, Common Green Magpie *Cissa chinensis*, Grey-headed Canary Flycatcher *Culicicapa ceylonensis*, Blue Nuthatch *Sitta azurea*, Puff-backed Bulbul *Pycnonotus eutilotus*, Black-headed Bulbul *Pycnonotus atriceps*, Puff-throated Bulbul *Alophoixus pallidus*, Stripe-throated Bulbul *Pycnonotus finlaysoni*, Ashy Bulbul *Hemixos avala*, Mountain Tailorbird *Phyllergates cucullatus*, Arctic Warbler *Phylloscopus borealis*, Large Scimitar Babbler *Megapomatorhinus hypoleucos*, Sooty-capped Babbler *Malacopteron affine*, Scaly-crowned Babbler *Malacopteron cinereum*, Puff-throated Babbler *Pellorneum ruficeps*, Black-capped Babbler *Pellorneum capistratum*, White-chested Babbler *Pellorneum rostratum*, Ferruginous Babbler *Pellorneum bicolor*, White-crowned Forktail *Enicurus leschenaultia*, Grey Bushchat *Saxicola ferreus* (male), Crested Myna *Acridotheres cristatellus*, Orange-bellied Leafbird *Chloropsis hardwickii*, Ruby-cheeked Sunbird *Chalcoparia singalensis*, Streaked Spiderhunter *Arachnothera magna*, Grey Wagtail *Motacilla cinerea*, Sunda Colugo *Galeopterus variegatus*, Smooth Otter *Lutrogale perspicillata*, Common Palm Civet *Paradoxurus hermaphrodites*, Tiger *Panthera tigris*, Eurasian Wild Pig *Sus scrofa*, Prevost's Squirrel *Callosciurus prevostii*, Horse-tailed Squirrel *Sundasciurus hippurus*, King Cobra *Ophiophagus hannah*

Dale Forbes: Crab-eating Mongoose *Herpestes urva*

Jon Hall: Asian Wrinkle-lipped Bat *Tadarida plicatus*

Sam Hopley: Wagler's Pit Viper *Tropidolaemus wagleri*

Neoh Hor: White-bellied Sea Eagle *Haliaeetus leucogaster*, Malayan Banded Pitta *Pitta irena*, Ferruginous Babbler *Pellorneum bicolor*, Asian Softshell Turtle *Dogania subplana*, Giant Leaf Terrapin *Heosemys grandis*

Robert Hutchinson: Red Junglefowl *Gallus gallus*, Silver Pheasant *Lophura nycthemera*, Lesser Frigatebird *Fregata ariel*, Yellow Bittern *Ixobrychus sinensis*, Pacific Reef Heron *Egretta sacra*, Javan Pond-Heron *Ardeola speciosa*, Black-shouldered Kite *Elanus caeruleus*, Changeable Hawk-Eagle *Nisaetus limnaeetus*, Eastern Marsh Harrier *Circus spilonotus*, Marsh Sandpiper *Tringa stagnatilis*, Wood Sandpiper *Tringa glareola*, Whimbrel *Numenius phaeopus*, Black- tailed Godwit *Limosa limosa*, Curlew Sandpiper *Calidris ferruginea*, Long-toed Stint *Calidris subminuta*, Oriental Pratincole *Glareola maldivarum*, Great Crested Tern *Thalasseus bergii*, Green Imperial-Pigeon *Ducula aenea*, Little Bronze Cuckoo *Chrysococcyx minutillus*, Great Eared-Nightjar *Lyncornis macrotis*, Collared Kingfisher *Todiramphus chloris*, Hooded Pitta *Pitta sordida*, Pied Triller *Lalage nigra*, Brown Shrike *Lanius cristatus*, Ashy Drongo *Dicrurus leucophaeus*, Mountain Bulbul *Ixos mcclellandii*, Mountain Tailorbird *Phyllergates cucullatus*, Arctic Warbler *Phylloscopus borealis*, Striated Grassbird *Megalurus palustris*, Asian Brown Flycatcher *Muscicapa dauurica*, Blue Rock Thrush *Monticola solitarius*, Pied Bushchat *Saxicola caprata*, Eastern Yellow Wagtail *Motacilla tschutschensis*, Grey Wagtail *Motacilla cinerea*, Olive-backed Pipit *Anthus hodgsoni ,* Dhole *Cuon alpinus*, Bearded Pig *Sus barbatus*, Plantain Squirrel *Callosciurus notatus*

Ayuwat Jearwattanakanok: Black Kite (in flight), Green-eared Barbet *Psilopogon faiostricta*, Small Minivet *Pericrocotus cinnamomeus,* Red-whiskered Bulbul *Pycnonotus jocosus*, Two-barred Warbler *Phylloscopus plumbeitarsus*, Rufous-fronted Babbler *Cyanoderma rufifrons*

Pitchaya and Rattapon Kaichid: Sunda Pangolin *Manis javanica*, Burmese Hare *Lepus peguensis*

Bill Kee: Irrawaddy Squirrel *Callosciurus pygerythrus*, Tropical Swallowtail Moth *Lyssa zampa*

Parit Kengsungnoen: Himalayan Swiftlet *Aerodramus brevirostris*

Jeremiah Loei: Fork-tailed Drongo-Cuckoo *Surniculus dicruroides*, Large-tailed Nightjar *Caprimulgus macrurus*

Bernard Master: Burmese Python *Python bivittatus*

Mohd Abdul Muin: Reticulated Python *Python reticulatus*, Spotted Gecko *Gekko monarchus*, Common Sun Skink *Eutropis multifasciata*, Blanford's Gliding Lizard *Draco blanfordi*, Green Paddy Frog *Hylarana erythraea*, Four-lined Treefrog *Polype- dates leucomystax*, Asian Grass Frog *Fejervarya limnocharis*, Common Mormon *Papilio polytes*

Yann Muzika: Lesser Mousedeer *Tragulus kanchil*, Rufous Piculet *Sasia abnormis*, Abbott's Babbler *Turdinus abbotti*

Susan Myers: Eastern Spot-billed Duck *Anas zonorhyncha*, Red Junglefowl *Gallus gallus*, Crested Fireback *Lophura ignite*, Siamese Fireback *Lophura diardi*, Great Argus *Argusianus argus*, Asian Openbill *Anastomus oscitans*, Woolly-necked Stork *Ciconia episcopus*, Lesser Adjutant *Leptoptilos javanicus*, Painted Stork *Mycteria leucocephala*, Indian Cormorant *Phalacrocorax fuscicollis*, Oriental Darter *Anhinga melanogaster*, Spot-billed Pelican *Pelecanus philippensis*, Grey Heron *Ardea cinerea*, Great Egret *Ardea alba*, Little Egret *Egretta garzetta*, Striated Heron *Butorides striata*, Black-crowned Night Heron *Nycticorax nycticorax*, Oriental Honey-buzzard *Pernis ptilorhynchus*, Crested Serpent Eagle *Spilornis cheela*, Shikra *Accipiter badius*, Lesser Fish Eagle *Ichthyophaga humilis*, Grey-headed Fish Eagle *Ichthyophaga ichthyaetus*, White-breasted Waterhen *Amaurornis phoenicurus*, Black-backed Swamphen *Porphyrio indicus*, Great Thick-knee *Esacus recurvirostris*, Beach Thick-knee *Esacus neglectus*, Black-winged Stilt *Himantopus himantopus*, Red-wattled Lapwing *Vanellus indicus*, Little Ringed Plover *Charadrius* *dubius*, Pheasant-tailed Jacana *Hydrophasianus chirurgus*, Common Sandpiper *Actitis hypoleucos*, Common Greenshank *Tringa nebularia*, Wood Sandpiper *Tringa glareola*, Common Redshank *Tringa tetanus*, Pintail Snipe *Gallinago stenura*, Small Pratincole *Glareola lactea*, Ashy-headed Green-Pigeon *Treron phayrei*, Mountain Imperial-Pigeon *Ducula badia*, Large Hawk Cuckoo *Hierococcyx sparverioides*, Moustached Hawk Cuckoo *Hierococcyx vagans*, Black-bellied Malkoha *Phaenicophaeus diardi*, Oriental Scops-Owl *Otus sunia*, Buffy Fish Owl *Ketupa ketupu*, Asian Barred Owlet *Glaucidium cuculoides*, Brown Wood Owl *Strix leptogrammica*, Savanna Nightjar *Caprimulgus affinis*, Glossy Swiftlet *Collocalia esculenta*, Whiskered Treeswift *Hemiprocne comata*, Red-naped Trogon *Harpactes kasumba*, Orange-breasted Trogon *Harpactes oreskios*, Common Kingfisher *Alcedo atthis*, Blue-eared Kingfisher *Alcedo meninting*, Black-backed Dwarf-Kingfisher *Ceyx erithaca*, Banded Kingfisher *Lacedo pulchella*, Stork-billed Kingfisher *Pelargopsis capensis*, White-throated Kingfisher *Halcyon smyrnensis*, Green Bee-eater *Merops orientalis*, Chestnut-headed Bee-eater *Merops leschenaultia*, Indian Roller *Coracias benghalensis*, Eurasian Hoopoe *Upupa epops*, Oriental Pied Hornbill *Anthracoceros albirostris*, Great Hornbill *Buceros bicornis*, Lineated Barbet *Psilopogon lineata*, Black-browed Barbet *Psilopogon oorti*, Rufous Woodpecker *Micropternus brachyurus*, Collared Falconet *Microhierax caerulescens*, Eurasian Kestrel *Falco tinnunculus*, Rose-ringed Parakeet *Psittacula krameri*, Red-breasted Parakeet *Psittacula alexandri*, Black-and-red Broadbill *Cymbirhynchus macrorhynchos*, Black-and-yellow Broadbill *Eurylaimus ochromalus*, Common Woodshrike *Tephrodornis pondicerianus*, Bar-winged Flycatcher-shrike *Hemipus picatus*, Green Iora *Aegithina viridissima*, White-browed Fantail *Rhipidura aureola*, Asian Paradise-flycatcher *Terpsiphone paradisi*, Barn Swallow *Hirundo rustica*, Striated Swallow *Cecropis striolata*, Sultan Tit *Melanochlora sultanea*, Chestnut-vented Nuthatch *Sitta nagaensis*, Velvet-fronted Nuthatch *Sitta frontalis*, Striated Bulbul *Pycnonotus striatus*, Flavescent Bulbul *Pycnonotus avescens*, Red-eyed Bulbul *Pycnonotus brunneus*, Black Bulbul *Hypsipetes leucocephalus*, Brownish-flanked Bush Warbler *Horornis fortipes*, Lanceolated Warbler *Locustella lanceolata*, Golden-headed Cisticola *Cisticola exilis*, Common Tailorbird *Orthotomus sutorius*, Ashy Tailorbird *Orthotomus ruficeps*, White-browed Fulvetta *Fulvetta vinipectus*, Chestnut-winged Babbler *Cyanoderma erythropterum*, Short-tailed Babbler *Pellor- neum malaccense*, Striped Wren Babbler *Kenopia striata*, White-cheeked Laughingthrush *Ianthocincla vassali*, Chestnut-capped Laughingthrush *Ianthocincla mitrata*, Black-headed Sibia *Heterophasia desgodinsi*, Spectacled Barwing *Actinodura ramsayi*, Chestnut-tailed Minla *Actinodura strigula*, Oriental Magpie Robin *Copsychus saularis*, White-rumped Shama *Copsychus malabaricus*, Blue Whistling Thrush *Myophonus caeruleus*, Snowy-browed Flycatcher *Ficedula hyperythra*, White-capped Redstart *Phoenicurus leucocephalus*, Grey Bushchat *Saxicola ferreus* (female), Mrs Gould's Sunbird *Aethopyga gouldiae*, Crimson Sunbird *Aethopyga siparaja*, Spectacled Spiderhunter *Arachnothera avigaster*, Oriental Pipit *Anthus rufulus*, Common Treeshrew *Tupaia glis*, Large Fruit Bat *Pteropus vampyrus*, Greater False-vampire *Megaderma lyra*, Fawn Leafnosed Bat *Hipposideros cervinus*, Lesser Sheath-tailed Bat *Emballonura monticola*, Banded Surili *Presbytis femoralis*, Sundaic Silvered Langur *Trachypithecus cristatus*, Dusky Leaf Monkey *Trachypithecus obscurus*, Northern Pig-tailed Macaque *Macaca leonine*, Small Asian Mongoose *Herpestes javanicus*, Leopard *Panthera pardus*, Asian Elephant *Elephas maximus*, Sambar *Rusa unicolor*, Common Barking Deer *Muntiacus muntjak*, Gaur *Bos frontalis*, Sunda Black-banded Squirrel *Callosciurus nigrovittatus*, Variable Squirrel *Callosciurus finlaysonii*, Cambodian Striped Squirrel *Tamiops rodolphii*, Three-striped Ground Squirrel *Lariscus insignis*, Dog-faced Water Snake *Cerberus rynchops*, Oriental Whip Snake *Ahaetulla prasina*, Jasper Cat Snake *Boiga jaspidea*, Gold-ringed Cat Snake *Boiga dendrophila*, Painted Bronzeback *Dendrelaphis pictus*, Common Mock Viper *Psammodynastes pulverulentus*, Yellow-lipped Sea Krait *Laticauda colubrine*, Common House Gecko *Hemidactylus frenatus*, Tokay Gecko *Gekko gecko*, Long-tailed Grass Skink *Takydromus sexlineatus*, Oriental Garden Lizard *Calotes versicolor*, Green Crested Lizard *Bronchocela cristatella*, Water Monitor *Varanus salvator*, Asian Giant Tortoise *Manouria emys*, Estuarine Crocodile *Crocodylus porosus*, Asian Toad *Duttaphrynus melanostictus*, Wallace's Flying Frog *Rhacophorus nigropalmatus*, Harlequin Flying Frog *Rhacophorus pardalis*, Four-lined Treefrog *Polypedates leucomystax*, Asian Grass Frog *Fejervarya limnocharis*, Golden Birdwing *Troides aeacus*, Rajah Brookes Birdwing *Trogonoptera brookiana*, Red-base Jezebel *Delias pasithoe*, Clipper *Parthenos sylvia*, Blue Pansy *Junonia orithya*, Tropical Swallowtail Moth *Lyssa zampa*, Cicada *Cicadidae*, Tropical Carpenter Bee *Xylocopa latipes*, Lantern Bug *Pyrops sp.*, Fulvous Forest Skimmer *Neurothemis fulvia*, Black-tipped Percher *Diplacodes nebulose*, Green Metalwing *Neurobasis chinensis*, Golden Orb-web Spider *Nephila pilipes*, Leeches, Giant Pill Millipede, Burma Chocolate Brown Tarantula *Chilobrachys dyscolus*

Parinya Padungtin: Bar-bellied Pitta *Pitta elliotii*, Limestone Wren Babbler *Turdinus crispifrons*, Black-headed Greenfinch *Carduelis ambigua,* Bengal Slow Loris *Nycticebus bengalensis*

Coke and Sam Smith: Sunda Colugo *Galeopterus variegatus*, Asian Wrinkle-lipped Bat *Tadarida plicatus*, Dusky Leaf Monkey *Trachypithecus obscurus*, Stump-tailed Macaque *Macaca arctoides*, Large Indian Civet *Viverra zibetha*, Common Palm Civet *Paradoxurus hermaphrodites*, Binturong *Arctictis binturong*, Leopard Cat *Prionailurus bengalensis*, Black Giant Squirrel *Ratufa bicolor*, Pallas's Squirrel *Callosciurus erythraeus*, Cambodian Striped Squirrel *Tamiops rodolphii*, Low's Squirrel *Sundasciurus lowii*, Red giant Flying Squirrel *Petaurista petaurista*, Malayan Porcupine *Hystrix brachyura*

Kaeryn Stout: Asian Golden Cat *Catopuma temminckii*

William Tan: Great Egret *Ardea alba*, Cattle Egret *Bubulcus ibis*, Brahminy Kite *Haliastur indus*, Collared Scops-Owl *Otus lettia*, Large-tailed Nightjar *Caprimulgus macrurus*, Scarlet-rumped Trogon *Harpactes duvaucelii*, Blue-bearded Bee-eater *Nyctyornis athertoni*, Blue-tailed Bee-eater *Merops philippinus*, Black Hornbill *Anthracoceros malayanus*, Greater Racket-tailed Drongo *Dicrurus paradiseus*, Pin-striped Tit Babbler *Mixornis gularis*, Short-tailed Babbler *Pellorneum malaccense*, Asian Fairy Bluebird *Irena puella*, Little Pied Flycatcher *Ficedula westermanni*, Asian Glossy Starling *Aplonis panayensis*, Orange-bellied Flowerpecker *Dicaeum trigonostigma*, Scarlet-backed Flowerpecker *Dicaeum cruentatum*, Olive-backed Sunbird *Cinnyris jugularis*, Little Spiderhunter *Arachnothera longirostra*, Gold-ringed Cat Snake *Boiga dendrophila*, Paradise Treesnake *Chrysopelea paradise*, Hawksbill Turtle *Eretmochelys imbricate*

Tom Tarrant: Gull-billed Tern *Gelochelidon nilotica*, Bay Woodpecker *Blythipicus pyrrhotis*

Wong Tsu Shi: Bushy-crested Hornbill *Anorrhinus galeritus*, Rufous-fronted Babbler *Cyanoderma rufifrons*, Sunda Pangolin *Manis javanica*, Asian Softshell Turtle *Dogania subplana*, Asian Giant Tortoise *Manouria emys*, Green Paddy Frog *Hylarana erythraea*

INDEX